LOW-WAGE WORK
IN DENMARK

LOW-WAGE WORK
IN DENMARK

Niels Westergaard-Nielsen, Editor

The Russell Sage Foundation Case Studies of Job
Quality in Advanced Economies

Russell Sage Foundation • New York

The Russell Sage Foundation

The Russell Sage Foundation, one of the oldest of America's general purpose foundations, was established in 1907 by Mrs. Margaret Olivia Sage for "the improvement of social and living conditions in the United States." The Foundation seeks to fulfill this mandate by fostering the development and dissemination of knowledge about the country's political, social, and economic problems. While the Foundation endeavors to assure the accuracy and objectivity of each book it publishes, the conclusions and interpretations in Russell Sage Foundation publications are those of the authors and not of the Foundation, its Trustees, or its staff. Publication by Russell Sage, therefore, does not imply Foundation endorsement.

Library of Congress Cataloging-in-Publication Data
Low-wage work in Denmark / Niels Westergaard-Nielsen, editor.
   p. cm. — (The Russell Sage Foundation case studies of job quality in
   advanced economies)
  Includes bibliographical references and index.
  ISBN 978-0-87154-896-2
  1. Unskilled labor—Denmark. 2. Wages—Denmark. 3. Minimum wage—
  Denmark. 4. Labor market—Denmark. I. Westergård-Nielsen, Niels C.
  HD8544.L69 2008
  331.7'9809489—dc22

2007045927

Text design by Suzanne Nichols.

RUSSELL SAGE FOUNDATION
112 East 64th Street, New York, New York 10021
10 9 8 7 6 5 4 3 2 1

Contents

About the Authors

NIELS WESTERGAARD-NIELSEN is professor of economics at the Aarhus School of Business, University of Aarhus, and is the director of the Center for Corporate Performance (CCP).

ANNE-METTE SONNE ANDERSEN is an assistant professor at MAPP, Department of Marketing and Statistics, Aarhus School of Business, University of Aarhus.

NUKA BUCK is research assistant at MAPP, Department of Marketing and Statistics, Aarhus School of Business, University of Aarhus.

TOR ERIKSSON is professor of economics at the Aarhus School of Business, Aarhus University.

LARS ESBJERG is assistant professor at MAPP, Department of Marketing and Statistics, Aarhus School of Business, University of Aarhus.

JACOB K. ESKILDSEN is associate professor at CCP, Department of Marketing and Statistics, Aarhus School of Business, University of Aarhus.

KLAUS G. GRUNERT is professor of marketing and director of MAPP— Center for Research on Customer Relations in the Food Sector, Aarhus School of Business, University of Aarhus.

JINGKUN LI is an economist at COWI A/S, and was earlier employed as project coordinator for the Danish low wage research project team.

ANN-KRISTINA LØKKE NIELSEN is a teaching assistant professor at the Department of Marketing and Statistics, Aarhus School of Business, University of Aarhus, and member of the Center for Corporate Performance.

ROBERT SOLOW is Institute Professor Emeritus at the Massachusetts Institute of Technology and a Nobel laureate in economics.

OLE HENNING SØRENSEN is a researcher at the National Research Center for the Working Environment.

INTRODUCTION

The Danish Story

Robert Solow

Ry any reasonable standard definition of "low-wage work," about a quarter of American wage earners are low-wage workers. The corresponding figure is smaller, sometimes much smaller, in other comparable advanced capitalist countries. This fact is not very good for the self-image of Americans. It does not seem to be what is meant by "crown(ing) thy good with brotherhood, from sea to shining sea." The paradox, if that is the right word, is the starting point for the extensive study of which this book is an important part. What are the comparative facts, what do they mean, and why do they turn out that way?

A foundation dedicated from its beginning to "the improvement of social and living conditions in the United States of America" has to be interested in the nature of poverty, its causes, changes, consequences and possible reduction. Low-wage work is not the same thing as poverty, still less lifelong poverty. Some low-wage workers live in families with several earners, and share a common standard of living, so they may not be poor even while working such jobs. Some low-wage workers are on a reasonably secure track that will eventually move them to better paid jobs, so they are not poor in a lifetime sense. But some low-wage workers are stuck with very low income for a meaningful length of time. For them, low-wage work does mean poverty in the midst of plenty.

Of course, the incidence of poverty can be reduced by transfer payments outside the labor market. Nevertheless, in a society that values self-reliance, and in which productive work confers identity and self-respect as well as the respect of others, income redistribution unconnected or wrongly connected with work is not the best solution except in special cases. In that kind of society, ours for instance, the persistence of low-wage work is felt as a social problem on its own. It first has to be understood if we are to find satisfactory ways to diminish its incidence or alleviate its effects.

One obvious basis for low-wage work is low productivity, which may be primarily a characteristic of the worker, as is often simply assumed, or may be primarily a characteristic of the job. If it inheres in the job, equity could be achieved by passing the job around, so to speak, like boring committee assignments or military service, but that would have no aggregate effect. Wherever low pay originates, however, raising productivity provides a double benefit: it diminishes the amount of low-wage work to be done, and it increases the useful output of the whole economy.

Low productivity, and therefore low-wage work, tends to reproduce itself from generation to generation. This is an important additional reason why a high incidence of low-wage work is a "social condition" that needs to be improved. Growing up in a chronically low-wage family limits access to good education, good health care, and to other ladders to social mobility. So a persistent high incidence of low-wage work, when confined to a relatively small group, contravenes the widely accepted social goal of equal opportunity.

These are among the reasons why, in 1994, the Russell Sage Foundation inaugurated a major program of research on the nature, causes, and consequences of low-wage work and the prospects of low-wage workers. This initiative replaced a successful but more conventional program of research on poverty. It was called, rather grandly, *The Future of Work*. One of its key motivations was the need to understand how poorly educated, unskilled workers could cope with an economy in which most jobs were becoming technologically advanced, and therefore more demanding of cognitive power and refined skills.

This formulation was intended to call attention both to workers and to jobs, the natural subtext being that low-end jobs might be disappearing faster than low-skilled workers. This potential disparity presented the danger that low-wage workers could be stranded in an economy that had no use for them. The research mandate was interpreted quite broadly.

The Future of Work program was, as a matter of course, focused on the United States. It produced a large body of useful and original research, some of which was collected and summarized in the 2003 volume *Low-Wage America: How Employers Are Reshaping Opportunity in the Workplace*, edited by Eileen Appelbaum, Annette Bernhardt, and Richard Murnane. One of the refreshing aspects of these studies was precisely that the needs and capacities of employers shared the stage in the low-wage labor market with the abilities and motivations of workers.

One interesting hypothesis that emerged from this work was the notion that employers have significant discretion about the way they organize their use of low-skilled workers and the value they put on the continuity and productivity of their work force. The extreme versions came to be labeled "low-road" and "high-road" modes of organization. At the low-road extreme lie employers such as the typical car-wash, whose workers are regarded as casual labor, interchangeable parts that can be picked up off the street freely under normal labor-market conditions. There is no advantage in doing otherwise. At the other extreme are employers who regard their unskilled workers as an asset whose productive value can be increased by more training and longer attachment to the firm.

The point of this distinction was the belief that in some market situations both styles can be viable. An employer's place on the continuum is not uniquely determined by technology and the intensity of competition in the product market. Satisfactory profits can be earned by somewhat higher- and somewhat lower-road modes of organization; in some industries, examples of both can be found coexisting.

Of course, the nature of the technology and the competitive intensity in the industry are important determinants of labor-market outcomes. That is not in doubt. In some situations, however, there may be scope for several levels of wages and job quality for unskilled workers. It is important here to note that job quality covers much more than the current wage and benefits paid; it includes the length and slope of the internal wage scale, the degree of job security, the training offered and the possibilities of promotion within the firm, small creature comforts, the pace of the work itself, the autonomy and ergonomic character of the work, and so on. Each of these has a cost to the firm and a value to the workers, and the two are not always the same.

It hardly needs arguing that these elements of job quality can be important for the satisfaction and self-respect attached to a job. It then becomes important to the researcher to understand the broad factors that govern the typical choices made by employers. These may include historical precedents, legislation, the working of the educational system, collective bargaining, and other "institutional" biases.

At this stage of the argument, the advantages of a comparative cross-country study stand out. Most of those broadly institutional factors cannot be studied empirically within the United States because they change so slowly in time, and because there is not much locational variation. One cannot actually see them at work in a still snapshot. One can speculate and make thought-experiments, but that is not the same thing. So the idea sprouted within the Russell Sage Foundation in 2003 that it might be very useful to observe systematically how the fate of low-wage labor differs across a sample of European countries. Not any countries will do: one wants countries with somewhat different but not radically different political and institutional histories; but they must be at the same level of economic development as the United States if lessons are to be learned that could be useful in the United States. In the end, the countries chosen included the three indispensable large countries—France, Germany, and the United Kingdom—and two small northern European countries—Denmark and the Netherlands. The choice was consciously limited to Europe in order to avoid the complication of drastically different sociopolitical systems. A competition was held, and a local team selected for each of these five countries.

The planners of the project framed it in such a way that would sharpen the inferences that could be made from cross-country comparisons. Most centrally, five target jobs were chosen as objects of close study, the same five in each country. They were nurses' assistants and cleaners in hospitals, housekeepers in hotels, checkout clerks and related occupations in supermarkets and retail stores specializing in electrical goods, packagers, machine tenders and other unskilled occupations in two branches of food processing, namely confectionary and meat products, and low-skilled operators in call centers. (This last choice took advantage of an already ongoing international study of the call-center industry.) These are all low-wage jobs in the United States. The fact that some of them are not low-wage jobs in some of the five countries is an example of the value of cross-country comparisons. The simple fact invites, or rather compels, the question: Why not?

Each national team was asked to compile a statistical overview of low-wage work in its country, with special but not exclusive attention to the five target jobs. The team was also asked to complement the routine data with a survey of the historical, legislative, educational and other institutional infrastructure that is believed to underlie its own particular ways of dealing with low-end jobs and low-skilled workers. The final part of each country report is a series of case studies of each of the target jobs, including interviews with employers, managers, workers, union representatives and other participants. (When temporary work agencies were used to provide some or all of the relevant workers, they were included in the interviews wherever possible.) The national teams met and coordinated their work in the course of the research. This book is the report of the Denmark team.

There will be one more stage to complete the project. A six-country group of participants, including Americans, will prepare an explicitly comparative volume, job by job. They will try to fathom what deeper attitudinal, institutional, and circumstantial factors might explain the sometimes dramatic differences in the way these six modern nations engage with the problem of low-wage work.

One big, somewhat unexpected, finding is the one mentioned in the first paragraph of this introduction. The six countries differ substantially in the incidence of low-wage work. ("Incidence" is defined as the fraction of all workers, in the country or in a specific sector, who fall into the low-wage category.)

There is an interesting and important definitional issue that arises immediately. Uniformly in Europe (and elsewhere), a low-wage worker is anyone who earns less than two-thirds of the national median wage (usually the gross hourly wage, if only for data-availability reasons). This obviously makes the incidence of low-wage work an index of the inequality or dispersion of the wage distribution: multiplying or dividing everyone's wage by ten leaves the number of low-wage workers unchanged. The same applies to the measurement of poverty. In the United States, the poverty line is an absolute income. It was initially chosen as an empirical compromise, never entirely appropriate and less so as time passes, but nevertheless an absolute income. The United States has no corresponding definition for low-wage work, but the same approach could be taken. There are arguments to be made on both sides of this issue; for the purposes of this project, the choice of a low-wage threshold makes little practical difference. We use the European definition because that is the way their data are collected.

There is yet another practical reason to use the European definition. As noted, the two-thirds-of-median index simply reflects the degree of wage dispersion: a low incidence of low-wage work means a relatively compressed wage distribution, at least in the lower tail. This measure makes international comparisons more meaningful. Comparing absolute real wages between the United States and other countries is problematic because pensions, health care, payroll taxes, employer contributions and other such benefits and deductions are handled differently in different systems. Relative comparisons are subject to similar distortions, but considerably less so.

Here are the basic facts. In 2005, the incidence of low-wage work was 25 percent in the United States, 22.1 percent in the United Kingdom, 20.8 percent in Germany (2004), 18.2 percent in the Netherlands (2004), 12.7 percent in France (2002) and 8.5 percent in Denmark. The range is obviously very wide.

In a way, that is helpful, because figures like this can not be interpreted to the last decimal. Here is one interesting example of an unexpected twist. It turns out that the Dutch are the part-time champions among these countries, with a significantly larger fraction of part-time workers than elsewhere. This appears to be a voluntary choice, not something compelled by the unavailability of full-time work. Part-time workers tend to be paid lower hourly wages than full-time workers in the same or similar jobs, even in countries where it is against the law to discriminate against part-timers. The incidence measures given in the preceding paragraph are based on a headcount: 18 percent of all Dutch workers earn less than the low-wage threshold. One could with reason ask instead what fraction of the hours worked in the Netherlands falls into the low-wage category; the answer is about 16 percent. The fact that the hours-based incidence is lower would be common in all countries, but the difference is particularly large in the Netherlands.

A key issue is the degree of mobility out of low-wage work that characterizes each country's system. The seriousness of the "problem" turns almost entirely on the transitory nature of low-wage work. It is impossible to be precise about inter-country differences, because the data are sketchy and definitions vary. It is clear, however, that there are substantial differences among the countries, although mobility is fairly substantial everywhere, if only because younger workers eventually propel themselves into better jobs. The Danes appear to have the shortest residence times in low-wage work. For Americans the take-away lesson is that the self-image of an extremely mobile society is not valid, at least not in this respect.

Of course, there are many uniformities—often just what you would expect—among these countries in the pattern of low-wage work. The "concentration" of low-wage work in any subgroup of the population is defined as the incidence in that subgroup divided by the incidence among all workers. For instance, any subgroup with a higher incidence than the country at large will have a concentration index bigger than 1. This is the case for workers in the service sector of the economy, for women, for young people, for part-timers, and for those with little education. In most instances, the particular sectors we have picked out for study have a high concentration index; together, retail trade and "hotels and catering" have a concentration ratio of about 3 in the Netherlands. The categories mentioned obviously overlap, but the data do not permit us to zero in statistically on young part-time secondary-school-only women working in supermarkets. Nevertheless, the odds are very high that they fall into the low-wage category.

The cross-country differences are more interesting, however, because they at least offer the possibility that we can find explanations for them in the circumstances, institutions, attitudes and policies of these basically similar economies. It is important that these are basically similar economic systems with broadly similar labor markets. They differ in certain historically established social norms, institutions and policies. One can hope to figure out which of these fairly small differences underlie the observed variation in the conditions of low-wage work. This would be difficult or even meaningless if we were comparing radically different economic systems.

Here is one example of commonality that illustrates the point. In some of the target jobs, in several instances and several countries, there has been a noticeable increase in the intensity of competition in the relevant product market. Low-cost German chains compete with Dutch food retailers. Large food retailers, domestic and foreign, put pressure on meat processing and confectionary prices in every country. The spread of international hotel chains—along with the availability of exhaustive price comparisons on the internet—has made the hotel business more competitive. In all such instances, business firms respond to intensified competition by trying to lower their own unit costs (as well as by product differentiation, quality improvement, and other devices).

The urgent need to reduce costs seems almost invariably—though not exclusively—to involve particular pressure on the wages of low-skilled workers. It is not hard to understand why this should happen in every country, precisely because they are all advanced capitalist market economies. The main reason is that low-wage workers usually have very little "firm-specific human capital." That is to say, since they have few skills of any kind, they have few skills that are difficult to replace for the firm that employs them. If they quit in response to wage reductions, they can be replaced with little cost, especially in a slack labor market. Low-wage workers have few alternatives, so they cannot defend themselves well. For similar reasons, they have little political power and usually little clout with their trade unions, if they have any union protection at all. Firms seeking profit will respond similarly, though not identically in every detail. Country-specific institutions can modify the response, but not entirely.

A closely related common factor has to do with "flexibility." Partly because technology now permits it, and partly because a globalized market now demands it, business firms find that their level of production has to fluctuate seasonally, cyclically and erratically. Sometimes it is not so much the total but the composition of production that has to change, often with short notice. Under those circumstances, it is an advantage if the firm can vary its employment more or less at will; otherwise, underutilized labor constitutes an unproductive cost. The low-end labor force is likely to bear the brunt of this adjustment, for the same reasons already mentioned in connection with wage pressure. Low-wage workers cannot do much to defend themselves against or prepare themselves for these vicissitudes, other than to try for even lower-wage part-time jobs or to resort to public assistance.

There is always a possibility that observed cross-country variation in low-wage employment practices are somehow "natural," in the sense that they can be traced to underlying differences that were not chosen and could not be changed, such as geographical or topographical characteristics, resource availability, or perhaps even some irreversible bit of historical evolution. That does not seem to be what is happening in these six countries. In many instances, cross-country differences are the result of legislation, with minimum wage laws being an obvious example. A more unusual example, at least to Americans, is the fact that many European governments, such as those in France and the Netherlands, can and do extend certain collective bargaining agreements to cover employers and workers in the industry who were not parties to the bargaining itself. In this way, even comparatively small union density can lead to much broader coverage by union agreements.

This need not be an unalloyed benefit to workers. Companies have been known to arrange to bargain with a small, weak union and then press for the resulting favorable agreement to be generalized. But the practice may also reflect a desire by employers to eliminate large wage differentials as a factor in inter-firm competition. It is interesting that when the abolition of this practice of extending collective bargaining agreements was proposed in the Netherlands, the employers' federation opposed the proposal. It is a toss-up which event seems more outlandish to an American: the practice of mandatory extension or that employers should oppose abolishing it.

Explicit legislation is not the only source of institutional differences that affect the low-wage labor market. All sorts of behavioral norms, attitudes, and traditions on both sides of the labor market can have persistent effects. The country narratives describe many such influences. For example, the German report outlines a distinctive system of wage determination and labor relations, based on diversified high-quality, high-value-added industrial production, along with "patient," mostly bank-provided, capital, and participation of employee representatives in company supervisory boards.

This system may be coming to an end, undermined by international competition—especially from the ex-communist countries of eastern Europe, including the reunification of Germany—and shifts in public opinion and political power. It is still a matter of controversy among specialists whether the traditional system had become unsustainable or simply unsustained. The German "mini-job," low wage, frequently incurring lower non-wage employment costs in practice, and limited to very short hours per month, is an example of a device to encourage both demand and supply for certain kinds of low-wage work.

This introduction is not the place for a detailed description of each national system. The individual country narratives will provide that. It is important, however, to underline the fact that the components of each national system often hang together in some way. It may not be possible to single out one component and think: "That looks clever; why don't we try it in our country?" The German mini-job, for example, is occupied mostly by women, and may work the way it does because the social welfare apparatus in Germany is still organized around the notion of the single-breadwinner family. The concept of a labor relations "system" may suggest tighter-fitting than the facts justify; a word like "pattern" might be more accurate. But the basic point remains.

The four continental countries in the study correspond in a general way to the common notion of a "European social model" in contrast with the more individual-responsibility oriented approach of the United States. The post-Thatcher United Kingdom probably falls somewhere in between. It would be a bad mistake, however, to ignore the differences among Denmark, France, Germany, and the Netherlands. To do so would be to miss the variety of conditions for low-wage labor that is possible for advanced capitalist market economies. Only the briefest characterization is possible here, but the individual reports are quite complete.

The Danish "flexicurity" system has achieved the status of a buzzword. The idea is to allow wages and job quality to be determined in an unregulated labor market (except for considerations of health and safety, of course) but to combine this flexibility with a very generous safety net, so that "no Dane should suffer economic hardship." For this system to be workable, the rules of the safety net have to push most recipients into whatever jobs are available. Even so, the system is likely to be expensive. Apparently the *lowest* marginal income tax rate is 44 percent (which is higher than the *highest* rate in the U.S.). One would need to know more about the details of the tax system in order to understand the content of any such comparison, but the details are unlikely to reverse the presumption that Danes are less tax-averse than some others.

To describe the Danish labor market as "unregulated" means only that there is very little intervention by the government. In fact, the labor market is regulated through centralized negotiations between representatives of employers and employees, who have very wide scope. For example, there is no statutory minimum wage, but a minimum labor scale is negotiated by the "social partners." It (almost) goes without saying that there is some evasion of this scale in traditional low-wage sectors, including some covered in the case studies. One reason why this is tolerated is that many of the affected workers are young people, especially students, who are only engaged in low-wage part-time work as a transitory phase. Denmark is a country that is low on university enrollments but high on vocationally-oriented post-secondary, non-university education.

There is a neat contrast here with France, which lives up to its reputation as a rather bureaucratically organized society. As the French report says, "Low hourly wages are fixed in France—perhaps more than in any other country—at the political level, not through collective bargaining agreements, and these wage rates are set in a centralized, not decentralized, manner. Thus, the legal minimum wage plays a crucial role in France." Since 1970, the SMIC (minimum inter-branch growth wage) is indexed not only to inflation but also to the growth of overall productivity and wages. The intent was specifically to resist what was felt to be a tendency in the market toward excessive wage inequality.

The SMIC has been set at a fairly high level, and one consequence of this has been the disappearance of some unskilled jobs, to be replaced by unemployment (especially long-term unemployment), participation in active labor market policies, and withdrawal from the labor force. Other forces have been at work, however—urban land-use regulation in food retailing, for example—so the simple-minded causal connection between the SMIC and high unemployment is not exact. France is also distinguished by having a trade union movement that is rather strong at the national level, but has very little presence on the shop floor. This may account for some evasion of labor market regulations at the low end.

The low-wage labor market in the United Kingdom is especially interesting because it is an example of changes in institutions and outcomes brought about in a relatively short time by deliberate acts of policy. The Thatcher government chose as a matter of principle to weaken or eliminate preexisting supports for the occupants of low-quality jobs, and to undermine the ability of the trade union movement to compress the wage distribution. As a result, the incidence of low-wage work increased in the late 1970s and after. The Blair government, looking for a work-based solution to the problem of poverty, undertook measures to increase the supply of low-wage workers, but it also introduced a (fairly low) National Minimum Wage in 1999. The net outcome appears to have been a steady increase in the incidence of low-wage work from the late 1970s until the mid-1990s, and a leveling-off since then.

In effect, the United Kingdom has changed from a system rather like the other continental European countries to something much closer to the United States. The incidence of low-wage work has then followed the same trajectory. Of course, other economic factors, common to many countries, were also at work.

The Netherlands occupies a position somewhere between the Nordic model and the United States model, but not in a simple average sense. Many of the institutions are peculiarly Dutch; together they are described as the "Polder" model. One of its features is the important extent to which organizations representing employers, the government, and labor act jointly to regulate the labor market and much else, sometimes in a very detailed way. For instance, the minimum wage for young workers is substantially lower than for adults. The proliferation of part-time jobs, many of them occupied by students and young people, may be a consequence of this in part, though it may have other roots as well.

It is striking to an outsider that these tripartite institutions are more than merely regulatory. They are described as "deliberative," and apparently much of the serious public discussion of issues underlying socioeconomic policy takes place within them. This fact may make fairly tight regulation palatable to the Dutch public. The system has had considerable success; for example, the national unemployment rate fell from over 10 percent in 1984 to under 4 percent in 2001, when the widespread recession supervened. As will be seen in the Dutch report, however, it has its problems.

The purpose of these brief vignettes is definitely not to provide a summary of the pattern evolved in each of these countries with respect to low-wage job quality. That information is to be found in each of the separate country studies. The goal of this introduction is to illustrate the important general point that there are several viable systems of labor-market governance, including the mode of management of the low-wage labor market. The issue is not uniquely determined by the needs of a functioning market economy, or by technology, or by the imperatives of efficient organization. The system in place in each country has evolved in response to historical circumstances, cultural preferences, political styles and fashion in economic and social ideas. One cannot avoid noticing that relatively small countries, like Denmark and the Netherlands in our sample, and the other Nordic countries, Austria and perhaps Ireland outside it, seem more able than large countries to create and maintain the amount of trust that is needed for tripartite cooperation. This observation begs the question as to whether successful policy aimed at improving the relative status of low-wage workers may require a degree of social solidarity and trust that may be beyond larger, more diverse populations.

There are certainly many common influences as well: the response to intensified competition; the role of women, immigrants, and minorities; limitations on productivity; and so on. But there is no unique or best pattern. It even seems likely that the same "principles" of organization, applied in different institutional contexts, would eventuate in quite different practices. Some of this may emerge in the detailed comparative volume that is still to come.

Denmark has the lowest incidence of low-wage work among all the countries involved in this study—a little over 10 percent for women and a little over 6 percent for men in 2002. In addition, mobility out of low-wage work is very high in Denmark, probably the highest we have observed. To top it off, after a bad patch of unemployment in the early 1990s, Denmark has brought its unemployment rate down to well below the French and German levels, and only slightly above the U.S. level. So the pillar of the Danish labor market model generally known as "flexicurity" is now much discussed and possibly the object of imitation.

The basic idea behind flexicurity is that the labor market should be as free of state interference as possible, and most especially that it should operate without job protection regulations. As compensation, the social safety net for losers in the job market offers wide coverage and generous benefits. The explicit goal in Denmark is to ensure that no Dane experiences economic hardship. To make this work, pretty obviously, recipients of benefits must be required to accept any reasonable employment when employment is available, with few excuses accepted.

A system like this is inevitably expensive, and income tax rates in Denmark are certainly very high by American standards. An outsider is naturally led to wonder whether this style of economic policy is limited to small countries, where feelings of social solidarity may outweigh more individualistic patterns of political and economic behavior. That is not really an answerable question. It is worth pointing out, however, that Denmark's real growth rate in recent years, after allowing for demographic differences, compares favorably with the rest of the European Union. Real GDP (purchasing power parity prices) per hour worked is about 10 percent less than in the United States, and average annual hours worked are, again, 10 percent below the U.S. figure, which is quite comparable to the major EU economies.

Although the absolute incidence of low-wage work is low, as already mentioned, the pattern of concentration in various subgroups remains fairly typical. The incidence is *relatively* high among women, the young, those with only lower secondary education, and workers in the retailing, hotel, and restaurant industries. The concentration of low-wage work among the young is more extreme than elsewhere among the study countries. This fact is closely related to the high rate of mobility out of low-wage work in Denmark. Student status is a strong determinant of low-wage status.

Indicators of mobility are given in the findings reported in this volume. As a quick preview: of every one hundred Danes who were low-wage workers in 1995, only about ten remained in that status five years later. If there is a chronically low-wage population, it appears to be quite small. Most of the remainder are working at normal wages, with small fractions relegated to temporary or permanent transfer incomes.

The incidence of low-wage work among (non-Western) immigrants in Denmark is almost twice as high as it is among Danes (and among migrants from elsewhere in Europe). It is noteworthy that all of this difference refers to nonstudents; Danish and non-Western immigrant students have similar exposure to low-wage work. Remarkably, the overall rate of mobility out of low-wage work is very similar for immigrants and Danes, but the destinations are different: many more of the immigrants move to unemployment or social assistance, are enrolled in a training or other labor market program, or leave the labor force.

As already mentioned, the Danish model is one in which there is very little direct government intervention in the labor market. Regulation of the labor market is the outcome of bargaining between the "social partners": the trade unions and the employers' organizations. Collective bargaining covers much more than wage scales. The social partners bargain over normal hours, overtime, and working conditions; there is no statutory minimum wage, but there is an agreed minimum, currently about $15 an hour at the current exchange rate. This seems very high, but direct comparisons with, say, the United States are not meaningful without careful attention to differences in tax rates and the provision of public services. This agreed minimum wage is certainly not low, and it is probably violated in some of the low-wage sectors.

As we would expect in such a system, union density is high—about 80 percent. Workplace representation comes mainly through the election of shop stewards, who are in principle responsible to both the local constituency and the union. Apparently many large firms include worker representatives as regular members of the board of directors.

The Danish system is certainly exposed to the same strains as others, as the industry case studies show. Firms seek flexibility and higher productivity. Bargaining has become more decentralized to allow adaptation to local needs and circumstances. Labor market policies are now oriented more toward training than income maintenance. The pressures of international competition, including the possibility of outsourcing to Asia and eastern Europe, have created a need in Denmark, as elsewhere, for cost reductions, and Danish industries have responded in many of the same ways as seen elsewhere. One of the advantages of the comparative approach adopted in this study, however, is that it gives us a look at not only how different modes of organization work but also at the different ways in which they respond to similar strains.

CHAPTER 1

Low-Wage Work in Denmark

Niels Westergaard-Nielsen

This book attempts to describe the functioning of the Danish labor market mainly from the perspective of a low-wage earner. In describing conditions for low-wage workers in Denmark, the contributors to this volume focus especially on labor market institutions.

There are many differences between being a low-wage worker in Denmark and a low-wage worker in the United States. The low-wage level in Denmark is measured in this book at and below two-thirds of the median earnings, which by coincidence is just at the level of the median hourly earnings in the United States. If we adjust for lower purchasing power in Denmark, the Danish low-wage threshold is of course reduced. The main reason for this equality is that the wage distribution in Denmark is much more compressed than in the United States, which means that the difference between being in the lowest earnings decile and being in the highest is much smaller in Denmark. There are other important differences between Denmark and the United States: all Danish low-wage earners are covered by health insurance, and the effective marginal tax even for low-wage income earners is about 44 percent. In the United States, low-wage earners do not pay federal tax, and they often receive an income subsidy when they have a family to support, the Earned Income Tax Credit (EITC). In Denmark, there is a small tax deduction that works in the same way; in addition, most public services are free of charge because they are paid out of the public budget and financed by high taxes. Most importantly, education and health care are almost always free in Denmark.

Although the wages of low-wage Danish workers are high compared to the median wage in the United States, the average American still earns more than the average Dane because he or she works longer hours—on average about one-fifth more. Danes work a little less than the average European, and in Europe only Germans work fewer hours. The low number of hours worked in Denmark is a result of gradual reductions of weekly hours and increases in vacation time. Moreover, Danes tend to retire later than the average European but earlier than the average American. However, the number of working hours for each Danish household is higher than in most European countries because of the high female labor force participation rate.

The first two chapters of the book describe Danish institutions and how they influence the conditions in Denmark's labor market. This first chapter introduces the themes we cover, and the next chapter goes into more detail about Danish institutions and legislation and their effect on outcomes for low-wage workers. These first two chapters are based on public statistics and government register–based statistics on individuals. The remaining chapters in the book are based on interviews with workers in selected industries that in other countries are known for employing many low-wage workers: the food industry, the retail sector, hotels, hospitals, and call centers.

LOW-WAGE WORK IN THE DANISH CONTEXT

Low-wage work has long been a central issue in Danish welfare policies at different levels. Trade unions, political parties, and a long succession of governments have contributed to the debate over this issue in different ways. The generally accepted policy has been to let the labor market pay the salaries that can be justified from the value of production while the government provides social assistance and makes other welfare transfers to people who cannot support themselves by working. Maintaining this welfare system has over time become a high-priority issue for most political parties, with the result that today no Danish political party is making serious attempts to limit welfare policies. The trade unions have been key advocates for low-wage workers; for many rounds of central bargaining, the unions' goal was to push up the lowest wages, in particular the wages of women. Related efforts were the introduction of a minimum tariff (wage) and the adoption of an equal pay act for men and women.

In the following, we take an introductory tour through the institutions that are important for low-wage Danish workers. More thoroughly documented in chapter 2, these institutions play important roles in the case reports in subsequent chapters.

BACKGROUND

Denmark has a long tradition through its welfare policies of supporting those who cannot make a decent living in the market. Thus, conditions for low-wage earners and the provision of income transfers through welfare policies aimed at them are closely related in Denmark. Before the end of the nineteenth century, the state was subsidizing old-age pensions at a low level and also subsidizing the sickness insurance systems that prevailed at the time.

The first public old-age pension was based on an applicant's need, which was evaluated by the authorities, but anyone over the age of sixty-five could apply, regardless of previous work experience and contributions. Finally, in 1957, everyone over the age of sixty-seven was granted the right to a minimum pension irrespective of their prior income or the income they might have been receiving along with the pension. The minimum pension could be supplemented with means-tested extra benefits related, for example, to health, housing and heating, and that system is close to what is still in place today.

Sickness insurance and unemployment insurance were originally organized as private insurance based on guild membership, so prior to the twentieth century it was available only to the few and mainly to high-wage workers. Sickness insurance specifically for the poor and mandatory work accident insurance was introduced before the turn of the century. In 1907 a law creating an unemployment insurance (UI) system was passed in the Parliament. The law included a state subsidy and provided for a substantial trade union influence on the management of UI funds. Indeed, because management of the UI funds was based on the old privately organized system, a strong relationship was maintained between the trade unions and the public UI system. Unemployment insurance has remained more or less the same over the years, with only two major changes: sickness insurance has been taken over by the state, and in the late 1960s daily pay was increased to a maximum of 90 percent of an individual's previous salary, though a relatively low upper absolute ceiling was also established. These benefit amounts have since been regulated according to either a wage index or the consumer price index. All benefit payments are now also subject to taxation.

For low-wage workers, this system has resulted in a relatively high replacement ratio in the event of unemployment or sickness.[1] However, it has also kept their incentive to seek work relatively low. At the same time, it is an important feature of the Danish system that income transfers for workers who are covered by the unemployment insurance system are not means-tested. This differs from the benefits for people between the ages of eighteen and sixty-five who are not insured and who may not take part in the labor force; all of their income transfers are means-tested. However, even their benefits are close to the level of unemployment benefits in the short term and close to the level of an old-age pension plus supplements according to need in the longer term. As discussed in greater detail in chapter 2, the result is that the lowest level of benefits sets a minimum standard for normal pay.

THE DANISH MODEL FOR ORGANIZING THE LABOR MARKET

In the thoroughly organized Danish labor market, labor market issues historically have been settled in centralized negotiations between employer and employee representatives without government interference. This is sometimes referred to as the "Danish model." The key ingredient in this model is the lack of government interference as the trade unions and the Danish Employers' Federation (DA)—the two so-called social partners—make agreements on most regulatory issues. The social partners not only bargain over wages and set wages but also make agreements on normal working hours and set rules, sometimes together with the government, to protect workers with respect to overtime and the work environment, including work-life balance issues.[2] Increasingly, these agreements are made at the firm or workplace level and advances are subsequently rolled out gradually over the whole organized labor market. An example of a difference between the Danish institutional structure and that of many other countries is that there is no minimum wage in Denmark, but the social partners negotiate a minimum tariff for all jobs at member firms, and as we shall see, most nonmember firms adhere to this minimum tariff as well.

The higher inclination in the European Union to legislate on rules is a constant challenge to the Danish system, and Denmark's trade unions and the Employers' Federation have had to expend much effort over the years in defending the Danish system of self-governance. The EU has made the pragmatic decision to accept the special

Danish nonlegislated solutions as long as a clear majority of workers are covered by union agreements. This resolution has given rise, however, to some problems in smaller corners of the labor market where relatively few workers are organized.

The negotiation of all issues related to the labor market by the labor market institutions without political interference is the defining feature of the so-called Danish model. However, two important caveats should be pointed out. First, both explicitly and implicitly, the government does interfere occasionally in labor market negotiations. Second, the social partners do not arrive at collective bargaining agreements independently of political considerations, as exemplified by how they agreed on a minimum tariff.

THE MINIMUM WAGE

One of the clearest consequences of the Danish model is that Denmark does not have a minimum wage law, as many other countries do. Nevertheless, employers responded to union pressure at the general wage bargaining in 1977 and agreed on a minimum tariff covering all employees of members of the Danish Employers' Federation. The employers made this concession because they expected wages to grow so much over the next couple of years that the bad effects of the minimum tariff on employment would quickly be offset as other wages increased even more. This expectation made sense because wage inflation in those years was substantial.

Though not all Danish employers are members of the Employers' Federation, the minimum tariff was quickly recognized by most employers, since the trade unions were quick to make it known if an employer did not pay the minimum agreed standard pay in areas where there was no collective agreement and to threaten strikes or work blockages. Register data show that there are still some substandard wages and employment conditions in the restaurant, retail, and cleaning industries, probably because unions are relatively weak in these areas and because they employ a lot of young people, among whom are many students (as demonstrated in chapter 2). In our case studies in chapters 4 and 5, and in the case studies on retail establishments and hotels in particular, we did not find substandard wages, though employment conditions were not always up to the union standard.

Equal Wages

The trade unions viewed the introduction of a minimum tariff as a victorious step in their ongoing struggle to raise the wages of low-wage workers, who were concentrated among women and low-skilled men. The new wage policy, called the "solidarity wage policy," negotiated the same absolute pay increase for female workers as for groups of higher-wage workers, such as metalworkers. Of course, the result was that soon after the contract went into effect, the much more strongly organized metalworkers negotiated a higher wage locally and thus reestablished the previous wage differentials. Some critics said that the unions used the solidarity wage policy as a tool to get higher wages for their insiders. However, over a number of years the wage gap between women and men actually narrowed, and by 1990 the wage differential had been reduced to about 18 percent.[3] Finally, in 1976, a bill was passed in the Parliament that forbade paying men and women differently for identical work.

Since then, gender differences with respect to wages have not moved much. The main difference now is that some types of work are still mainly considered female work, such as cleaning rooms in hotels and hospitals, as demonstrated in the case studies in chapters 5 and 6. Furthermore, the low-paying public sector is still dominated by female employees, while the opposite is true in the higher-paying private sector. Unlike in the United States, however, low-skilled workers in the Danish public sector generally do not earn more than their counterparts in the private sector. In Denmark, work conditions in the public sector used to be better and the working hours more flexible, with the result that low-skilled new mothers tended to move from the private sector whenever they could get a job in the public sector. This has changed somewhat over the last ten years, so that now many private jobs have the same or better work conditions to offer. Nevertheless, many consider even low-paid jobs in the public sector attractive because job content and the work environment are more meaningful than is found with similar work in the private sector.

Union Strength

Judging from the very high membership rate on the workers' side—86 percent of all Danish workers are members of unions—one might get the impression that unions are strong in Denmark. Unions also have had a large influence on welfare policy, both as a labor market institution and as a close ally of the Social Democratic Party, which has been in the government more than any other party since the 1930s.

Unions are important for most workers since their shop steward is usually their representative with management. Thus, trade unions play an everyday role at many workplaces and are generally well accepted among employers and non-organized workers as well. Unions in Denmark operate differently from unions in both Germany—where the works councils can have representatives who do not represent the union because they are elected at the firm level and can be independent of the union—and France, where trade unions may not be represented at the firm or plant level at all.

In more recent years, wage bargaining has become much more decentralized in Denmark, and though this shift has weakened both the Employers' Federation and the trade unions as organizations, the unions now seem to be stronger at the firm level. Nevertheless, the recent ruling by the European Human Rights Court outlawing closed-shop agreements has given some workers, especially those in retail and food production, one less reason to be union members.

Unions have had difficulty recruiting young workers in recent years, and perhaps because they have apparently not been active in youth labor markets, there is an increasing concentration of low-wage jobs in those markets. This change is reflected in the case studies, which show that more and more jobs in the retail, hotel, and call center industries have been taken over by young people, especially students. Many of these workers do not expect to stay in the business and are therefore less likely to become union members. It should be noted that younger workers do not seem to have squeezed out older workers from these industries. If any group has suffered from the influx into these industries of young workers it is immigrants, who have difficulty retaining employment (see chapter 2). Furthermore, the steep union membership fee is yet another deterrent to membership among young low-wage workers. The youth labor market is discussed in more detail in chapter 2.

EMPLOYMENT PROTECTION RULES

Denmark has one of the lowest levels of employment protection in Europe. Blue-collar workers can usually be laid off on very short notice. The law gives white-collar workers and salaried employees in some occupations a period of notice before layoffs, depending on tenure (one month per year of employment, up to a maximum of nine months). There is no similar law for blue-collar workers, but some unions have negotiated a short period of notice in case of a lay-off as part of their contract. This system of little or no notice of layoff for many workers has been widely accepted among unions and legislators because it creates a flexible labor market that allows for the most efficient use of labor. For the trade unions, the compensating arrangement is probably the relatively high and readily available UI benefits.

Thus, Danish workers are clearly not as well protected as workers in the rest of Europe, and in some ways they are as unprotected as American workers, but the Danish income replacement system is much more generous. The result is that worker turnover is of the same magnitude as in the United States. Furthermore, workers always receive sickness pay, health insurance, unemployment benefits, and pensions independent of their employer and thus do not lose any coverage by moving from job to job.

The policy of combining flexibility and social security has in recent years been dubbed "flexicurity" and hailed in many European countries as a model conducive to job creation, structural change, and growth; the fact that Denmark has a low unemployment rate by international standards is taken by some as evidence in support of the virtues of this model. There is no doubt that the flexicurity model has some attractive properties. However, some caution should be taken in interpreting its supposed virtues (see, for example, Andersen and Svarer 2006). The elements of flexicurity have remained basically unchanged over several decades and were therefore in place during the period from the mid-1970s to the early 1990s when there were double-digit unemployment rates in Denmark. There may be other equally important explanations for Denmark's low unemployment rate related to the decentralization of wage bargaining and the close cooperation between employers and local trade union representatives, helped by a general sense of mutual trust in Danish workplaces. The fact that the Danish system has been more successful in recent years could also be related to changes in the administration of unemployment benefits: they have become less lenient, and the duration of benefits has been reduced from 9.4 years to 4 years. And finally, it should be mentioned that business cycles have been much better of late.

The interesting point, however, is that the Danish combination of United States–style flexibility and an extended welfare model can produce a relatively efficient labor market valued on the GDP per capita and the rate of unemployment. This finding is investigated further in chapter 2.

LOW-WAGE WORKERS AND LABOR MARKET INSTITUTIONS

The Danish welfare system is based on the principle that no citizen should suffer any economic hardship; thus, welfare benefits are intended to cover everybody. The system is probably itself an important institutional structure in that, compared to less generous welfare systems, it discourages many people from taking low-wage jobs because the option of getting UI or welfare benefits increases their reservation wage. This argument is strengthened for people with low earnings capacity (owing to low education, immigrant background, and so on). Hence, according to this view, only those who expect to move out of low-wage work relatively quickly are likely to accept a low-wage job.

The system of unemployment benefits is the other institution that may influence the number and behavior of low-wage earners. The UI system is different from the welfare system in that it is based on voluntary membership. Nevertheless, the majority of Danish workers are members and pay the premium, owing in large part to the state subsidy that enables members to pay only a fraction of the costs. When workers have been members and employed for a year, they gain eligibility for unemployment benefits. This waiting period is probably why some of the low-wage hotel and retail workers we met (see the case studies in chapters 4 and 5) are not members of the UI system. They simply do not expect to be in the same job one year later.

The unemployment system provides benefits for all periods of unemployment regardless of the household's income and wealth (unlike welfare benefits). For establishments, the system works like a subsidy for those who are temporarily laid off. For members, it could work like a subsidy that lowers the hours they work, as suggested in chapter 2. If productivity fluctuates over the year, employers have an incentive to hire low-productivity workers only for the periods when they are most productive and to lay them off during other periods. The result is fewer working hours for employees at the lower end of the wage scale. This system may actually mask low productivity: had there been no provisions for short-term unemployment, these workers might have received lower wages owing to their lower productivity, and they might have been characterized as low-wage workers.

The welfare system provides many other forms of temporary or permanent income transfers from the state, most of which are means-tested; these income transfers go only to people who are in demonstrable need. The main exception to the rule of means-testing is a program for early health-related retirement that provides income comparable to an old-age pension, so it is a very low amount for a young person. There is little doubt that this program may provide especially low-productivity workers with another exit, partly because they have the least to lose in qualifying for this program. Chapter 2 investigates whether this is really the case.

Another institution that could explain the high mobility of low-wage earners is the system of company-provided and government-supported training programs, both those related to existing jobs and those for the unemployed.

REGULATIONS AT THE WORKPLACE

It is probably typical of the Danish labor market model that there is often a local consensus, or even a more general consensus, about how to implement and improve on workplace regulations, even if this consensus is not explicitly formulated. Sometimes that consensus leads to a revision of the regulations. There are several examples of such revisions in the case studies, such as the ergonomic work conditions practiced in the call centers (chapter 7). Though it is not required that the desks in offices be electrically adjustable, most employees in the call center studies do have desks that can be adjusted this way. The reason is undoubtedly to show appreciation for workers so that they will stay longer. The bad workers can be laid off anyway. Working time and hours are also regulated by local agreements. In this area of regulation, there is a wide span of self-governance, and employees and employers make their own rules if necessary. In principle, this system is not much different from Germany's (see Ilsøe 2006), but the outcome often seems to be completely different because the Danish local arrangements have been made in an atmosphere of trust that helps all parties see that a particular ruling is a benefit for everyone.

TRUST

Trust is without a doubt an important condition for Danish local agreements. The local shop steward is instrumental: when he has a cooperative relationship with both management and the trade union, consensus is likely to be the outcome. In other cases, workers and management are less fortunate. The case studies provide several examples of how trust can be used. Another area in which trust is important is in decentralized wage bargaining, a process that has become more and more important recently. Trust in this context means that workers know that the employer's statements are honest.

Why should trust be any more important in Danish workplaces than in other, similar countries, such as the other Nordic countries? We can only speculate. First, Denmark has a long tradition of seeking peaceful solutions. The rules for handling labor conflict were established as early as 1899, and most of the country's labor market institutions were established at the beginning of the twentieth century. Denmark has also had no revolutions or civil wars, unlike Finland, for example. And unlike Sweden in the 1920s and 1930s, Denmark has had no labor uprisings. Furthermore, Denmark was only lightly influenced by the two world wars.

Second, Denmark encourages small firm structures, so that it has no big dominating firms as Sweden and Finland do. Small firms are probably much more dependent on good labor relations than big firms, and both management and workers are well aware of this.

Third, until recently the population has been very homogenous. People are more willing to share resources with less fortunate citizens when their commonalities remind them that it could be their own family in distress. This willingness to share leads to a greater acceptance of high taxes to pay for the extended welfare system than there would be in a less homogenous population.

More recently, as the number of immigrants has grown to 10 percent of the population, the cohesion of the Danes has clearly been challenged. The rising number of immigrants has spawned a right-wing political party that defends the welfare system for low-income groups even as it vigorously works to limit the number of immigrants and cut their benefits. The views of this party are supported to some extent by many other political parties, and as a result, Danish laws have been changed on a number of issues. This development is not unique to Denmark and can be found in many European countries. The core idea of this political movement is to maintain the present level of benefits but keep out immigrants so that welfare benefits are not diluted by distribution to too many people. This idea has long kept company with a trade union view that immigrants should not be allowed to take work away from Danes. Both arguments are hollow: the fact of the matter is that Denmark needs to reform its welfare system and also needs to recognize that, with its aging population, it needs the labor of immigrants because labor shortages will be the norm rather than the exception in the future.

This short discussion of labor market institutions has demonstrated that, even though institutions are an important factor in workplace conditions, what really matters is the input of workplace agents and the manner in which they manipulate conditions to benefit employers or employees. That said, it is probably also the case in Danish workplaces that the agents have trust in each other. The uniqueness of the Danish labor market also illustrates why it is so difficult to transplant so-called good institutions from one workplace to another or from one country to another.

LIVING STANDARDS

The interrelationship between low wages and the Danish welfare system makes it difficult to infer that to be a low-wage worker in Denmark is to be poor. In fact, low-wage workers are generally eligible for various in-kind and means-tested benefits, such as child subsidies, extra child subsidies if the parent is alone with the child, lower day care tuition payments, and certain housing benefits. These benefits (described in more detail in chapter 2) are also uniquely Danish in that they are given independently of the job and thus do not show up in the industry studies.

In addition to these benefits, Danish low-wage workers receive the free services of a welfare society: public schools that are free of charge, as are institutions of higher education; student grants to all students older than eighteen; subsidized child care; free health care (except dentists); and a pension system that gives a share to everybody. All these services and benefits are described and quantified in chapter 2.

The cost of Denmark's welfare society, of course, is a tax burden that is among the highest in the world. Even low-wage earners in

Denmark pay high taxes compared to their counterparts in most other countries.

The Jobless in Denmark and the "Penniless" in the United States

Owing to the high minimum standard of wages in Denmark, wages there are somewhat compressed in the bottom of the wage scale. However, the high minimum standard also means that many workers who should have been in the lowest part of the wage distribution are not: as explained earlier in the chapter, they have been priced out of the market because their productivity is not high enough to become employed. These are the workers who get by for shorter periods on unemployment benefits or who rely on social assistance if they are not eligible for unemployment benefits. Most of these unemployed Danes actually get a job after a while on benefits, because even if to an employer their productivity is not worth the wage all year, it may be in peak periods. In this way, the benefit works as a subsidy to both workers and employers.

If unemployed workers do not succeed in getting a job within a year, the unemployment system requires that they start on "activation" measures, perhaps in the form of education or training and perhaps in combination with a subsidized job. The benefit stops after a maximum of four years. (For youth below age twenty-five, the maximum duration of full benefits is six months.) If an unemployed worker cannot find a job after the expiration of unemployment benefits, the next step is social assistance, provided that the applicant and his or her spouse have no other income or wealth. From there the worker can apply for early retirement. In the next chapter, we look at how many Danes actually end up taking early retirement.

Another reason for not being able to meet productivity demands is poor health. A worker who is unemployed for this reason can apply for a health-related pension, which is provided by the state. About 22 percent of the total potential labor force (those age eighteen to sixty) are either on a disability pension or receiving other transfer income, and their situation is very different from that of the working poor in the United States. In chapter 2, we show that low-wage earners do receive early retirement benefits more frequently than other workers, though we are not able to state the direction of causation.

However, some people fall through the cracks and fail to receive any unemployment benefits, such as part-time workers, students, youth, and immigrants. These people are very likely to become low-wage workers, as we will see in chapters 4 (retail) and 5 (hotels). But they may not continue earning low wages for long, as demonstrated in chapter 2.

The main difference between unemployment benefits in the United States and in Denmark seems to be that Danes can receive benefits for four years whereas the period is only twenty-six weeks in the United States. Furthermore, the benefits are high in Denmark. On the other hand, though subsidized jobs are available for Danes who are handicapped or otherwise long-term unemployed, Denmark does not really have in-work-benefit programs such as those in the United States and the United Kingdom.[4] However, there are many other means-tested benefits in Denmark that are related to having a low in-come and that make the lives of low-earning Danes very different from the lives of low-wage Americans. These benefits are briefly dis-cussed in chapter 2.

Furthermore, it is hard for immigrants, who on average have lower skills than the Danes, to earn a living in Denmark because of the high threshold of earnings created by the welfare programs. As we would expect, the result is that the labor force participation and employ-ment rates of immigrants are much lower in Denmark than in the United States and the United Kingdom.

Overall, we might say that the low-skilled tend to be jobless in Denmark but not penniless, whereas in the United States the low-skilled tend to have a job but to be penniless. This characterization is not entirely accurate, however, because relatively more people are working in Denmark than in the United States and the unemploy-ment rate is lower in Denmark. Thus, this opposition between the penniless and the jobless does not work in absolute terms.

One of the more important features in this comparison between the United States and Denmark is the fact that jobs that tend to be low-wage in the former are not always low-wage in the latter. This is true, for instance, in the food-processing industry. The reasoning in Denmark is undoubtedly that offering low wages would attract only low-productivity workers and the result would be that the industry could not be run in a profitable way. The alternative is to use more capital and more expensive and more productive workers. The facts seem to support this view. Within the hotel cleaning and retail indus-tries, conditions seem to be more similar between the two countries, both of which offer low wages to workers in these industries. The interesting difference, however, is that Danes do not keep these jobs for long. One reason is that many of these jobs are taken by students who are working part-time. But turnover among even the nonstudents who take these jobs tends to be high. Most go to higher-wage jobs, but some leave for a life on transfer income, which is not possible in the United States. In chapter 2, we go into more detail about this transition.

With their high labor force participation rate, despite all the ways in which they make it possible to receive welfare or unemployment benefits, and with few low-wage workers, few high-wage workers, and vast homogeneity in the population, have the Danes really created the best of all possible worlds? Before attempting to answer this question, there are some critical issues to address. First, the income tax and the total tax level in Denmark are among the highest in the world. This undoubtedly has consequences for the labor supply, at least as measured in hours compared to other countries, as is demonstrated in chapter 2. With the high level of welfare and unemployment benefits, people are not very eager to get a job. Both of these issues—high tax levels and disincentives to work—have become more and more problematic for the growing group of immigrants who become discouraged workers (though on benefits) because their relatively low productivity makes it difficult for them to find jobs. The result is that only about 40 percent of all non-Western immigrants in Denmark work. Perhaps one of the worst consequences may be that their children do not grow up under the same conditions with working fathers and mothers as most other Danish children do. Indeed, even second-generation immigrants have a lower labor force participation rate than Danes.

Denmark's high income taxes and relatively high level of benefits are probably both issues in need of reform. Any discussion of those issues would be premature, however, without the detailed descriptions presented in the next chapter, which brings into relief other aspects of the Danish welfare society and provides more details on the economic conditions of low-wage workers in Denmark.

NOTES

1.   The replacement ratio is calculated as the UI benefit per hour divided by the previous wage per hour.

2.   One example is time off for a child's first day of sickness. This benefit
     is part of the general bargaining and is not subject to legislation. As a
     result, 7 to 8 percent of all Danish parents do not receive it. See chap-
     ter 5 for interviews with some hotel workers in this situation.
3.   This is lower than in the United States, where the wage differential be-
     tween men and women is 23 percent (Blau and Kahn 2000), but
     higher than in Sweden, where it is 16.5 percent.
4.   Denmark provides a small tax deduction for earnings compared to
     transfer income, as well as programs that give handicapped people a
     subsidy to work fewer hours.

REFERENCES

Andersen, Torben M., and Michael Svarer. 2006. "Flexicurity—den danska
   arbetsmarknadsmodellen" ["Flexicurity—The Danish labor market
   model"]. *Ekonomisk Debatt* 1: 17–29.
Blau, Francine D., and Lawrence M. Kahn. 2000. "Gender Differences in
   Pay." *Journal of Economic Perspectives* 14(4, Fall): 75–99.
Ilsøe, Anna. 2006. "Flexicurity paa virksomheden" ["Flexicurity at the establishment level"]. Working paper. Faos, University of Copenhagen.

CHAPTER 2

Statistical Analysis and History of Low-Wage Work in Denmark

Niels Westergaard-Nielsen

A t first sight, an outside observer might find that the Danish labor market looks like other labor markets in Europe and North America, but closer inspection would reveal a number of features that differentiate Denmark from other countries and sometimes even make it look more like one of the states of the United States—and sometimes the very opposite.

Perhaps the most prominent of those features is the central idea of the "Danish model": compared with many other countries, agreements between employers and trade unions in Denmark are more important as regulatory mechanisms than legislation and government interventions. These institutions also have more of an impact on incentives and work for low-wage earners than for other wage earners. Second, Danish labor market institutions date back to the beginning of the twentieth century or even earlier, a long history that has given rise to a strong tradition of seeking peaceful solutions to conflict and given all labor market parties an incentive to create resolutions that benefit everyone. A third important feature of the Danish labor market is the growing decentralization of wage bargaining, even as union membership remains high. Fourth, Danish welfare policies are comprehensive, and state expenditures on labor market programs are high; as a result, Denmark spends more on these programs than any other country. Finally, the level of employment protection is low in Denmark; with a level of employment protection comparable to that of the United States, Denmark consequently experiences worker turnover that is in the same league as the United States.

This chapter explains the role of Denmark's labor market institutions and presents evidence and statistical analyses that undergird the following chapters on specific industries. Furthermore, it explains how Denmark's welfare system and labor market institutions set the conditions for the low-wage labor market. After a brief introduction to the Danish economy, the chapter describes the Danish labor market and industrial relations before going on to discuss its labor market institutions in some detail. After that is a discussion of how low-wage employment has developed in Denmark over the last twenty years, followed by a section on mobility out of low-wage work and the interaction between mobility out of low-wage work and the welfare system. The last section discusses the costs of Danish labor market policies and possible reforms.

THE DANISH ECONOMY

Throughout most of the twentieth century, Denmark has experienced relatively high and stable GDP growth and maintained a remarkable record of staying among the countries with the highest GDP per capita. Today Denmark's GDP per capita is about 81 percent of the American level, using purchase power correction (see table 2.1). This GDP per capita is due to an annual work effort measured in hours that is 89 percent of the level in the United States and productivity that is also 89 percent of the American level.

As in many other industrialized countries, growth in Denmark became relatively more unstable after the oil crisis of the 1970s. The 1980s started with low growth, which quickly led to an overstimulation of consumption, a subsequent overheating of the labor market, and a deterioration of the balance of payment. A genuine recession ensued, partly created by an austerity policy intended to improve the balance of payment and curb the expectations of wage inflation. The balance-of-payment problems disappeared slowly during this period because firms became more competitive, but unemployment soared. The turning point came in 1994, when employment and economic growth started rising again. From then on, the balance of payment turned positive—partly because of oil revenue from the Danish North Sea sector and partly because of the expansion of markets in Germany and eastern Europe after the fall of the Iron Curtain—the wage drift expectations were curbed, and unemployment started coming down again.

The role of oil revenues in the Danish economy has been like a sweetener: oil's share of GDP increased from less than 1 percent in 1990 to 3 percent in 2004. The important point is that oil and gas revenues have created a nice buffer on the trade balance, accounting for 8 percent of total exports in 2004. On the tax side, 2 to 3 percent of

Table 2.1 GDP per Capita in Denmark Compared with
          the United States (Purchase Power Corrected),
          2005

	Denmark	United States
GPD per capita (national currency)	DKK270,304	US$39,732
GDP per capita (ppp)	$32,141	$39,732
GDP per capita (ppp), index USA = 100	81	100
Annual hours worked (average)	1,540	1,731
Annual hours worked, index USA = 100	89	100
GDP per hours worked, index USA = 100	89	100

Source: OECD (2006).

all taxes are collected through the production of crude oil and natural gas. What is new, however, is that Denmark has not allowed these advantages to slip away in the form of higher wages and inflation, as usually happened in the past when the economy grew. In 2006 Denmark still had a trade surplus, the government had not raised taxes, and it had been able to run a surplus on the budget; as a result, public debt had been reduced significantly. One explanation for Denmark's surpluses is that the labor market seems to run more smoothly

Table 2.2 GDP Growth in Denmark, EU-15, and the
          United States, 1992 to 2005

	1992 to 2001	2003	2004	2005
Denmark				
GDP	2.3	0.7	2.4	2.4
Employment	0.4	−1.1	0.1	0.3
Labor force	0.0	−0.1	0.3	0.1
EU-15				
GDP	2.2	0.9	2.0	1.4
Employment	0.8	0.3	0.8	0.6
Labor force	0.7	0.7	0.7	0.8
United States				
GDP	3.2	3.0	4.4	3.6
Employment	1.4	0.9	1.1	1.6
Labor force	1.2	1.1	0.6	1.2

Source: OECD (2005a).

with more decentralization of wage bargaining and a tightening of unemployment policies, as discussed in chapter 1.

As is clear from its more recent growth patterns, Denmark cannot match the United States in GDP growth, partly owing to its smaller labor force and lower population growth, but Denmark more than keeps up with EU-15 in GDP growth. Furthermore, like the United States, Denmark has seen its employment rate grow more than its labor force, which confirms the decline in unemployment in the period from 1992 to 2001.

EMPLOYMENT IN DENMARK COMPARED TO THE UNITED STATES

From an international perspective, Danish labor force participation is high even compared to the United States (see table 2.3). More than 80 percent of Danes between the ages of fifteen and sixty-four participate in the labor force, whereas the comparable number is almost 5 percent lower in the United States. The main difference is seen among women: with its high-quality child care facilities, Denmark has enjoyed a long tradition of female participation in the labor force. If we look at differences by age group, we see that more young and middle-aged Danes participate in the labor force than their American counterparts, but that this difference becomes somewhat smaller for the older group. One reason for high labor force participation among Danes is that the welfare system provides incentives to work (as explained later in the chapter), but participation is especially high among young people because of a strong tradition of high school graduates taking a job before entering university, combined with a large apprenticeship program that employs about 40 percent of Danish youth. These factors also have a great impact on the youth unemployment rate.[1] Finally, it is worth noting that the labor force participation rate for people with less than an upper secondary education is relatively low in Denmark, and only slightly higher than in the United States. The reason for this low rate is that this group tends to find low-wage work and the welfare system in Denmark provides low-wage workers with relatively attractive alternatives to working.

In recent years, the unemployment rate has become relatively low in Denmark; in fact, it is now among the lowest in Europe and even lower than the unemployment rate in the United States. Around 1992, however, it was in double digits and among the highest in Eu-

Table 2.3 Labor Force Participation, Employment, and
Unemployment in Denmark and the United
States, 2004

	Labor Force Participation		Employment Rate		Unemployment Rate	
	Denmark	United States	Denmark	United States	Denmark	United States
Whole population (fifteen to sixty-four years old)	80.2%	75.4%	76.0%	71.2%	5.3%	5.6%
Gender						
Men	84.2	81.9	79.9	77.2	5.2	5.7
Women	76.1	69.2	72.0	65.4	5.5	5.5
Age						
Fifteen to twenty-four years old	66.4	61.1	61.3	53.9	7.8	11.8
Twenty-five to fifty-four years old	88.2	82.8	84.0	79.0	4.7	4.6
Fifty-five to sixty-four years old	65.5	62.3	61.8	59.9	5.6	3.8
Education (2003)						
Upper secondary school or less	65.4	64.1	60.7	57.8	7.2	9.9
Upper secondary school	83.6	78.0	79.9	73.3	4.4	6.1
Tertiary education	89.4	85.1	85.2	82.2	4.7	3.5

Source: OECD (2005a).

rope. Since then, Danish economic growth has stepped up and the government has tightened up its labor market policies. These are not, however, the only reasons for the improved unemployment figures; as we will see later in the chapter, Danes' growing participation in labor market programs and the increase in the rate at which they exit the labor force to take early retirement have also played significant roles in reducing Denmark's unemployment rate.

Comparing the unemployment distribution across age groups, we find that institutional policies are partly responsible for different unemployment rates at different ages. Thus, the lower Danish unemployment rate among the young is partly due to limited access to unemployment benefits up to the age of twenty-five; in addition, the

Danish apprenticeship system keeps the young employed. For the older group, institutional policies work the other way around. The Danish unemployment benefit rules and the so-called post-employment wage, which can be obtained after the age of sixty, keep people in the labor force until the age of sixty and then give them an incentive to retire quickly after they reach that age.

THE DANISH WELFARE SYSTEM

The Danish welfare system covers everybody in the country because it is based on the principle that no citizen should suffer any economic hardship. As an important institutional structure, this system probably discourages many people from taking a low-wage job; a less generous welfare system would not provide UI or welfare benefits that increase each individual's reservation wage. The argument that the Danish welfare system provides disincentives to take low-wage work is even stronger with respect to workers with a low earnings capacity (because of low education, immigrant background, and so on). Hence, according to this view, only those who expect to move out of low-wage work relatively quickly are likely to accept a low-wage job.

One important effect of this disincentive is that low-wage jobs in Denmark rely on a much higher minimum skills standard in workers compared to the equivalent jobs in, for example, the United States. Even though the formal educational level is higher in the United States, the minimum skill level among employed individuals is likely to be higher in Denmark, simply because the bottom of the Danish skill distribution never reaches the labor market. This fact probably explains the strategies observed with several of the case study firms (see especially chapters 3, 4, and 7 on the food-processing industry, the retail sector, and call centers), namely, that many employers choose to upgrade their skill demands for low-wage jobs and create a career path for these employees.

INDUSTRIAL RELATIONS

Taken at face value, the Danish labor market has more in common with the United States labor market than with those of the central European countries because of the lack of direct government intervention in rules and functioning. One major difference between Denmark and the United States, however, is that Danish trade unions play a big role in deciding how workers are treated and remunerated at the workplace level. This pattern differs from, say, France, where unions play a role at the central level but not at the workplace level. Another difference from the United States is that the Danish government pays a relatively high benefit when people are out of work, and if needed, it supplies training for those who are out of work.

The key ingredient in the "Danish model" is that Danish trade unions and the Danish Employers' Federation (the social partners) negotiate over most of the regulatory issues, and the role of the government is to "pay the bill." The social partners are responsible for wage bargaining and wage setting. They also make agreements concerning normal working hours and set rules for labor protection with respect to overtime and work environment. Another feature of the Danish model is the lack of minimum wage laws. Nevertheless, the social partners have agreed that no member firm will pay less than €12.00 (DKK 89.50, or about US$16.20) [2] per hour (2005). To the basic wage is added the vacation pay of 15 percent, which is set by law; altogether the effective minimum wage is about €13.80 (US$18.64) per hour. The Employers' Federation does not include all Danish employers, but the unions are quick to identify companies that pay less than the minimum tariff. Anecdotal evidence has it that this happens most often in the unorganized parts of the retail sector and at hotels and restaurants. However, the case studies did not provide any firm evidence of wages lower than the tariff.

The role of the Danish government is to provide unemployment benefits and to retrain workers who have lost their jobs owing to low productivity. The government also provides health care and disability pensions. In other words, the government provides the safety net. Those who are not covered by unemployment insurance are usually eligible for social assistance, which is equal to the UI benefit at its lowest level, the main difference being that all payments are means-tested.

Because the Danish and Swedish labor market models have many features in common, they are sometimes termed the "Nordic labor market model." The main idea is that whenever companies find that they are unable to keep workers productive in their current jobs, it is the role of the government to take over and retrain those workers. Having gone through retraining, workers are assumed to be more productive and thus more attractive to a new firm; thus, overall productivity is increased. The efficiency of this turnaround, however, is questionable. It is a fact that a substantial number of workers find it hard to reenter employment after they have lost their job (Ibsen and Westergaard-Nielsen 2005).

Despite their similarities, there are also differences between the Danish and Swedish models. One of these is that the Danish model allows layoffs, whereas the Swedish model is considerably more restrictive in this respect. The Danish model holds that companies should not be forced to maintain a large workforce if it is no longer profitable to do so and that when workers are rehired where their productivity is higher, society at large benefits because overall flexibility and productivity are increased. Of course, this policy also puts a burden on workers in the form of income loss and search time for a new job.[3] That burden is probably the main rationale for the relatively high unemployment benefit in Denmark (at least for low-wage earners). Another difference is that the Swedish model builds even more on a tripartite cooperation among government, unions, and employers.

EMPLOYEE ORGANIZATIONS

In Denmark, about 80 percent of all employees are members of a trade union. This high membership rate is partly a consequence of a close informal relationship between the UI benefits system and the unions (the so-called Ghent system), though there is no direct legal connection between the two systems. However, union membership and unemployment insurance coverage are usually solicited as a joint package. Furthermore, many individuals have worked as both trade union officials and administrators in the UI system, and these roles are often related. Thus, potential union members often consider UI coverage part of the package of union membership. High membership rates are also found in four other countries that have a similar relationship between unions and their UI system: Belgium, Sweden, Iceland, and Finland. By contrast, the union rate is only about 50 percent in Norway, where unemployment insurance is part of the welfare system (Neumann, Pedersen, and Westergaard-Nielsen 1991). Besides this mechanism, some trades have closed-shop contracts that restrict the jobs to members of a particular trade union. Such agreements have been quite standard within some industries, especially the food-processing industry (see chapter 3). In 2006, however, closed-shop agreements were outlawed by the European Human Rights Court.

Among the case study target groups, we find that the union membership rate among hotel housekeepers is particularly low and that only a few are members of the unemployment insurance system. The union membership rate is much higher for all other kinds of workers in the industry studies except students.

Danish unions are traditionally organized by trade (skills and level). Skilled workers (those who served an apprenticeship) used to have their own union separate from nonskilled workers within the same industry. To some extent this traditional division of members is also related to wage differentials in the sense that some unions have more low-wage members than others.

Almost all workers' unions are members of the umbrella organization Landsorganisationen i Danmark (LO, the Danish Confederation of Trade Unions). Thus, LO represents about 53 percent of all wage earners. LO used to be a powerful, overarching union that did most of the bargaining on the workers' side, but it has now handed over much of that power to member unions as part of a general decentralization. Most non-LO unions are unions for supervisors at various levels, university graduates, and civil servants. The primary unions representing low-wage workers are the United Federation of Danish Workers (3F), the Danish Union of Public Employees (FOA), and the Union of Commercial and Clerical Employees in Denmark (HK), and they are all members of LO. These unions represent workers in the meat industry, hospitals, and the retail industry, among many others.

Instead of works councils, as in Germany, Denmark has a system of shop stewards at all large workplaces. The trade union members at a workplace elect or appoint a shop steward as their spokesperson and negotiator in dealings with management. The shop steward also represents the local workers by representing the trade union. This arrangement is different than in Germany, where a shop steward would not necessarily represent the union, and different from France, where workplaces have a local union representative. In Denmark, if a workplace employs workers from many trade unions, one of the shop stewards may be elected to represent all of them.

Furthermore, employee representatives serve on the boards of most large shareholding companies in Denmark. Although they represent the employees, they are clearly governed by the same set of norms and bylaws as other board members, especially those having to do with confidentiality, personal integrity, and responsibility.

Employers' Organizations

Employers also have a number of their own organizations. The umbrella employer organization is the Danish Employers' Federation (DA). DA consists of individual employers and industry-related employers' federations. The most important of these are the Confederation of Danish Industries (DI) and Danish Trade and Service. Danish employers are significantly less organized than Danish workers.

Collective Agreements

Wage setting in Denmark has undergone huge changes in recent years. Wage bargaining in the manual labor market used to be highly centralized, with biannual wage bargaining sessions between LO and DA and between the unions of the public employees and the government. Though some groups still use the old system, the new system is much more decentralized; the central level deals only with nonwage issues such as pensions, working hours, and vacation. All wage bargaining has been moved to lower-level organizations, to the company level, or even to the individual level. This transformation has happened gradually, but it picked up speed at the negotiations in 1993.

Over the last few two-year contract periods, the wage bargaining system has increasingly become a "minimum pay system": typically only the lowest wage is negotiated, and the employee negotiates additional pay directly with his or her employer with the assistance of the union representative. Thus, in 2004, 22 percent of all contracts in the organized labor market did not mention workers' wages at all (Danish Employers' Federation 2005); in those cases, the wage had to be agreed upon between the employer and the employee. In about 60 percent of all contracts, the lowest pay was specified, it being explicitly assumed that additional pay was going to be negotiated.

The result has been increased possibilities for agreeing on special local wage systems and for introducing new performance-related pay packages, including bonuses. In theory, the newly decentralized wage bargaining system could be used to lower the base wage and put a larger part of the business risk on the worker. This seems not to be the case, however, though there are clearly now more groups of workers and more firms in Denmark that have negotiated performance-related pay (Eriksson and Westergaard-Nielsen 2003).

Though many employees nowadays are "salaried" and thus paid

by the month, especially supervisors, managers, and others who work in administration, wages for most manual workers are calculated by the hour. This means that overtime is normally remunerated at a higher rate. (It is worth noting that because of the shorter work-week in Denmark, the overtime rate kicks in earlier there than in the United States.) Overtime for salaried employees is remunerated with extra pay, no pay, or time off. However, the whole concept of overtime is also gradually changing: most local agreements now define the workweek as thirty-seven hours on average, counted over one year or more. We see this change in our case studies of the retail industry (chapter 4) and the food-processing industry (chapter 3); hospitals (chapter 6), by contrast, have always had varying work schedules.

While wage setting has been decentralized in the private labor market, public-sector wage bargaining is still highly centralized, with central negotiations every two years (covering the hospitals in our industry cases). However, a new wage system has been introduced into the public sector. Called "new-wage," it has decreased the number of steps on the wage ladder, and it allows for local agreements and also, on a fairly limited scale, for various sorts of individual wage premiums related to performance. Nevertheless, since the public sector has always had a career system—promotions have always been dependent to some extent on performance—these changes may not be that significant.

Employment Protection

Denmark has one of the lowest levels of employment protection in Europe. Most blue-collar workers can be laid off at very short notice, which could be anywhere from a few days to three months, depending on the length of tenure and the union contract. By law (the Salaried Workers Act), white-collar workers and salaried employees in some occupations are secured a period of tenure-dependent notice in case of layoffs (one month per year of employment up to a maximum of nine months). There is no comparable law protecting blue-collar workers in that respect, but as part of their contracts some unions have negotiated for longer periods of notice in case of a layoff. However, short or nonexistent notice has been widely accepted among unions and legislators because it creates a flexible labor market that permits the most efficient use of labor. For the trade unions, the compensation is probably the high UI benefit, which is relatively lower for higher-wage salaried employees, and this is probably also one reason why there is slightly better legal protection for white-collar workers. The other reason may be that presumably it takes a white-collar worker somewhat longer to find a new job.

One of the immediate costs of low employment protection is undoubtedly higher turnover. Danish turnover is as high as 27 percent on average (Ibsen and Westergaard-Nielsen 2005) and in general is of the same magnitude as in the United States. The major difference between the two countries, however, is that Danish labor market institutions are attuned to this high turnover rate to a much higher degree than American institutions. First, health insurance is administered independent of the workplace; vacation pay and pension are also independently administered; and finally, unemployment benefits provide a much better cushion for workers who cannot find new employment immediately.

Turnover is somewhat higher for young people and in particular for people with less than two years of employment. In fact, the probability that an individual who has worked in the same job for five years will stay in that job for another five years is 50 percent (Eriksson and Westergaard-Nielsen 2007). Turnover does not differ much across occupational groups. Turnover is also remarkably lower for people who are members of the UI system than for those who are not, owing to the type of people who become insured (Ibsen and Westergaard-Nielsen 2005.) This difference in turnover rates is clearly seen when we compare employees at hotels and in the food industry in the following chapters. Job changes are also found to be closely related to wage growth. For instance, Paul Bingley and I (Bingley and Westergaard-Nielsen 2006) have found that about one-third of all wage growth for fifty-year-old employees is related to changing employers. Another interesting aspect of Denmark's high turnover rate is its connection to the high rate of mobility out of low-wage jobs. Workers do this by using the UI system to cover many short spells of unemployment, the cost of which is that Danes work a relatively low number of hours.

Thus, on the one hand, young people seem to carry the immediate burden of low job protection. On the other hand, it is probably also one of the reasons why youth unemployment is as low as 3 percent, compared with more than 20 percent in many EU countries. Of course, there are other reasons for low unemployment among Danish youth, the most important being the Danish apprentice system; that alone probably explains why young Danes have a lower unemployment rate than young people in the United States. But we may conclude that greater employment flexibility (and higher turnover) in Denmark does not lead to higher unemployment. And interestingly enough, there is less concern about job security in Denmark than is the case in Great Britain, which also has fairly high worker turnover (Kristensen and Westergaard-Nielsen 2004).

In recent years the Danish labor market has become internationally famous for its "flexicurity" model: as discussed in chapter 1, this model combines *flexible* hiring and firing rules for employers and a social *security* system for workers. As previously mentioned, many observers have taken flexicurity as a model conducive to job creation, structural change, and growth, and they look at Denmark's low unemployment rate as evidence in support of the model. However, the flexicurity model has basically been in place over several decades, including the period of extremely high unemployment rates from the mid-1970s to the early 1990s. It should also be noted that the main change made since that period was the introduction of new labor market policies during the 1990s, including in particular a shorter duration for unemployment benefits. Moreover, despite the reduction in the official unemployment rate, there has been no corresponding fall in the number of people who are dependent on public transfers. Hence, the "road back to a job" has not been sufficiently well marked, and a substantial number of Danes continue to have difficulties getting back into employment if they lose their job (Ibsen and Westergaard-Nielsen 2005).

SOCIAL CONTRIBUTIONS AND TAXES

In Denmark, tax payments cover all contributions to publicly provided health care, pensions, benefits, schooling at all levels, and other social services. The first tax rate is 8 percent of all gross earnings. This tax is deductible from the taxable income. The second type of tax is an income tax, with a tax-free allowance of about €5,000 (US$6,700). After the 8 percent tax on the first €5,000, marginal tax rates then progress in three steps: 44 percent from €5,000 to €25,000 (US$33,500); 50 percent from €25,000 to almost €40,000 (US$53,700); and 63 percent on incomes above €40,000. Low-wage workers—those earning close to the effective minimum wage—thus have a marginal tax rate of 44 percent. The only other contribution a worker makes to the public coffers is the tax-deductible contribution to unemployment benefits, which is about €900. UI membership is tax-deductible, and though not compulsory, about 80 percent of the labor force are members. For people with an income close to the minimum wage (about DKK 150,000, or €20,000 (US$26,900)), the payment of the UI insurance premium effectively adds another 3 percent to their taxation. Including the UI premium in total taxes, the marginal tax rate for the lowest incomes is 47 percent. However, low-income earners do receive the Danish version of the United States' Earned Income Tax Credit (EITC), a credit of 2.5 percent, and they are also more likely to receive UI benefits as well as housing and other benefits. Besides the income tax, a 25 percent VAT is levied on almost all traded goods, including food. This is distinct from the practice in many other EU countries where the VAT differentiates between food and nonfood. Furthermore, Denmark levies a number of other taxes on items like cigarettes, tobacco, wine and spirits, beer, soft drinks, electricity, lightbulbs, and cars. Altogether, these taxes are relatively more burdensome for the low-wage earner than for those with higher incomes.

Compared to American low-wage earners, however, Danish low-wage earners have their taxes partly offset by benefits, which to some extent are means-tested. Sickness insurance is administered through a national health insurance system that covers all medical care except dental work; housing is subsidized for the poorest residents; child care facilities are subsidized; and education is free. In addition, Denmark offers child support that is higher for single parents and a state-organized pension system. (See the appendix to this chapter for more details on these benefits.)

THE UNEMPLOYMENT BENEFIT SYSTEM

The unemployment benefit system is still partly organized according to "Bismarckian" principles. Thus, workers can voluntarily choose to become a member of one of more than thirty different unemployment insurance funds, according to their occupation. Eligibility for unemployment benefits is conditional on the worker having had a job for at least one year and having been a member of a UI fund for the same period. The unemployment benefit is 90 percent of the previous wage, with a maximum of €1,800 per month. Consequently, low-wage workers have a replacement rate of 90 percent, whereas it is lower for higher-income earners. Unemployment benefits are taxed, but the special tax rate of 8 percent on all work income does not apply to unemployment benefits. Together, the high income replacement rate and the asymmetric tax treatment create an incentive problem for low-wage workers: they earn little by working compared to being unemployed. It has been demonstrated that 23 percent of all employed women and 12 percent of all employed men actually earn €80 or less per week by working relative to what they would receive in unemployment benefits (see Smith 1998).

Unemployment benefits are obtained from the third day of unemployment and are paid for one year without any other obligation than seeking work. The employer who lays off an employee is by law obliged to pay for the first two days of unemployment; according to surveys, however, this happens only in about half of all cases. Consequently, there is a small element of experience rating in the Danish system. After one year of unemployment, the UI recipient has to become active in a labor market program.

A high income replacement rate coupled with the fact that there is almost no experience rating for either employers or workers leads to many short spells of unemployment. Even in years of low unemployment, more than 20 percent of all wage earners experience at least one spell of unemployment. A high proportion of these spells are concentrated around the Christmas holiday period and other vacation periods and have the character of temporary layoffs. As a result, low-pay workers' total working hours are about 80 percent of the total normal hours described earlier. The use of temporary layoff is not limited to low-wage earners.

The UI system is based on modest membership fees, with the government paying the deficit. As described earlier, UI funds are unofficially connected to the trade unions, with the result that membership in the UI system and union membership are considered a package. About 80 percent of the labor force are members of the UI system, and about 85 percent are members of trade unions. It is interesting that the hotel case studies show that there are few members of the UI system among Danish room attendants, probably because many work in the hotel sector only briefly and do not find it necessary to become members of the system. Another issue is the membership fee, which comes to about 3 percent of a low-wage income after taxes.

The unemployment benefit system is different from the welfare system in that, unlike the welfare system, it provides benefits for all periods without employment *irrespective* of a household's income and wealth.

OUTCOMES OF DANISH LABOR MARKET POLICIES AND INSTITUTIONS

These different systems and institutions have a number of outcomes. In this section, we look at some basic statistics that shed some light on how the Danish system works. We start with unemployment and end with the consequences of globalization.

UNEMPLOYMENT

Unemployment generally increased in Denmark through the 1970s and 1980s, with a few periods of brief improvement. At its maximum in 1993, the measured unemployment was almost 12 percent of the labor force. The year 1994 was a turning point for the Danish economy. Over the next four to five years, unemployment was reduced by almost 200,000, employment rose by the same amount, and the rate of unemployment fell from 12 percent to 5 percent. What these simple statistics overlook is the fact that the potential labor force (the age cohorts between eighteen and sixty-five) also grew during that period. Thus, closer inspection shows that a substantial number of the unemployed did not go directly into employment but entered into different types of labor market activities in the period after 1994.

The major reasons for the improvement in the Danish unemployment rate lay in a fortunate combination of domestic fiscal policies and growth in Europe. Furthermore, the fall of the Iron Curtain increased demand from Germany in the aftermath of the reunification. The positive development of Danish oil production, along with the reduction of international interest rates, laid a solid foundation for balance-of-payment surpluses in subsequent years. Increasing incomes made it possible to start reducing the public debt, and that made it relatively easy to comply with the Maastricht criteria for joining the single European currency. In the end, and after a referendum, Denmark decided not to use the euro. Nevertheless, the Danish krone was pegged to the euro. Interest rates have also approached the euro interest rate, so the international monetary markets clearly believed in a steady and firm relationship with the euro.

Figure 2.1 Unemployment as a Percentage of the Full-
Time Labor Force, 1980 to 2003

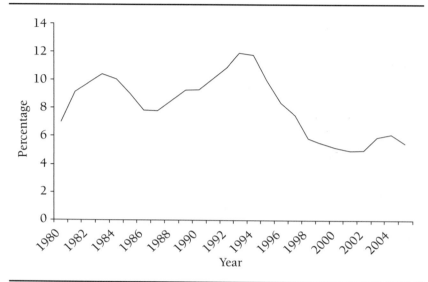

Source: Author's calculations from Statbank Denmark data.

JOBLESSNESS AND UNDEREMPLOYMENT

Joblessness and underemployment have a special status in a welfare
system that provides an almost universal income support system.
The problem with such a system is that people who cannot get a job
with an acceptable wage may fall back into receiving income support
of some sort. The income support programs are available in order of
accessibility: unemployment, sickness pay, welfare payment, and disability pension (see the appendix for details on the entire social safety
net). With a large and comprehensive welfare system that provides
benefits close to the lowest wages, there are relative weak incentives
to work for those with the lowest incomes. Peder Pedersen and Nina
Smith (2002) show, for example, that in 1996, for around 16 percent
of all employed UI fund members, the difference per month between
what they would have earned from working and what they would
have received in UI benefits was less than DKK(2001) 500. Figure 2.2
shows the composition of full-time-equivalent persons on unemployment and labor market programs (LMP), welfare, and sickness

Figure 2.2 The Proportion of the Labor Force (Age
Eighteen to Sixty-Six) on Income Transfer,
1988 to 2004

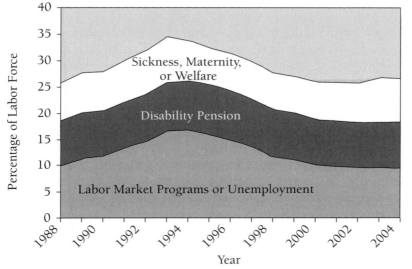

Source: Author's calculations from Statbank Denmark data.

and maternity leave. The envelope curve reflects to a large degree the
movements in unemployment and labor market programs. However,
it is remarkable that the proportion of the population depending on
sickness, welfare, and disability benefits seems to grow somewhat in
years when unemployment goes down. Furthermore, it is remarkable
that more than 25 percent of the labor force is on some sort of income
transfer.[4] Both observations tell us that the total number of welfare
dependents does not go down as much as the unemployment rate
goes down, simply because there is a tendency to move people to
other arrangements; as a result, the total cost to labor market programs and related programs does not go fully down when business
cycles improve.

Another dimension of this development is, of course, determining
whether low-wage earners are indeed more likely than other wage
earners to take up welfare transfer payments. In figure 2.3, we have
looked at the annual rate of transition from employment into welfare
and disability pension for low-wage earners and other wage earners.

Figure 2.3 Transfers from Active Labor Market
             Participation to Permanent Transfer Income
             Among Eighteen- to Fifty-Nine-Year-Olds

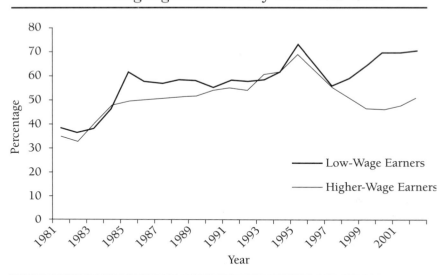

Source: Author's calculations from Center for Corporate Performance/Integrated Database for Labor Market Research (CCP/IDA) data.

We would have expected the transition rate of low-wage earners to be somewhat above that of higher-wage earners, because the relative income loss on these welfare transfer arrangements is lowest for low-wage earners. The reality, however, is somewhat more complicated. In most years the annual transfer rate from active participation in the labor market to permanent transfer income (pension, early retirement, and so on) has been about 0.6 percent among eighteen- to fifty-nine-year-olds. The figure shows that each year about 0.5 percent of all wage earners in this age group transfer to some sort of permanent early retirement. There appears to be little difference between low-wage and higher-wage workers except for the years after 1997, when low-wage workers tended to leave the labor market more frequently than higher-wage workers. The reason might be that unemployment declined in these years and labor market policies were tightened to provide more "sticks" and fewer "carrots," with the result that more people—and especially those with the lowest incomes—tried to move from employment and unemployment into programs that did not require that an individual hold a job or be actively searching for

Table 2.4 Hourly Wages (in 2002 Euros) for Eighteen- to
Sixty-Year-Olds, by Decile, and 90/50 and
50/10 Ratios

Year	10 percent Decile	50 percent Decile	90 percent Decile	90/50 Ratio	50/10 Ratio	Number of Observations
All						
1980	€13.00	€18.50	€28.10	1.517	1.429	1,813,315
1990	14.80	20.90	32.40	1.550	1.412	2,046,360
2002	15.10	21.90	34.90	1.595	1.455	2,206,092
Men						
1980	14.80	20.70	31.20	1.507	1.396	974,651
1990	16.40	23.20	36.40	1.571	1.415	1,066,656
2002	16.30	24.20	39.70	1.639	1.488	1,127,755
Women						
1980	12.00	16.40	22.90	1.396	1.359	838,664
1990	13.90	19.00	26.30	1.385	1.363	979,704
2002	14.40	19.90	29.00	1.459	1.383	1,078,337

Source: Author's calculations from Center for Corporate Performance/Integrated Database for Labor Market Research (CCP/IDA) data.

one. A similar but weaker phenomenon was observed around 1985, a period that also saw an upswing in the economy.

DISTRIBUTION OF WAGES AND EARNINGS

Denmark is known for a highly compressed wage structure. This is clearly seen in table 2.4, which shows that the median hourly wage for the entire working population is less than 50 percent above the wage of a person in the tenth percentile. Similarly, those in the ninetieth percentile earn just 60 percent more than those at the median. However, it is remarkable that inequality has been rising since as early as 1980.

The entire wage distribution for 2002 measured in euros is shown in figure 2.4. The figure shows the cutoff point at two-thirds of the median hourly wage, under which we classify people as belonging to the low-wage group. This group comprised 8.5 percent of all wage earners age eighteen to sixty in 2002, or 188,095 individuals. The minimum tariff is marked with a lower line, which shows that some workers actually earn below the minimum tariff (to be discussed later).

Figure 2.4 Wage Distribution, All Danish Wage Earners, 2002

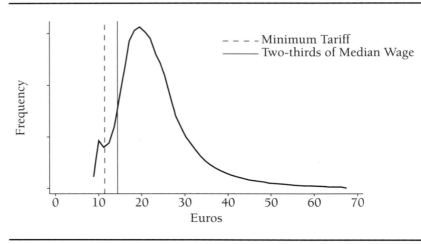

- - - - Minimum Tariff
——— Two-thirds of Median Wage

Source: Author's calculations from Center for Corporate Performance/Integrated Database for Labor Market Research (CCP/IDA) data.

The proportion of low-wage workers has changed somewhat over the years, as described in figure 2.5. In general, more men have become low-wage earners, while the share of women working in low-wage jobs has remained unchanged. The Danish low-wage threshold is around €14 per hour, which, incidentally, is a little less than the median wage in the United States. But this is a somewhat misleading comparison because the Danish wage is subject to a high marginal taxation of at least 44.5 percent.[5] Moreover, the fact that working hours differ between Denmark and the United States shifts the American annual wage distribution somewhat upward compared to the Danish. On the other hand, the low-wage earner in Denmark receives free health insurance and a number of other services from the state paid by general tax revenue.

FEMALE PARTICIPATION IN THE LABOR FORCE

The high rate of female participation is an important characteristic of Denmark's labor force. Interestingly, women now participate almost as much in the United States as they do in Denmark, but the conditions are different. In Denmark, female participation grew simultane-

Figure 2.5 Proportion of Male and Female Low-Wage
              Workers, 1980 to 2002

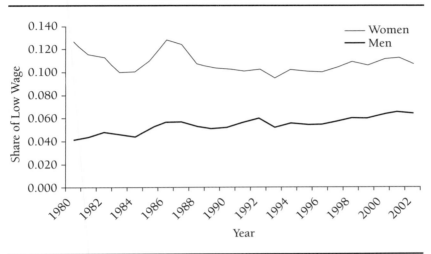

Source: Author's calculations from Center for Corporate Performance/Integrated
Database for Labor Market Research (CCP/IDA) data.

ously with a massive growth in child care facilities that started in the
late 1960s. Child care is provided largely by the public sector in Denmark: six out of ten children between the ages of one and six are in
publicly provided day care. Day care used to be highly subsidized but
is now less so. The growth of female participation in the labor force
was closely related to the growth of the public sector and the creation
of the present welfare state. In fact, the influx of females into the labor market was a precondition for the creation of Denmark's welfare
state, and many jobs, particularly in the public sector, started as part-
time jobs. Now, only 8 to 9 percent of all women between the ages of
twenty-five and fifty-five work part-time. Young women tend to work
part-time, as do older women, probably because they are combining
a job with some other activity. The different sectors of the economy
do not differ anymore with respect to part-time work. The frequency
of part-time work is about 24 percent for all women in Denmark, according to the Organization for Economic Cooperation and Development (OECD). However, this number includes students, many of
whom work part-time, as is also seen in the case studies. Furthermore, the number is based on a threshold of thirty hours per week,

which is high compared to a full-time workweek of thirty-seven hours. Similar OECD statistics for the United States show a part-time rate for women of 18.8 percent and 31.2 percent for EU-15.

It is remarkable that female participation in the Danish labor force started as part-time employment in the 1970s and has gradually turned into predominantly full-time employment. This pattern is unlike that of the many other European countries where part-time work for women still plays a significant role. A number of factors have undoubtedly contributed to this development. First, taxation is separate from work in Denmark. Second, maternity leave was extended from fourteen weeks prior to 1983 to twenty-six weeks around 1990, and then to fifty-two weeks in 2006.[6] Third, trade unions have fought ardently against part-time work. Fourth, day care facilities are designed for full-time child care, and there are hardly any part-time centers; moreover, there are only a few places that offer discounts for picking up children early.[7] Fifth, although schools end early in the day for the younger grades, they provide after-school care. Sixth, today's young women are better educated than young men and want to exploit their education and compete for careers.

The lowest wages are still earned by females. Despite passage in 1976 of the Equal Pay Act, a law requiring that men and women receive equal pay for equal work, the difference is still 7 to 8 percent, after controlling for personal characteristics. Raw female median earnings divided by median earnings for men for only full-time work was .82 in 2002. This was only a slight improvement from .80 on 1980, and indeed it had been stalled at .82 since 1992.[8] Several studies have shown that the main gender difference with respect to wages is now in the allocation on jobs (Datta Gupta and Rothstein 2005).

Regular Workweeks and Average Weekly and Annual Hours Worked

One of the main differences between the United States and Europe is that hours worked have been gradually reduced in most European countries. In Denmark, so-called normal hours are set during the general wage bargaining between the trade unions and the Employers' Federation. The normal thirty-seven-hour workweek covers literally everyone and can be interpreted as the maximum normal hours for the majority of hourly workers and a good number of salaried workers. Hours worked beyond the normal hours are nor-

Figure 2.6 Change in Annual Normal Hours Worked,
1966 to 2004

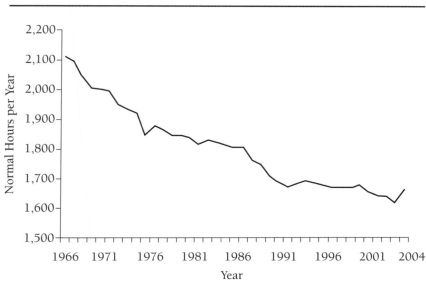

Source: Andersen et al. (2005).

mally paid as overtime, and jobs with fewer than twenty-eight weekly
hours are classified as part-time.

As elsewhere, normal hours have been gradually reduced in Denmark as a consequence of trade union pressure and the general increase in purchasing power. The reduction has averaged about 0.7
percent per year (Andersen et al. 2005) as a result of various causes.
In the late 1960s and early 1970s, efforts to reduce hours focused on
hours worked per week; then a period came when vacation time was
increased from four to five weeks; and in the 1990s weekly hours
were reduced again, from forty to thirty-seven hours. Vacation time
has been extended gradually since the first legislation on vacation
was passed in 1938. Recently, Denmark has started extending vacation time from five to six weeks. According to the original law, vacation is both a right and an obligation. In 2004 this meant that a total
"normal" working year was about 1,658 hours. The change over the
years in the number of annual statutory (normal) hours is shown in
figure 2.6.

Normal hours worked in Denmark are among the lowest in the

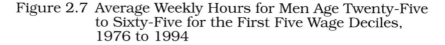

Figure 2.7 Average Weekly Hours for Men Age Twenty-Five to Sixty-Five for the First Five Wage Deciles, 1976 to 1994

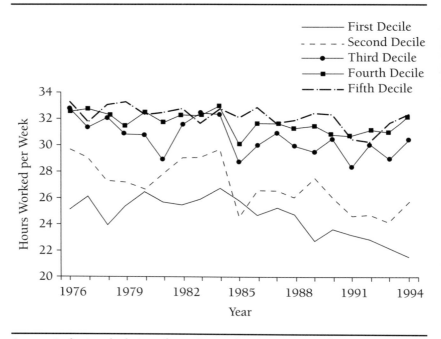

Source: Author's calculations from Center for Corporate Performance/Integrated Database for Labor Market Research (CCP/IDA) data.

world. Only German and French manufacturing workers worked fewer hours per year in 2004 (Bundesvereinigung der Deutschen Arbeitgeberverbände 2005). Additionally, on average people do not even work the prescribed number of normal hours. Low-wage earners in particular work less. Danish low-wage earners worked an average of only 1,140 hours in 1994; the comparable number for low-wage workers in the United States in the same period was 1,700 hours (Westergaard-Nielsen 1999).

Figure 2.7 shows clearly that the lower earnings deciles in Denmark work less than the higher deciles, as is the case in many countries. The difference between Denmark and most other countries is undoubtedly that Danes are more likely to receive unemployment or sickness benefits to make up the difference between hours actually

Table 2.5 Distribution of Daily Hours, 1990 to 2003, for Every 1,000 Persons (Survey-Based)

Year	1 to 19 Hours	20 to 29 Hours	30 to 34 Hours	35 to 39 Hours	40 Hours or More	Total Number of Persons (in Thousands)
1990	11	9	5	60	14	2,471
2000	11	7	10	55	18	2,370
2003	11	7	10	55	18	2,413

Source: Author's calculations from Statbank Denmark data.

worked and normal hours. (This is also the reason why there is a difference between the number of persons working and the number of full-time equivalent persons on unemployment or other transfer payments.) Figure 2.7 shows the average weekly hours worked for men age twenty-five to sixty-four who are working a positive number of hours and have an income.[9] Each curve represents one wage decile.[10] The low number of hours worked is of particular interest to the study of low-wage work because it shows that low wages are also correlated with a low number of hours and probably a relatively heavy dependence on transfer income in the form of housing benefits, extra child benefits, and other means-tested benefits. We see the same pattern between wage deciles in the United States, but there the gaps in working hours are not filled with unemployment benefits and other transfer pay. Thus, we can establish the fact that low-wage persons tend to work fewer hours. The picture is probably even more pronounced if we also include women, youth, and students, even though some of these groups are not covered by the UI system. In chapter 5, we will see that this indeed is the case for hotel room attendants.

Normal daily hours lie between seven and eight hours. The distinction between normal hours and overtime depends on each bargaining unit and its contract. The distribution of actually worked hours appears in table 2.5.

The table shows clearly that short part-time hours have been declining and longer hours have actually been increasing in recent years. The reason may be related to a gradual decentralization of the bargaining process that has allowed for local agreements on working hours.

Figure 2.8 Labor Force Participation of Immigrants and
Ethnic Danes

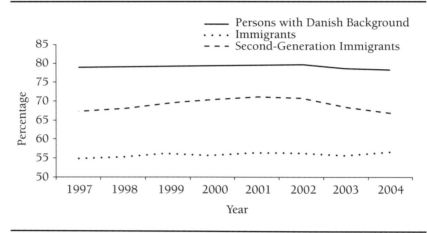

Source: Author's calculations from Statbank Denmark data.

EMPLOYMENT AND UNEMPLOYMENT AMONG IMMIGRANTS

The number of immigrants and second-generation immigrants in Denmark has risen sharply over the last twenty years. In 1980 there were about 150,000 immigrants in Denmark; by 2004, the number had risen to almost 500,000, or about 10 percent of the population. The high influx of immigrants, however, has not been followed by a similar increase in their labor force participation, as can be seen in figure 2.8. As a matter of fact, the labor force participation rate among Danish immigrants is as low as 55 percent. This has led to less integration of immigrants and is undoubtedly one of the underlying reasons for the increasingly restrictive immigration policies.[11] The main explanation for low labor force participation among immigrants is that the slow rate at which they adopt the Danish participation pattern combines with their relatively easy access to welfare payments. Another problem, of course, is the language barrier. Unemployment is also higher among immigrants: over the years unemployment has been a little more than twice as high for immigrants as for ethnic Danes.

Another important issue is that immigrants from non-Western

Figure 2.9 Relative Income Distribution Among Couples at Least
One of Whom Is Parent to a Fourteen-Year-Old Child,
Depending on Immigrant or Ethnic Status, 2003

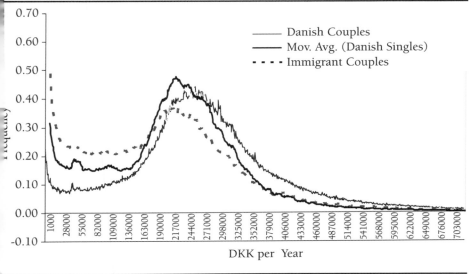

DKK per Year

Legend:
——— Danish Couples
——— Mov. Avg. (Danish Singles)
- - - - Immigrant Couples

Source: Author's compilation from Center for Corporate Performance/Integrated Database for Labor Market Research (CCP/IDA) data.

countries are clearly receiving lower incomes than Danes of similar characteristics. Figure 2.9 shows the income distribution for individuals who are parents of children age zero to fourteen given that they have a positive income. (Forty-five percent of immigrant parents have no work-related earnings at all, compared to 11 percent of Danes.) The figure shows that non-Western immigrants are also twice as likely to be in the low-income category below DKK 166,000 (€22,300) per adult parent living as part of a couple. This finding may have a serious negative impact on the children of immigrants and their possibilities for getting out of low-income settings.

Regional Disparities in the Labor Market

The regional disparities are small in Denmark, mainly owing to the size of the country. One way of demonstrating the regional disparities is to look at the rate of unemployment in different areas of Denmark (see figure 2.10). There are some zones of high unemployment and

Figure 2.10 Regional Rates of Unemployment, 2003

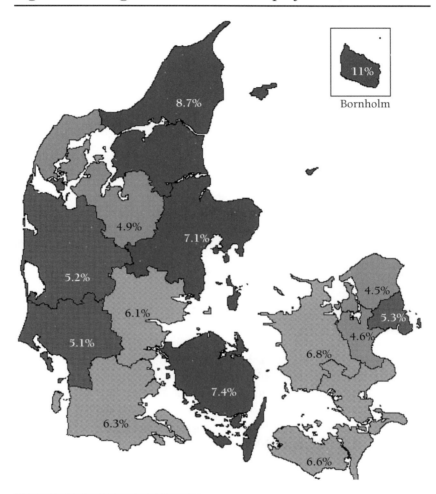

Source: Author's compilations from Statbank Denmark data.

low economic activity, but they are relative small. As such, it has been difficult to find any substantial differences across regions in the case studies. However, there are small differences. Thus, chapter 5 shows, for example, that there are more immigrants in the hotel workforce in the capital than outside the capital.

SKILL COMPOSITION

The Danish skill distribution is dominated by a large fraction of skilled workers who have served as apprentices (53 percent of the workforce). Apprentice training in Denmark is organized much as it is in Germany, Austria, and Switzerland: under a so-called dual training system, the apprentice works for a master for a low wage and goes to technical school at the same time.[12] Apprentice training takes between three and a half and four and a half years and can start only after normal school has been completed. Apprentice training is organized by the Ministry of Education in cooperation with the trade unions and the Employers' Federation, which is another example of the cooperation between the social partners mentioned in chapter 1. This ensures the quality of the training. Apprentice training is undoubtedly one of the decisive factors that keep youth unemployment rates down in the "apprentice countries" (Germany, Austria, and Switzerland).

At the same time, Denmark has a relatively modest proportion of highly educated people: 27 percent have completed postsecondary education in Denmark. This rate is much lower than in the United States, as shown in table 2.6.

The main reason for the low share of people with a postsecondary education is that to some extent the apprentice system "crowds out" further education. It may be that those who have been through an apprentice training find it too difficult to add extra years of education on top of their apprentice training. The same pattern is seen in the other big apprentice countries, Germany, Austria, and Switzerland, but not in most other countries. Another reason for the relatively low rate of postsecondary education in Denmark is that the average return to one extra year of education is among the lowest within the OECD area: about 6 percent in 2003. (A couple of years earlier the return was even lower in the Netherlands, and the Scandinavian countries were in the same league [Harmon, Walker, and Westergaard-Nielsen 2001].) The low return to education is probably caused by a compressed wage distribution that, again, is related to the fact that the public sector at one time was the main employer of the college-educated. In recent years, the private sector has employed more of these workers, and that shift, as expected, has been accompanied by higher returns to education.

Table 2.6 Education Levels Among Twenty-Five- to Sixty-Four-Year Olds, 2002

	Lower Secondary Plus Primary	Upper Secondary	Postsecondary
Australia	39%	30%	31%
Austria	22	63	14
Canada	17	40	43
Czech Republic	12	76	12
Denmark	20	53	27
Finland	25	42	33
France	35	41	24
Germany	17	60	23
Greece	47	34	18
Ireland	40	35	25
Japan	16	47	36
Korea	29	45	26
Netherlands	34	42	24
Norway	13	55	31
Portugal	80	11	9
Spain	58	17	24
Sweden	18	49	33
Switzerland	15	59	25
United Kingdom	16	57	27
United States	13	49	38
Country Mean	33	44	23

Source: OECD (2004).

The third group of workers consists of those who receive no formal vocational training after their basic schooling (20 percent). Many of these do have some sort of training, but compared to the apprentices, their skills are more firm-specific and less general. The skilled workers (those with apprentice training) are clearly those in the manual labor market who have the best jobs, the highest wages, and so on. Though the difference in income for different educational groups is small, the type of work, the working conditions, and expected work-life are all lower for the less-educated.

While most countries tend to increase average educational levels, this is so far not happening in Denmark, since the young genera-

Table 2.7 Postsecondary Education, by Age Group, 2003

Twenty-Five to Thirty-Four	Thirty-Five to Forty-Four	Forty-Five to Fifty-Four	Fifty-Five to Sixty-Four	Twenty-Five to Sixty-Four
28%	28%	29%	21%	27%

Source: OECD (2004).

tions are not getting more education than the older generations (see table 2.7).

Occupational and Internal Labor Markets

The Danish labor market is characterized by extremely high worker turnover. As a consequence, internal labor markets are probably weaker compared to those of other economies. Nevertheless, higher worker entry rates in the bottom parts of the wage distribution and higher exit rates in the higher parts confirm the existence of internal labor markets.

Figure 2.11 shows the entry and exit rates in the top and bottom quartiles of the wage distribution. Not surprisingly, mobility is substantially higher in the lowest quartile, where entry rates exceed exit rates by a wide margin, whereas these rates are reversed in the top quartile. This finding reflects, of course, the fact that workers tend to get hired at the bottom and to leave from positions further up the wage ladder. It is generally found that mobility is high in low-paid work. However, as shown by Iben Bolvig (2005), one-third of all transitions out of low-wage jobs are out of the labor force. The other two-thirds are transitions to higher-paid employment within the same firm and to jobs in other firms, respectively. Notably, Bolvig also finds that firms with a higher-than-average share of low-wage workers have lower turnover among their low-wage workforce than other firms. The entry rates in the bottom quartile vary procyclically and are quite volatile. Entry into the top quartile displays the same pattern, but the variation is less pronounced.

Thus, there are internal labor markets in which workers earn their way up through the hierarchy; at the same time, low-wage employees tend to stay within one firm to a greater extent than their American counterparts (Bolvig 2005).

Figure 2.11 Exit and Entry Rates, by Earnings Quartile

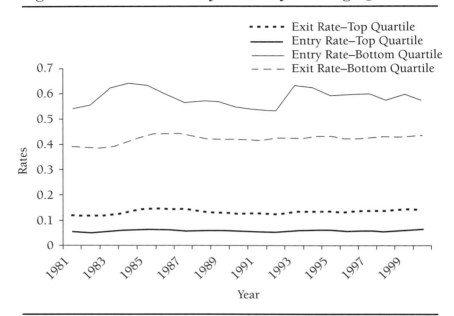

Source: Author's calculations from Center for Corporate Performance/Integrated Database for Labor Market Research (CCP/IDA) data.

The Impact of Globalization on the Danish Industrial Structure

As in other countries, there has been a strong drift in Denmark from manufacturing to service jobs. Over the last twenty years, almost 200,000 jobs have been created in the service industry. At the same time, manufacturing has witnessed a reduction of almost 20,000 jobs. In manufacturing, some subsectors have created jobs, while others have experienced net losses of jobs. The big losers are the food industry, the shipyards, and the textile and clothing industries. The winners are trade, hotels and restaurants, and various types of business services. Adjustment to this shift has been facilitated in part by the high turnover rate of Danish workers, and in general it has taken place without mass unemployment in the industries and regions most affected (see Eriksson et al. 2006).

Karsten Bjerring Olsen, Rikke Ibsen, and I (Olsen, Ibsen, and Westergaard-Nielsen 2004) have carefully studied this development in the textile and clothing industry. Using data collected from our sample since 1980, we show that the whole industry has been virtually dismantled over the last thirty years. What had the greatest impact on the workers was that the factories almost stopped employing young workers and also that workers who lost their jobs when one factory closed got new jobs in one of the remaining factories. As a result, textile and clothing workers were actually more loyal to the industry than workers in other industries. Most workers affected by the factory closings thus continued doing what they were best at until they retired or found another job. At the same time, the design and marketing of clothes became more active elements of the industry, but with a different composition of workers. Tor Eriksson and his colleagues (2006) demonstrate that the same has happened in other industries that eliminated jobs, but no other industry has done so as dramatically as the clothing industry. However, this study also shows that there are substantial losses to workers in the form of unemployment and subsequent lower wages when they are caught in a firm closure.

TRENDS IN LOW-WAGE EMPLOYMENT

In this section, we look at measures of low wages and trends in who works for low wages, followed by an analysis of the industries in which most of the low-wage work is found. Third, we investigate the role of different factors in explaining which jobs are low-wage and who fills them. Finally, we look at low-wage work in the industries and occupations that we discuss in the case study chapters.

MEASURES OF LOW-WAGE WORK

The OECD defines low wage as a wage less than or equal to two-thirds of the median wage. This measure is used, for purposes of comparison, in all five of the European countries associated with this project. Because the Center for Corporate Performance/Integrated Database for Labor Market Research (CCP/IDA) data are drawn from administrative records, the earnings variables come from annual earnings at the individual's main employer that year. With the help of pension contributions, which are a function of hours worked, we have calculated a monthly or hourly wage for use throughout this chapter.

In the national statistics, total employment consists of all types of jobs, irrespective of their origin or who fills them. When we want to characterize some jobs as low-wage jobs, it seems to be appropriate to distinguish between primary jobs and secondary jobs. Another issue is that some job holders may not be dependent on their job for very long because they are students.

The role of students in the labor market varies from one country to the next and from one industry to the next. In Denmark, it is common for students to work part-time, and so to some extent they are an important part of the labor force, especially in some industries, as is shown in subsequent chapters. During the last decade, 5 to 7 percent of the Danish workforce was registered as more or less active students. In the retail and hotel sectors, more than 20 percent of the labor force is students, and that share has been increasing over the years. These trends are clearly seen in the case studies. Students do manual work for a few years for the lowest wages, accepting irregular work hours, and then most of them quickly move away from these jobs as soon as they finish their schooling.

In this chapter, we generally treat students like all other kinds of employees, thus following the general statistics convention. However, we assess their impact so as to check for the robustness of our findings. For example, in the hotel sector over 50 percent of low-wage workers are students, and our case studies tend to confirm this finding.

All Danish students receive a grant from the State Education Grant and Loan Scheme (SU) for the normal duration of their study. For students who have their own household, the grant was €651 (US\$874) per month in 2007, before tax. For single parents, the grant is twice as much. Since this amount is less than most students feel they can survive on, many of them work while they are students. The rule from the student grant administration is that they can earn up to €9,950 (US\$13,400) annually without any reduction in their grant. A few students choose not to receive grants at all but to rely fully on their own income.

These restrictions give students clear incentives to work but also to work relatively few hours. If we use student status as provided by the registry data and also designate as students those whose work income falls below the grant allowance, we end up with 8.5 percent of the labor force having student status. Of these, 36 percent work in retail, 12.3 percent in hotels and restaurants, and 7 percent in food manufacturing. The rest are spread out across many other industries.

The industries studied here are of different sizes; thus, students constitute 27 percent of hotel and restaurant workers and 13 percent of retail workers. Students play only a minor role in all other industries. We have met a number of students working in retail and in hotels, restaurants, and call centers. Young people with student status appear to be an important group of workers in these areas, not the least because they are willing to work at odd hours and for relatively modest pay.

A factor related to these observations is that a large proportion of young people in Denmark spend one or more years after high school working and traveling before they start vocational training. Young people in this stage of their lives are like the students who are willing to take low-wage jobs, and they do not become members of trade unions or unemployment insurance funds, probably because they do not expect to stay for long in the trade.

Together with some groups of immigrants, students—both those currently enrolled and those spending time before vocational training traveling and working—are probably responsible for the relatively low trade union membership in the hotel, restaurant, cleaning, and retail trades, as we see in the case studies.

WHO WORKS FOR LOW WAGES?

Most low-wage jobs are in service and sales and in "elementary occupations."[13] These areas account for about 60 percent of all low-wage work. Service and sales work covers personal service (housekeeping and restaurant service, personal care) and protective service (firefighters, police officers, and prison guards), modeling, retail sales and stall or market sales. Workers in elementary occupations are street service workers, helpers, and cleaners, caretakers and janitors, messengers and doorkeepers, agricultural, fishery, and mining laborers, and manufacturing and transport laborers. A small portion of managerial and professional work is also low-wage, especially in small firms or family-owned companies that employ only one or a few persons, such as restaurants and kiosks.

Later we describe the proportion of different low-wage groups as defined here. First, we look at the age composition, which clearly shows that the fraction of low-wage young people has almost doubled over the investigated period, reflecting the observation in the last section about student workers. Furthermore, our analysis shows

Figure 2.12 Low-Wage Work by Age Group, 1980 to 2002

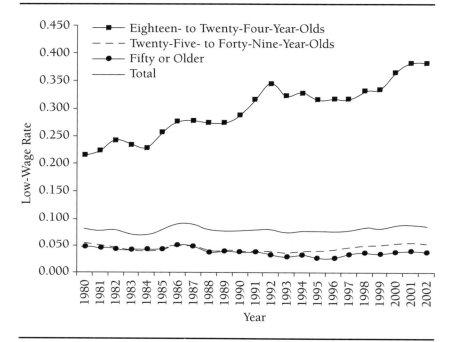

Source: Author's calculations from Center for Corporate Performance/Integrated Database for Labor Market Research (CCP/IDA) data.

that the fraction of workers age twenty-five and older is almost constant but has a tendency to move a bit upward when the business cycle improves, probably reflecting that a better overall job situation causes authorities to insist that more unemployed accept relatively low-paid jobs. High upward mobility makes this a highly sensible policy, as is shown later in the chapter.

One interesting point is that the share of young low-wage workers goes up but does not increase for the other age groups, suggesting that low-wage jobs have become more concentrated among young people over the years (see figure 2.12). This trend also means that to a large extent low-wage work has become a problem that one outgrows. The increasing number of youth earning low wages after 1997 should probably be seen as a consequence of the so-called youth package introduced in 1996 and the stop to unconditional welfare benefits to youth. Both changes lowered the reservation wage for youth. The youth package changed the rules for youth below age twenty-six; now they can receive unemployment benefits for only six months. After that age, they receive just 50 percent of the usual unemployment benefit if they do not start vocation training. Before the rule change, young people who had no dependents and were not members of a UI fund were eligible for welfare if they had no other means. That benefit was stopped at the same time.

One explanation for the rise in the youth share of low-wage workers beginning in the mid-1980s may be the centralized admission system to postsecondary education. Since the beginning of the 1980s, high school grades have been used to allocate students to different educations; if students cannot meet the requirement of their chosen education, they can improve their standing by working for a limited period and in that way make up for low grades. The result of this policy has been to lower the reservation wage for youth as more youth take low-wage jobs. This trend was then reinforced by the changes in the youth package. The system has gradually been reformed in recent years so that work does not count so much in the admission process; thus, we can expect to see a decline in the youth share of low-wage workers in the coming years.

Women are still concentrated in low-wage work, as can be seen in figure 2.13. This is the case for both young women and older women. The difference between men and women is five to twelve percentage points and is lowest for the oldest group. The difference seems to diminish for those age twenty-five or older, while it tends to increase slightly for the young.

Looking at the educational groups in figure 2.14, we see that the largest share of low-wage workers is found in the group with only a secondary education (those who left school by age sixteen) (15 percent); fewer are found among those with upper secondary schooling (those who did not leave school until age nineteen) (8 percent), and only about 2 percent of college- or university-educated workers earn low wages. It is remarkable that the humps around the upswings are found in all educational groups and that there is a clear upward trend, which is strongest for the lowest-educated group. This last finding should be seen in conjunction with the age pattern discussed earlier; thus, it is safe to conclude that low wages are most prevalent among young people with low education.

Figure 2.13 Low-Wage Work by Gender and Age, 1980 to 2002

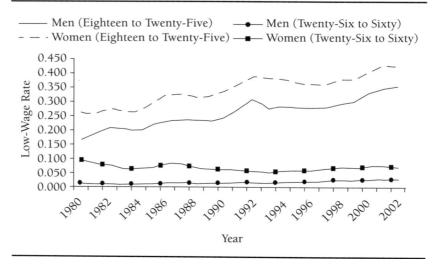

Source: Author's calculations from Center for Corporate Performance/Integrated Database for Labor Market Research (CCP/IDA) data.

Figure 2.14 Low-Wage Work by Education

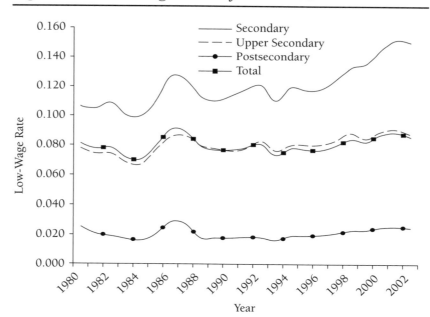

Source: Author's calculations from Center for Corporate Performance/Integrated Database for Labor Market Research (CCP/IDA) data.

Where Do People Work for Low Wages?

There is relatively little low-wage work in Denmark, though the proportion of low-wage income earners has increased slightly from 5 percent in 1996 to 8 percent in 2001. Table 2.8 shows that low-wage work is concentrated among the young, among women, and in the bakery, retail, and hotel industries, in contrast to a high-wage industry like meat processing. These shares have remained more or less unchanged over the last six to seven years. The age dimension is interesting, of course, because the high concentration of young people in low-wage work implies that such work is only temporary; another implication is that a high proportion of the population will have been low-wage earners at some time in their lives. Such an experience, of course, has a great impact on the social cohesion of a society.

Table 2.8 Proportion of Workers Age Eighteen to Sixty Earning Less Than Two-thirds of the Median

	1996	2002
Overall	7.6%	8.5%
Gender		
Men	5.5	6.4
Women	10.0	10.7
Age		
Eighteen to twenty-five	28.6	35.0
Twenty-six to thirty-five	5.3	6.8
Thirty-six to forty-five	3.0	4.0
Forty-six to fifty-five	2.8	3.6
Fifty-six to sixty	3.1	4.2
Education		
Secondary	11.8	15.0
Eighteen to twenty-four	40.1	49.0
Twenty-five to fifty-four	5.8	8.0
Fifty-five to sixty	4.6	6.7
Upper secondary	8.0	8.7
Eighteen to twenty-four	26.9	31.6
Twenty-five to fifty-four	4.5	5.7
Fifty-five to sixty	2.8	4.1
Postsecondary	2.0	2.4
Eighteen to twenty-four	18.4	22.4
Twenty-five to fifty-four	1.7	2.3
Fifty-five to sixty	1.3	1.5

Table 2.8 (continued)

	1996	2002
Occupation		
Managers	1.0	0.6
Supervisors and foremen	1.7	1.8
White-collar	3.4	3.8
Blue-collar	8.7	10.6
Other employees	9.1	10.5
Nonclassified employees	22.6	16.5
Industry		
Manufacturing	4.5	4.6
Meat industry	3.0	3.7
Confectionary	26.6	32.8
Construction	6.3	8.4
Service	8.3	9.1
Retail	22.0	23.3
Supermarket	24.2	26.2
Department store	29.4	27.5
Hotels with restaurants	24.6	24.6
Hotels without restaurants	21.9	19.2
Health	8.3	9.7
Hospitals	5.0	4.2

Source: Author's calculations from Center for Corporate Performance/Integrated Database for Labor Market Research (CCP/IDA) data.

DECISIVE FACTORS IN BECOMING A LOW-WAGE WORKER

To investigate the multidimensional factors that are decisive in becoming a low-wage worker, we have run a logit on the probability of being observed as a low-wage worker during a full year. This is done on more than 43 million observations over the years 1980 to 2000, so the significance is high. Table 2.9 shows that students, women, and immigrants are more likely than others to become low-wage workers. Furthermore, the table shows a clear age dimension, implying that the low-wage propensity is reduced with age.

The industry controls shown in table 2.10 reveal that some industries are more prone to low-wage work than others. The industry least likely to pay low wages is the stone and clay industry, followed by the chemical industry, and the most likely sector for low-wage work is the agricultural industry sector.

Finally, the variation over time confirms our previous results

Table 2.9 Logit Estimates of the Probability of Being
Observed as a Low-Wage Earner Among
Eighteen- to Sixty-Year-Old Workers, with
Controls for Year and Industry

	Coefficient	Standard Error
Intercept	1.79	0.01
Immigrant	0.17	0.01
Women	0.91	0.00
Education		
Secondary	0.08	0.00
Vocational	−0.46	0.00
Upper secondary	−0.77	0.01
College	−1.50	0.00
Postgraduate	−1.93	0.01
Student	1.05	0.00
Age		
Age	−0.27	0.00
Age-squared	0.00	0.00
Number of observations	43,848,504	
Number of low-wage cases		1,979,986

Source: Author's calculations from Center for Corporate Performance/Integrated Database for Labor Market Research (CCP/IDA) data.

showing that low-wage work became more and more likely over the period from 1980 to 2000, with a relatively low probability at the beginning of the 1980s, a high probability in 1986 and 1987, and a decreased probability from 1998 to 2000.

Table 2.10 The Rank Order of Industries in Probability of
Having Low-Wage Workers

Least Likely	Medium	Most Likely
Stone and clay	Machine	Textile
Chemistry	Food industry	Other industry
Postal service	Iron and metal	Construction
IT	Wood	R&D
Plastic	Auto	Social service
Electricity	Finance	Rental business
	Furniture	Primary sector
	Paper	
	Transportation	
	Business service	

Source: Author's compilation from Center for Corporate Performance/Integrated Database for Labor Market Research (CCP/IDA) data.

Figure 2.15 The Fraction of Low-Wage Earners Within the Target Industries

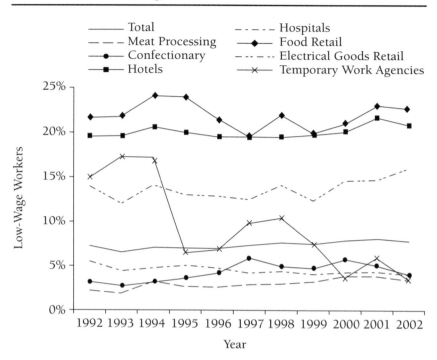

Source: Author's calculations from Center for Corporate Performance/Integrated Database for Labor Market Research (CCP/IDA) data.

Low-Wage Work in the Target Industries and Occupations

Using the definition of low-wage earnings as two-thirds of median earnings, we can now assess the number of low-wage earners within the target industries and occupations. Figure 2.15 shows that both the hotel and food retail industries have a low-wage share just above 20 percent, followed by electronic goods retail with 13 to 15 percent. The meat-processing, confectionary, and hospital industries are all below 5 percent. Call center employees cannot be identified in this context.

An interesting example is temporary work agencies (TWAs), which started by having a relatively large share of low-wage earners and ended up having a small share. The main reason is that TWAs have become dominated by nurses and other hospital employees who earn extra money working for hospitals at higher-than-usual wages.

Altogether, the selected industries cover 8 to 10 percent of all low-wage jobs in Denmark.[14]

THE DYNAMICS OF LOW-WAGE EMPLOYMENT: EARNINGS MOBILITY

In this section, we look at how long low-wage earners continue to earn low wages and whether they eventually get a higher wage or end up receiving some sort of welfare payment. We also analyze whether immigrants have a different mobility pattern compared to the Danes. Finally, we investigate the relationship between poverty and low wages.

DO LOW-WAGE WORKERS REMAIN LOW-PAID?

Looking at the period of time an individual spends earning low wages is, of course, important to any assessment of the impact of low wages. We have seen that young people in particular take low-wage jobs more frequently than others do and that the unskilled are also more likely to be found in the low-wage group. The first finding indicates that most people stay in low-wage employment for only a short while.

In this section, we look at how long a cohort of low-wage workers actually remain low-wage workers. This can be done in several ways. We first look at the cohort of workers who earned low wages in 1995 and follow them year by year and report the share of them who were still earning low wages in 2002. Table 2.11 shows that seven years later only a low percentage of the cohort remained in the low-wage group. One explanation for this might be that the 1995 cohort includes a number of people who found themselves in the low-wage group by chance. Therefore, we repeat the analysis with the group of people who remained in the low-wage group for three consecutive years. This reduces the sample from 145,000 to 17,000, but with little effect on the pattern of relative propensities.[15]

Conditioning on three years earning low wages makes it more dif-

Table 2.11 The Proportion of Low-Wage Earners in 1995 Who
Remained in the Low-Wage Group for One Year or
Three Years Consecutively, Up to Seven Years

	One Year in Low-Wage Group			Three Years in Low-Wage Group		
Year	Total	Exit	Share in Low-Wage Group	Total	Exit	Share in Low-Wage Group
1995	144,810		100.0%	17,365		100.0%
1996	77,584	67,226	53.6	8,740	8,625	50.3
1997	44,075	33,509	30.4	5,243	3,497	30.2
1998	24,803	19,272	17.1	3,520	1,723	20.3
1999	14,590	10,213	10.1	2,422	1,098	13.9
2000	8,780	5,810	6.1	1,790	632	10.3
2001	5,145	3,635	3.6	1,375	415	7.9
2002	2,950	2,195	2.0	1,106	269	6.4
Size of initial group	157,371			19,735		
Missing persons	12,561			2,370		

Source: Author's calculations from Center for Corporate Performance/Integrated Database for Labor Market Research (CCP/IDA) data.

ficult, of course, to leave the low-wage group than conditioning on only one year earning low wages, simply because the former measure contains only those who have been seriously affected by low wages.

The most likely explanation for high mobility out of the low-wage group is that a large fraction of those in low-wage jobs actually accepted them in the first place as part of a job training program, as a step on a job ladder, or as a temporary situation, as happens with many students and other young people. Therefore, we also see that young people and people with the lowest educational levels dominate the low-wage group. These findings are fully in line with our impressions from the case studies. Several of the young low-wage informants working in retail and at call centers, for example, stated that they considered their job a temporary position and that they did not expect to stay for a long time. Hence, the register data seem to indicate that their expectations will prove true.

The interesting question then becomes whether low-wage jobs are a stepping-stone to better or at least higher-paid jobs, or whether they lead to welfare dependence.

UPWARD AND DOWNWARD MOBILITY AND WORKER CHARACTERISTICS

To answer this question we now turn to the issue of where people move after having at least one period in low-wage work. Do they remain in low-wage work or do they move to jobs that pay higher wages? Are they unemployed for a time? Do they receive welfare benefits temporarily or permanently? Figure 2.16 shows what happened, year by year, to the cohort of 157,000 workers who earned low wages in 1995.[16]

With the least restrictive definition of the sample, only 30 percent remained low-wage workers the following year. Forty-five percent found better-paying jobs, and only 15 percent were on temporary welfare (a status that includes being unemployed). A negligible share had already ended up on permanent welfare by the end of the first year. That share of the sample increased over time, but only to a few percentage points of the sample. Figure 2.16 shows the remarkable fact that low-wage workers continued moving to the group of better-paid or normal-wage workers, while the number moving into welfare programs did not change at all after the first two years. As expected, the distribution between those receiving temporary welfare benefits and those receiving permanent benefits changes slightly over time as more people's transfer income becomes permanent.

Finally, it should be noted that about 10 percent of all low-wage earners are in a group whose wage is poorly measured, mostly because hours are poorly measured, and thus they are classified as "missing."

Figure 2.16 confirms that low-wage work is mostly a temporary phenomenon in Denmark. It also shows that about 10 percent of all low-wage earners receive unemployment benefits or some sort of short-term welfare payments. The figure is based on the status of workers in November of each year, so the proportion of individuals affected by unemployment or temporary welfare during each year most likely is higher. This finding is fully in line with our discussion of figure 2.7, which reported the hours of work for different income groups and showed that a low wage was correlated with having few hours of effective work. Both figures also show, however, that relatively few low-wage workers "give up" and apply for permanent welfare payments. A statistical model taking different initial conditions

Figure 2.16 Where Do the Low-Wage Workers Go?

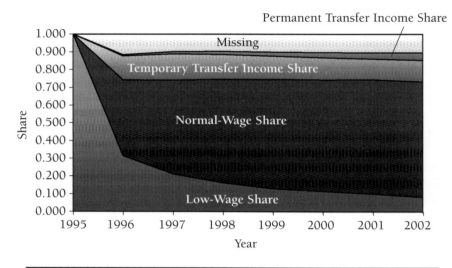

Source: Author's calculations from Center for Corporate Performance/Integrated Database for Labor Market Research (CCP/IDA) data.

and outcomes into consideration is presented by Rita Asplund, Peter J. Bingley, and Niels Westergaard-Nielsen (1998).

LOW-WAGE MOBILITY AND IMMIGRANTS

Next, we examine the impact of low-wage work on immigrants, by which we mean immigrants from non-Western countries. We have shown that low-wage status in Denmark is usually short-lived and that students and immigrants are more likely to be low-wage workers. While the status of students and other young people changes over their lives, that of immigrants does not.

Table 2.12 shows the proportion of different occupational groups with jobs in the low-wage category. The share of low-wage workers is increasing for both immigrants and non-immigrants, but much more so for immigrants. While the fraction of working students in the low-wage group is identical for the two groups, twice as many of all immigrants in the private and public sectors are low-wage workers.

If we track those who held low-wage jobs, both immigrants and non-immigrants, and record how many were still low-wage workers

Table 2.12 Low-Wage Immigrant and Non-Immigrant
Workers, 1980 to 2001

	1980	1990	2000	2001
Non-immigrants	3%	4%	5%	5%
Students	18	34	38	40
Public job	3	4	4	4
Private job	3	4	5	5
Immigrants	2	4	9	9
Students	18	23	37	40
Public job	3	4	9	9
Private job	1	4	9	9

Source: Author's calculations from Center for Corporate Performance/Integrated Database for Labor Market Research (CCP/IDA) data.

five years later, we find that there is no difference between immigrants and non-immigrants (see table 2.13).

We also looked at the share of former low-wage workers who were either employed or on an income transfer program. It appears that immigrants were much less successful at maintaining their employment than non-immigrants (see table 2.14). They were also more likely to be out of the labor force and supported by their families, on social assistance, unemployed, or involved in activation measures.

Thus, we can conclude that the reason we find more immigrants among low-wage workers is simply that Denmark has received more immigrants. Those who maintain a job seem to move out of low-wage work exactly as fast as non-immigrants. There are several major differences, however, between immigrants and non-immigrants: immigrants are less likely to retain a job compared to non-immi-

Table 2.13 Low-Wage Share Five Years After Being
Observed as a Low-Wage Worker, Conditioned
on Being Active in the Labor Force, 1980
to 2003

	Immigrant	Non-Immigrant
Low-wage	9%	9%
Not low-wage	91	91

Source: Author's calculations from Center for Corporate Performance/Integrated Database for Labor Market Research (CCP/IDA) data.

Table 2.14 Low-Wage Immigrant and Non-Immigrant
Workers Five Years Later, 1980 to 2003

	Immigrant	Non-Immigrant
Education	3%	5%
Job	57	79
Out of labor force	11	4
Social assistance	2	0
Activation	5	1
Pension	2	2
Unemployment	19	8

Source: Author's calculations from Center for Corporate Performance/Integrated Database for Labor Market Research (CCP/IDA) data.

grants, more will end up receiving some sort of transfer income, and more will probably be supported by their families. We can also conclude that there is no indication that immigrants are taking over Denmark's low-wage jobs, as has happened in many other countries. Instead, they have adopted the habits of non-immigrants—namely, becoming dependent on the welfare system and developing a relatively high reservation wage that discourages them from taking low-wage jobs.

Finally, we have also looked at the possibility that immigrants escape low-wage work by becoming self-employed. Immigrants are somewhat more likely to be self-employed than non-immigrants, but the numbers are very small.

LOW WAGES AND POVERTY

The last empirical question we try to answer is the extent to which low-wage status also indicates that a person is poor. We follow the Danish Economic Council (2006) in defining poverty in Denmark as having a household income per person that is less than 60 percent of the median income. By this definition, we find that around 35 percent of all low-wage earners live in a household that can be characterized as poor. Furthermore, this fraction seems to be constant, even when we follow a cohort of low-wage earners from 1996, as graphed in figure 2.17.

We conclude that there is a link between earning low wages and living in a poor household, but the link is relatively weak and poverty tends to disappear over time, together with low wages.

Figure 2.17 Poverty Among Low-Wage Workers, 1996 Cohort

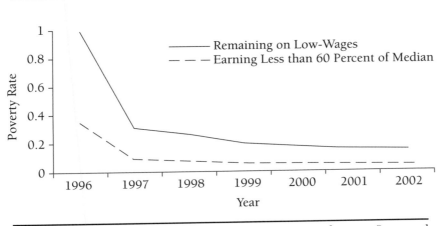

Source: Author's calculations from Center for Corporate Performance/Integrated Database for Labor Market Research (CCP/IDA) data.

LABOR MARKET POLICIES

One of the main elements of the Danish model is the government's support of the Danish labor market. There are both active and passive labor market policies, and most of them affect low-wage earners. The main policies underwent major changes in 1994 and in subsequent years. Since many people were affected by these changes, we distinguish between the periods before and after this reform. It is important to realize that the programs enacted after 1994 affect both high- and low-wage earners, but the incentives to participate in various elements of Denmark's labor market policies vary between income groups owing to the ceiling built into the benefit system.

Active Labor Market Policies

Until 1994, active labor market policies consisted of a job offer and a training program, an educational subsidy system, the Danish vocational education and training system (AMU), and a subsidy program for the newly started self-employed. The job offer program offered the long-term unemployed—individuals with a total unemployment duration of more than two years—seven- or nine-month subsidized jobs. These jobs counted toward eligibility for yet another period on unemployment benefits. At that time, the maximum duration of benefits was 9.4 years. Participants in the job offer program were paid the normal unemployment benefit. Finally, there were AMU courses, which taught unemployed as well as employed workers specific skills, for example, how to operate specific equipment.

After the labor market reform of 1994, unemployed recipients of UI benefits were obliged to take part in some type of "activation" program. At first this obligation was initiated after four years of passive unemployment, but that period has been gradually shortened; today activation is initiated after one year of passive unemployment. The first twelve-month period contains no other obligation than looking for a job. The activation period may then last for up to three years, during which time the unemployed person must be activated more than 75 percent of the time. The unemployed person will receive unemployment benefits for the duration of the four years, though the wage when he or she is in job training may be higher according to the type of job.

As a result of the 1994 reform, the subsidized job training periods under the labor market programs no longer count toward eligibility for future unemployment benefits. However, this policy shift did not change the number of people who exhausted their benefits, probably because the labor exchange offices began to put more effort into providing jobs for this group. Health-related retirement may be another reason why people stop receiving unemployment benefits, but this possibility has not been investigated thus far.

The main activation measures are job training and education. The purpose of the first is to give the unemployed an opportunity to get a job by going through a job training period with a private or public employer. A private employer receives a fixed subsidy of about half a normal low salary for a six-month period and has to pay the usual wage for that particular job, whereas a public-sector employer pays a fixed, relatively low wage. The ratio between private and public job training has been around one-to-four both before and after the reform. Furthermore, individual job training can be arranged for people who have difficulties getting a job because of long-term unemployment or poor educational background. In addition, activation can take place in so-called pool jobs in the public sector.

Another type of activation is education, both programs of study at ordinary educational institutions and courses designed for the unemployed. Ordinary educational courses must be ones that appear on a list issued by the Ministry of Employment. Unemployed individuals who are enrolled in education can receive unemployment benefits for a period of up to five years. Ordinary educational courses have become very popular in recent years: four out of five people in the activation program choose ordinary educational courses.

The other major labor market program that provided education was the education leave program, which was in effect from 1992 to the end of 2000. The education leave program made paid leave from a job conditional on the employer's consent. Even the unemployed could get educational leave for a number of prespecified courses, and in the meantime they would not be offered jobs. Unemployed individuals on educational leave were eligible for full UI benefits. In the beginning, there were few constraints on the number and variety of education leaves, but they became more and more limited until the program was abandoned altogether at the end of 2000. It was replaced by a system that supports unemployed individuals who want to take courses at ordinary education institutions. There are almost as many people enrolled in the new program as there were in the education leave program.

Finally, it should be mentioned that two other programs were enacted that never really attracted large numbers of participants—job rotation and the home service program. Job rotation, which was introduced in 1992, supported education and training programs for employed people provided they were replaced by an unemployed person. It was probably improved business cycles that made this program redundant. The home service program was an arrangement by which certified companies could receive state subsidies to employ people to do household work. This subsidy enabled firms to compete with black market activities. This program was terminated in 2004.

A special youth program was enacted in 1996, with no introductory period, for those under age twenty-five, and this program is still in effect. The initial period on normal UI benefits runs for only six months for young people. After that, they have the right and the obligation, if they have no prior vocational training, to take an education course of at least eighteen months' duration. Those who do have vocational qualifications must undergo job training. For both groups, the benefit is 50 percent of the UI benefit. Noncompliance brings all benefits to a complete stop.

The main labor market programs have been evaluated on several occasions. The most successful one has been the youth program, which has been shown to have a positive impact on the unemployment of young people (see Jensen, Rosholm, and Svarer 2003). But the relatively high growth rate in the economy has also had a positive impact on the demand for young employees in particular because when total demand for labor is increasing, demand for new entrants is even larger. Among other programs that have been evaluated, subsidized job training programs in the private sector have been found to have a positive impact when they match employers and employees. If the program participant does not stay with the employer after the training period, the effect is rather dubious. Similar effects are found for public-sector jobs. It is hard to find a clear positive effect of the educational programs. At face value, some of the programs look beneficial, but most look less so when we take into account their relatively long duration and the length of the period during which participants are not actively looking for a job (see Arbejdsministeriet 2000). More recently, a substantial effect from activation has been found to result from the mere threat of becoming activated (see Rosholm and Svarer 2004). In all these respects, the Danish activation policy does not seem to be better or worse than experiences elsewhere.

Passive Labor Market Policies

The so-called passive labor market programs consist of rules for early retirement, leave programs, and unemployment benefits. Figure 2.18 shows the total composition of active and passive labor market policies. The predominant passive labor market policy in this figure is early retirement; unemployment is shown as a separate curve. Though it is obvious that unemployment has declined since its peak in 1993, it is also obvious that passive and active labor market programs have absorbed some of the formerly unemployed; however, the total number of people on some sort of labor market program assistance is still higher than it was before 1990.

One of the main factors in the UI system is, of course, the replacement ratio of UI benefits compared to wages. The purpose of the high replacement ratio is to prevent a possible loss in welfare if a person becomes unemployed. The incentive problem arises because the high replacement ratio makes the income from finding a job only slightly better than the UI benefit. If the unemployed person is eligible for other transfer payments, the problem is aggravated. Many other

Figure 2.18 Active and Passive Labor Market Policies and
Unemployment, 1980 to 2003

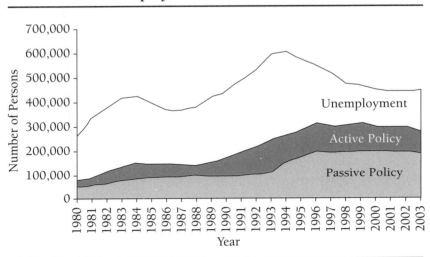

Source: Andersen et al. 2005.

countries experience similar incentive problems, but they are probably more serious in Denmark because benefits for low-wage earners
are so high (90 percent) and because benefits are not reduced over
time, as they are in most other countries. Furthermore, the Danish
income tax is high: extra income is taxed by a minimum tax of almost
50 percent.

Similarly, employers have only a small incentive to limit their use
of unemployment as a means of adjusting their demand for labor to
temporary business downturns and seasonal fluctuations with the
two days of employer payment. However, chapter 3 on the food-processing industry provides evidence that employers even find these
low costs too high and hence prefer to hold on to employees during
downturns, which is also the intention. Labor market statistics show
that temporary layoffs are nevertheless still a widespread feature of
the Danish labor market.

One reason is that a number of people choose to leave their jobs
with benefits if possible. Another is that the number of workers measured in hours by low-wage groups becomes smaller if they are members of the unemployment fund, as we demonstrated in figure 2.7.
There we saw that the actual average annual number of work-hours

by men in the lowest decile of the wage distribution is less than two-thirds of a full working year. Another reason for temporary layoffs is that many people become unemployed in connection with vacations (Christmas, New Year's, and summer). Even with low overall unemployment in 2004 (6.4 percent), 20 percent of the employed received unemployment benefits at some time during the year. At the peak of unemployment in 1993, this figure was 32 percent.

There are, of course, incentive problems with most public transfers. Incentive problems might even be more serious for those who are not insured in the event of unemployment and who receive welfare payments. Since welfare benefits are means-tested and include the income of a spouse, labor income is taxed at 100 percent up to the maximum income for eligibility for welfare benefits. This means that when both members of a couple are unemployed, one spouse must actually have a relatively high income if their total income is to exceed their previous welfare payment. The incentive problems are especially serious for workers with low skills, low-wage earners with high replacement ratios, and those for whom working entails high opportunity costs. Thus, the groups most affected are immigrant families in which both spouses are on welfare, low-skilled workers, and, especially, single mothers.

A reform in 2002 decreased the maximum welfare payment in order to reduce the incentive problems for welfare recipients, and in 2004 the employment allowance of 2.5 percent for earned income was introduced to increase the incentives to work.

The Cost of Labor Market Programs

Finally, it should be noted that the costs of Danish labor market programs are very high, especially when compared to other countries (see figure 2.19). OECD (2001) found that the total Danish expenditure on labor market programs was 5 percent of GDP. This high cost is one of the most critical elements of the Danish labor market and has implications for the sustainability of the whole welfare society.

Other Regulating Mechanisms

Though most of the regulation of the Danish labor market happens through the bargaining process between the trade unions and the Employers' Federation, the state has enacted a number of regulations

Figure 2.19 Total Costs of Labor Market Programs in
OECD Countries, 2001

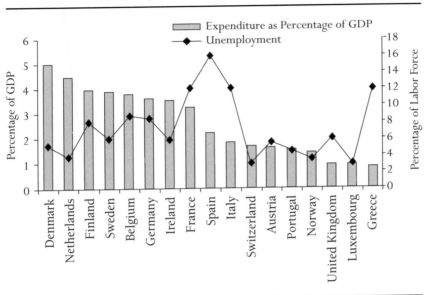

Source: OECD, *Economic Outlook*, 2001.

on health and safety standards in the working environment. Because some of Denmark's health and safety standards originate from the EU Council of Ministers, many of its regulations are almost identical to those in other EU countries.

Each workplace is obliged to have its own safety organization, which must plan and execute safety plans for the workplace. The Working Environment Agency sets rules for safety, and it is management's responsibility to enforce them. These regulations are extremely important for several of our industry studies. In the call centers, there are regulations on the minimum number of desks and chairs in the workplace and rules specifying, for instance, how many windows there should be in the room and the level of artificial light. In the food industry, rules governing how work is organized are intended to prevent accidents and exposure to substances, enforce health standards, and prevent ergonomic overload.

The regulations intended to protect workers from physical and psychological overload originated with the EU Commission. One example is the regulation prohibiting weekly working hours from exceeding forty-eight hours over a four-month period. Denmark did pass the EU Health and Safety at Work Act, but all other working regulations of working laws are part of the collective contracts.

Two final examples of regulation are the Salaried Workers Act, which regulates employment contracts for white-collar workers and includes rules on dismissals and hirings, and the Vacation Act, which sets minimum rules for how much vacation workers should have. All wage earners are granted five weeks of vacation, but some contracts allow for more vacation weeks.

Recent National Developments

Three recent developments may affect the prospects of low-wage earners.

Outsourcing   Since the fall of the Iron Curtain, Denmark has regained its market in the Baltic area. This has clearly increased competition among low-wage earners, not only because it has allowed more free trade, but especially because it has made it possible for companies to move production to countries in the Baltic area and in central and eastern Europe, where the wages of industrial workers are one-sixth of Danish wages and safety and environment regulations are much less restrictive. On the other hand, the opening of this market has been one of the main explanations for a strong demand for Danish goods and services and has thus contributed to strong economic development in Denmark.

The net effect is uncertain, though relatively low Danish unemployment and the high surplus in Denmark's trade balance, even in a period of recession, are signs pointing to the benefits of the opening of this market. At the same time, Denmark has also steadily increased the outsourcing of all sorts of manufacturing to China and of clothing manufacturing to the Baltic area, Ukraine, China, Bangladesh, and other Far Eastern countries. In Olsen, Ibsen, and Westergaard-Nielsen (2004), my colleagues and I describe the effects of outsourcing on Danish clothing and textile employment. We conclude, based on our own research and on more recent research on the effects on the whole economy (Eriksson et al. 2006), that outsourcing will have a depressing effect on wages and work conditions in a number of Danish firms. Outsourcing has already led to a shift in labor demand toward more skilled and educated workers. Similarly, the gradual opening of the Danish labor market to workers from the new EU member countries will undoubtedly have the effect of making low-wage jobs in the service sector available to temporary workers from these countries to a larger extent than we have seen so far. When this happens, we will once again see increasing competition and a downward pressure on wages and working conditions. In the food-processing industry, outsourcing has led to the shift of the most labor-intensive processes to Germany, which employs Polish workers, or to the mechanization of these processes.

Wage Bargaining   Wage bargaining used to be centralized and binding for at least the low-skilled workers, whose wage rates were semi-fixed for a two-year period. This system was widely believed to be an advantage for low-wage earners. However, it also created an element of inflexibility: since firms (and workers) were bound by the wage contract, changes in product demand and technological changes sometimes resulted in layoffs. Since 1993, more and more wage bargaining has been done at the firm and individual levels. The impact on employment remains unclear, but it is likely that this change in policy has made the Danish labor market more flexible, and it may also have contributed to fewer layoffs, because it is now a bit more feasible for firms to adjust wages instead of laying off workers. Similarly, the policy change gives firms more options in paying higher individual wages in response to outside wage offers, thus diminishing quits.

Labor Market Programs   Since the mid-1990s, labor market policies have become more oriented toward activation of the unemployed; previously the emphasis had been on income maintenance (Layard et al. 2003). This shift has probably also had an impact on low-wage earners.

Possible Reforms

Today the Danish economy is working relatively well, partly because of macroeconomic factors and partly because of what seems to be a beneficial structure. Nevertheless, there are a number of areas ripe for reform. The most prominent issue remains that of weak incentives to work. Incentives to work remain weak for everyone who is receiving some type of benefit and not participating in the labor market. Some of these individuals are, of course, clearly sick and unable to work; economic incentives should certainly not be expected to work for them. For others, however, the low incentive to work is attributable to the relatively high benefit level combined with the high rate of taxation. Many people find that they would have prohibitively high tax rates if they started working and at the same time would lose their means-tested benefits.

Many working people have similarly little incentive to work more than about 1,100 hours a year because UI benefits and the tax on earned income make it not worthwhile to work too many hours at a low wage. There are two solutions to this disincentive: limiting the use of unemployment benefits to even shorter periods of unemployment and lowering UI benefits or putting a tax premium on earnings. The government has begun to address this situation by introducing a work allowance of 2.5 percent of earned income. This tax allowance is presently limited to a little less than €1,000, so it provides only a marginal incentive to low-wage earners. But we believe that the idea is a good one and that the allowance should be increased substantially.

The incentive problem is serious for everyone in Denmark, but it is probably especially serious for immigrant families, because many of them earn low wages. High welfare payments and relative high minimum tariffs lead to little attachment to the labor market, and that undoubtedly has consequences for immigrant children and their ability to build a labor market career. One way to target this group would be to increase the earnings allowance for wage earners with dependents, in the manner of the Earned Income Tax Credit in the United States or the Family Tax Credit (FTC) in the United Kingdom.

Another issue of concern in Denmark as well as in other European countries is the early retirement age. It seems obvious that increases in expected lifetimes should lengthen working lives as well. Thus far, however, the Danes have put off changing the early retirement system, which allows people to retire at age sixty; the median retirement age, with public support, is around sixty-one.

CONCLUSIONS AND PREVIEW OF THE INDUSTRY STUDIES

This study shows that there is high mobility out of low-wage work in Denmark. Danish labor market institutions clearly support this mobility, in the sense that low-productivity workers tend to work less and are compensated for working fewer hours if they do not leave the labor force. Most of the institutions are constructed to ensure that low-wage workers have relatively high coverage. This means that low-wage workers are also likely to either increase their wage or become dependent on early pensions or other income supports. As a consequence, the tax pressure on all Danes is high, and the country's labor market policies are very expensive.

Furthermore, young people have tended to take over most of the low-wage work, primarily during the period of a couple of years after they finish high school and before they start university, and again during their studies. As a consequence of their short-term job horizon, they do not become members of the UI system and do not acquire the security of insured workers. However, they are highly flexible in the sense that they shift easily between jobs. The institutions for covered workers help them either to get better-paid jobs or to leave the labor force temporarily or permanently with income support. Many immigrants seem to be stuck between the two groups of workers: they are not covered by unemployment benefits, and they are not as productive as the young natives. As a result, many immigrants tend to drop out of the labor market after trying for a couple of years to get a foot in the door. Those who succeed, however, do as well as the Danes.

In the next chapters, we illustrate and contextualize a number of the findings from chapters 1 and 2. We have visited more than forty workplaces within the food-processing, retail, hotel and restaurant, hospital, and call center industries. We have interviewed persons at different levels, from top to bottom, where we expected to find most low-wage employees. In all cases, we wanted to investigate the work conditions for the occupational groups that are low-wage in some countries. We hope that these studies will fill in the reality behind the statistical framework presented in chapters 1 and 2 and give the reader an impression of the real working conditions of low-wage earners in Denmark.

In chapter 3 on the food-processing industry, we report our finding that workers can influence work routines and work organization if doing so improves efficiency. Furthermore, we find that work organization can differ between plants within the same company, illustrating the decentralization discussed earlier. However, we also find that good relations between companies and managers, on the one side, and unions, employee representatives (shop stewards), and workers, on the other, have been strained in some workplaces by companies' efforts to lower labor costs to defend themselves against globalization. This strain did not happen because employee representatives and workers were unwilling to cooperate and work toward lowering labor costs, but because management often initiated this change without consulting with employee representatives and workers.

The general finding from the study of the food-processing industry, however, is that workers and employee representatives do accept that their workplaces cannot survive if no effort is made to improve efficiency by changing work practices whenever necessary. They express a willingness to contribute and make sacrifices, including reductions in the number of workers, if their sacrifices help the company and ensure its long-term survival. They argue that management's failure to make use of their competencies and knowledge of production processes often creates what could have been avoidable problems, such as difficulties installing and using new machinery. Furthermore, by failing to involve workers in change projects, managers miss an opportunity to motivate workers and transfer "ownership" to workers.

The food-processing industry is special because it employs relatively many immigrants, who constitute around 10 percent of its workforce. In one of the workplaces we visited, about 30 percent of the production workers were immigrants. Language seems to be one of the prime problems in hiring more immigrants, and lack of Danish-language skills is believed to be a potential hazard. Some firms have now adopted a language policy of hiring only people who can communicate in Danish.

The food-processing sector is the only one in which we encountered closed-shop agreements limiting employment to members of a specific trade union.[17] This arrangement, of course, keeps up the union membership level; in other industries, however, this stipulation has been creating conflicts between workers, because some do not want to become members of a particular union. This apparently has not been the case in the firms we investigated.

In chapter 4 on low-wage work in the retail industry, we see that, as with the hotel sector, many low-wage workers are young people, including many students. The turnover rate is high, not because the low-wage jobs in this industry are bad, but rather because many young people want to try other things or concentrate on their studies. Most of the employees we interviewed for our case studies were happy with their jobs and put much emphasis on the social side of their jobs and on having good colleagues. Some employers specifically use workers' preference for a friendly workplace to build company spirit and supportive teamwork. This industry is characterized by good career possibilities for those who want to stay in the industry. There are two reasons for such opportunities: the industry suffers from a labor shortage because of its low prestige, and to a large extent it is occupied by individuals who do not wish to have a career in retail, either because they do not want to stay in the sector or because they do not want to invest in a career at all. As a result of these factors, there are a lot of very young Danish shop managers.

Chapter 5 on the hotel industry reveals that hotels may be the only investigated industry in which large numbers of low-wage workers are outside the supportive system of unemployment benefits, sickness insurance, and so on. Only 27 percent of full-time low-wage workers are covered by unemployment insurance, and the majority of part-time low-wage workers are not covered by the system. The main explanation is that membership in an unemployment fund is relatively expensive, especially for those who work only part-time. Furthermore, students make up about 50 percent of all low-wage workers in hotels, and most of them are employed on a part-time basis. Employment of immigrants in the hotel sector has increased in recent years, especially in the 1990s, owing to the overall increasing flow of immigrants to Denmark during that period. Immigrants made up 14 percent of the hotel industry's labor force in 2003; this figure had increased from 8 percent in 1992. Still, the immigrant proportion in the hotel sector is lower in Denmark than in the United Kingdom, Germany, France, and the Netherlands.

We have found that a substantial fraction of hotel industry employees lack income security from membership in a UI fund. Some employees may simply need less security, probably because they only want temporary employment. For some employees, on the other hand, especially immigrants, lack of insurance is due to ignorance of the Danish social security system. It is important to note that neither immigrants nor students lack formal access to the Danish social security system. In any event, the hotel sector is one in which the Danish flexicurity system is not fully operative. However, our interviews revealed that to some extent hotel managers and workers have replaced official flexicurity with the flexibility to change work hours and with cooperation between employees to cover sick days.

In chapter 6, we see that the hospital occupations we investigated are all highly organized, as are most Danish public employees. Furthermore, the unions that organize hospital workers have a long tradition of cooperating with employers about work organization, training programs, new ways of organizing work, and working hours. The hospital sector, like the public sector generally, has a tradition of peaceful bargaining. Employers are cooperative because they fully accept union dominance and influence in the workplace. As a result, hospitals pay reasonably well at the lowest levels, while there is more discontent with salaries higher up in the wage hierarchy. Employees seem to be happy with their jobs and tend to stay in them for long periods. In more recent years, there has been pressure on hospital employees and management to increase efficiency; this pressure has mounted at the same time that the structure of treatment at hospitals has changed: treatment regimens characterized by nursing with many days of hospitalization have been replaced with much shorter spells of hospitalization. This situation could have been solved by shifting large groups of personnel to the care sector now operating outside hospitals. Instead, the solution has been typically Danish: upgrading the present personnel to take over new multitasking job types. Furthermore, new and longer educations have been created to prepare workers for these new roles. The whole process seems to go fairly well, with cooperation between the local trade union representatives, the employees, and management.

Chapter 7 covers two types of call centers: those operated by the financial sector, and those operated by the utility sector. It is clear from the case studies that students occupy many of the low-wage jobs in the call center industry and generally have the jobs with the lowest job quality. But there are exceptions to the rule: in some call centers, students are highly trained and paid accordingly. All Danish call center employees are covered by the Work Environment Act, the Vacation Act, and the Salaried Workers Act. But Danish call centers appear to follow a set of "institutional norms" that surpass these regulatory requirements. The relatively high level of wages and work conditions at Danish call centers puts these centers in a class of their own compared to call centers in many other countries. One reason could be the higher degree of unionization in Denmark. But even if unionization becomes more common, it appears that unions actually have had a hard time getting call center employers and workers to make collective agreements. Another reason could be that it has been important for employers and employees to avoid creating "factories like those in the U.K." As a result, a new "collaboration agreement" between unions and employers is now being promoted. This agreement, which does not involve wage negotiations, is part of the general drive to decentralize wage bargaining, as explained earlier. The central element in the agreement is the naming of a shop steward who represents the workers. The company also has to pay a fee to an education fund that can be used by the company's employees. The company promises to adhere to a certain code of conduct and to contact the trade union to solve conflicts. Such agreements have become attractive to companies partly because of the negative press treatment of the call center industry and the coming shortage of labor. It seems plausible that regulation, high UI benefits, and an organized labor market are what prevent the erosion of job quality and pay in the call centers.

Overall, the Danish labor market model seems to work very well, with only a few groups excluded from receiving all the benefits of the system. In most workplaces, the model promotes high worker involvement in daily routines. Management respects the people who do the manual work, and the workers respect the managers, who have the financial responsibility. In a similar way, trust between management and workers in Danish workplaces seems to be mutual. Unions and the Employers' Federation have always played a big role in Denmark and still do. More recently, however, these two social partners have been decentralizing their efforts; in particular, the trade unions have reconfigured their role vis-à-vis companies as that of a partner in improving production, profitability, and the conditions of workers.

This shift clearly builds on a firm foundation of many years of cooperation and trust between workers and management. One of the foundations of this system is the government's provision of a social safety net and its reluctance to interfere too much in labor markets without the involvement of the social partners. This hands-off role for the government is also necessary to maintain high union membership, because members must feel that they get something for their union fees. In its present form, however, the role of the government appears to be very expensive, which of course could compromise the future of the model.

Outsourcing and immigration remain serious challenges. Outsourcing has been dealt with very efficiently through high worker flexibility. Immigration, however, poses a bigger problem; the labor market by and large has not been able to integrate all of the immigrants, partly because of a high implicit minimum wage, low productivity, and low language skills. Instead, the social welfare system has had to take care of the immigrants. That has added to the already high costs of the social security system and created political movements built on antagonism toward immigrants.

Can the Danish model be copied by other countries? This book will demonstrate that the Danish model is so intricate that it would be difficult to transfer to other countries. Other countries could copy some elements, however, without subscribing to the whole package.

APPENDIX A: THE SOCIAL SAFETY NET

This chapter demonstrates clearly that the social safety net is important for everybody in Denmark, and especially for low-wage earners since most transfer payments, except for UI benefits, are means-tested and provide an alternative to continued low-wage work in those cases where there might be a choice.

Old-Age and Disability Benefits

For many years, Denmark has had a pension system that is not limited to the working population but covers the entire population and provides an old-age pension after the age of sixty-five. (Before 2005, the age was sixty-seven for men and sixty-five for women.) This is a pay-as-you-go system in which the Parliament regulates benefits, which are taken from current tax revenue. Pensions are granted depending on the extent of other income after retirement and are independent of income before retirement.

In 1979 an early retirement program was introduced that gave all members of the UI system the option of receiving a benefit equal to the UI between the ages of sixty and normal retirement age. Consequently, this benefit is called "post-employment wage." The early retirement program has become important for the labor market situation of senior workers because it has created a dilemma for workers in their mid- to late fifties who lose their jobs: new employers are reluctant to hire them because they fear that they will take early retirement at the age of sixty.

Researchers have tested whether employers use the early retirement program to get rid of older workers. Paul Bingley and Gauthier Lanot (2004) have shown that the program has no effect on firms; their research indicates that employers do not systematically push senior employees into early retirement. It seems that other factors are important, such as the spouse's work situation. In 2006 the government decided to increase the early retirement age to sixty-two after 2017 in order to increase the labor force.

There is also a publicly provided disability pension for all age groups. Eligibility is determined on health grounds. In 2000 the proportion of Danes receiving a disability pension was about 10 percent of the labor force. One especially noteworthy effect of the early retirement program has been the gradual decline in the average retirement age. In 2001, 50 percent of a cohort had retired at the age of sixty-one. Furthermore, unskilled laborers tend to transfer to disability pensions before other groups.

MATERNITY LEAVE AND SICKNESS PAY

Maternity leave that covers all women is paid by the sickness benefit system, and the minimum extent of compensation and amount of leave time is determined by legislation. Since 2002, the total maternity leave period has been fifty-two weeks. Some collective contracts provide for greater compensation and longer leave periods. The mother has the right to fourteen weeks of maternity leave following birth. In the same period, the father has the right to two weeks of paid leave. From the time the child is fourteen weeks old, the father and the mother can share thirty-two weeks of leave. Mothers still take most of this time.

Every worker is eligible for sickness pay while on maternity leave. Sickness pay is taxable and amounts to €430 (US$580) per week. The employer pays for the first two weeks, after which time the public sickness benefit administration takes over. Usually high-salaried employees and all public employees get extra benefits according to their contracts, and many salaried employees are paid their usual salary when on maternity and sickness leave. The employer is reimbursed the minimum benefit from the sickness benefit administration. There are similar arrangements for employees who want to take leave for nursing terminally ill relatives or close friends. Doctors and hospitals are free for everyone, as described here and in the hospital study (chapter 6).

Family Allowance

All families receive a quarterly subsidy for each child under eighteen. It is highest for children between the ages of zero and two (€452 per quarter) and lowest for children between seven and eighteen (€322). These amounts are not means-tested and not taxable. Single parents and parents on disability or other pensions receive an extra child subsidy of €145 per quarter. If only one parent is alive, an even higher subsidy may be granted.

Child Support and Child Care Subsidies

Absent parents have to pay child support of €1,674 per year, which is tax-deductible for the absent parent and not taxed with the receiving parent. If support is not paid directly between the parents, the municipality can collect it by withholding it from wages and advancing the amount to the receiving parent.

All child care institutions receive a substantial subsidy from the local municipality that amounts to about two-thirds of all costs (the amount varies across municipalities). In 2006 the cost of full-day child care ranged from €260 per month to €470, depending on age. For those whose household income is below €54,000, there is a means-tested subsidy that reduces these amounts. Moreover, substantial sibling discounts are available.

Health Insurance

Health insurance is nationally provided and paid out of the general public budget. Medical treatment is free. Insurance covers all hospital and physician treatments but covers only a small part of dental costs. Doctors, most medical specialists, and all dentists are private but heavily regulated, while hospitals are mainly public.

Housing Subsidies

Housing subsidies are granted on a means-tested basis to low-income families, depending on the size of the family, the size of the apartment, and the rent. The subsidy works like a cap on the relative costs of housing. Furthermore, major cities still have rent control, and community housing receives a large subsidy to keep rents down. There are also indirect subsidies to owners of apartments and houses: the tax-deductibility in the lowest bracket (33 percent) of mortgage interest; the lower rate at which user costs are taxed; and the fact that capital gains on owner-occupied housing are not taxed. As a consequence, the type of housing chosen is dependent on income.

Income Support

Denmark has a weak version of the direct income support of the EITC in the United States. In 2007 it was given as a tax credit of 2.5 percent of the wage up to a maximum of €100. This gave low-wage earners of up to €40,000 a marginal incentive to work more. Again in comparison with the United States, it should be noted that everyone in Danish society pays taxes, though all low-income earners are eligible for various subsidies, some means-tested and others not.

APPENDIX B: DATA SOURCES

For this study, we used OECD data for the comparative part and register-based data where it was more appropriate.

The basic register data are longitudinal in nature and permit us to follow individuals on an annual basis. This amounts to 4.5 million persons each year from 1980 onward and covers the whole population age fifteen to seventy-four. The data contain individual-level information covering areas such as income and employment, detailed demographic information, and information on workplaces. These data come from Statistics Denmark and are part of the so-called IDA (Integrated Data Base for Labor Market Statistics) database. The sample of variables is selected and maintained by the Center for Corporate Performance (CCP) at the Aarhus School of Business, University of Aarhus (and before that, by the Centre for Labour and Social Research [CLS]).

These data were extended with different sets of surveys using the common population ID number as the merge key. A special feature of the CCP data is that we have linked these data with elaborate information on workplaces that can be aggregated to firms. The firm data also contain accounting information on all companies. As such, the data offer the unique feature of tracking personal movements over time with respect to jobs, firms, and earnings. In future, the data will be well suited for a full-scale analysis of the incidence of low-wage employment from the point of view of workers and firms.

NOTES

1. Apprentices are included in the labor force.
2. All currency conversions noted in this volume were made at the prevailing rate for August, 2007.
3. It should be noted that the circumstances under which people lose their jobs have an important impact on that loss. If the job loss is the result of a workplace closure or major restructuring, it is considered to have less of an impact (Ibsen and Westergaard-Nielsen 2005).
4. This 25 percent does not add up with the labor force participation rate of 80 percent in table 2.3 because the latter by convention counts heads irrespective of how much they work and the statistics in this section count full-time-equivalent persons.
5. Because taxes and, in particular, received benefits depend on individual factors, calculating after-tax and benefit income is a very complicated procedure. But because of progression in taxes and digression in benefits, the resulting distribution is more compressed than before taxes and benefits.
6. A mother is given leave of four weeks before birth and fourteen weeks after birth. During that period, the father has leave of two weeks. Thereafter, thirty-two weeks can be used by the father or the mother. The general pay is the same as unemployment insurance pay, but many white-collar workers are compensated during parental leave at near normal pay, as per their contract. It is possible, but unusual, to get part-time maternity leave.
7. The relative lack of part-time child care may be related to the full-time nature of government subsidies and to the contracts negotiated by the trade unions for day care employees.
8. Similar ratios for female/male earnings are .76 for the United States, .76 for the Netherlands, and .84 for Sweden (Blau and Kahn 2000).
9. Figure 2.7 is based on register data on contributions to an obligatory pension system in which contributions until 1994 were proportional to hours worked.
10. The five upper deciles are not shown.
11. For example, the "twenty-four years rule" prevents people below the age of twenty-four from getting immigration status for a spouse from abroad. And for married couples, an entrant visa is not automatically granted to a non-Danish spouse. Furthermore, refugees are turned back in large numbers.

12. Apprentices are not counted as low-paid in this study.
13. The 1988 International Standard Classification of Occupation (ISCO-88) codes are used in the study.
14. We cannot identify call centers in the registers because they are embedded in other industries.
15. Another issue is whether we allow those who have left the low-wage group to return to the sample and then count all observations as low-wage, or whether we delete them from the sample when they get a non-low-wage job, as we do in table 2.11. We have tried both approaches, and the difference is minuscule.
16. This total now includes the "missings" cited in table 2.11.
17. As described earlier, the European Human Rights Court outlawed closed-shop agreements in 2006.

REFERENCES

Andersen, Torben M., Hans Linderoth, Valdemar Smith, and Niels Wester-gaard-Nielsen. 2005. *Beskrivende Dansk Økonomi* [*Descriptive Danish Economy*]. Risskov, Denmark: HandelsVidenskab Bogforlaget.

Arbejdsministeriet (Danish Ministry of Labor). 2000. *Effekter af Aktiverings-indsatsen* [*Effects of Activation Policies*]. Copenhagen: Danish Ministry of Labor.

Asplund, Rita, Peter J. Bingley, and Niels Westergaard-Nielsen. 1998. "Wage Mobility for Low-Wage Earners in Denmark and Finland." In *Low Pay and Earnings Mobility in Europe*, edited by Rita Asplund, Peter J. Sloane, and Ioannis Theodossiou. Cheltenham, England: E. Elgar.

Bingley, Paul, and Gauthier Lanot. 2004. "Employer Pay Policies, Public Transfers, and the Retirement Decisions of Women in Denmark." *European Economic Review* 48(1): 181–200.

Bingley, Paul, and Niels Westergaard-Nielsen. 2006. "Job Changes and Wage Growth over the Careers of Private-Sector Workers in Denmark." In *Structural Models of Wage and Employment Dynamics*, edited by Henning Bunzel, Bent J. Christensen, George R. Neumann, and Jean-Marc Robin. Vol. 275 in Contributions to Economic Analysis series. Amsterdam: Elsevier.

Blau, Francine D., and Lawrence Kahn. 2000. "Gender Differences in Pay." *Journal of Economic Perspectives* 14(4, Fall): 75–99.

Bolvig, Iben. 2005. "Within- and Between-Firm Mobility in the Low-Wage Labor Market." In *Job Quality and Employer Behavior*, edited by Stephen Bazen, Claudio Lucifora, and Wiemer Salverda. London: Palgrave Macmillan.

Bundesvereinigung der Deutschen Arbeitgeberverbände (Federal German Federation of Employees). 2005. "Deutschland bleibt - Freizeit weltmeister" ["Germany remains leisure time world champion"]. KND Nr 13, April 2005.

Danish Economic Council. 2006. "Dansk Økonomi Efteraar" ("Danish Economy, Fall 2006"). Copenhagen: Economic Council.

Danish Employers' Federation. 2005. *Arbejdsmarkedsrapport* [*Labor Market Report*]. Copenhagen: Employers' Federation.

Datta Gupta, Nabanita, and Donna S. Rothstein. 2005. "The Impact of Worker and Establishment-Level Characteristics on Male-Female Wage Differentials: Evidence from Danish Matched Employer-Employee Data." *Labor: Review of Labor Economics and Industrial Relations* 19(1): 1–34.

Eriksson, Tor, and Niels Westergaard-Nielsen. 2003. "Resultatløn i Danske virksamheder" ("Performance Pay in Danish Companies"). *Ledelseshåndbogen* (*Total Quality Management*) April 2, 2003.

———. 2007. "Wage and Labor Mobility in Denmark, 1980–2000." Working paper 13064. Cambridge, Mass.: National Bureau of Economic Research.

Eriksson, Tor, Rikke Ibsen, J. Li, and Niels Westergaard-Nielsen. 2006. *Globalisering og det danske arbejdsmarked* (*Globalization and the Danish Labor Market*). Copenhagen: Jurist og Økonomforbundets forlag.

Harmon, Colm, Ian Walker, and Niels Westergaard-Nielsen. 2001. Introduction to *Education and Earnings in Europe*, edited by Colm Harmon, Ian Walker, and Niels Westergaard-Nielsen. Cheltenham, U.K.: E. Elgar.

Ibsen, Rikke, and Niels Westergaard-Nielsen. 2005. "Job Creation and Destruction over the Business Cycles and the Impact on Individual Job Flows in Denmark 1980–2001." *Journal of the German Statistical Association* 88(2): 183–206.

Jensen, Peter, Michael Rosholm, and Michael Svarer. 2003. "The Response of Youth Unemployment to Benefits, Incentives, and Sanctions." *European Journal of Political Economy* 19(2, June): 301–16.

Kristensen, Nicolai, and Niels Westergaard-Nielsen. 2004. "Does Low Job Satisfaction Lead to Job Mobility?" Discussion paper 1026. Aarhus, Denmark: Aarhus School of Business, Institute for the Study of Labor (February).

Layard, Richard, Stephen Nickell, Jaap de Koning, and Niels Westergaard-Nielsen. 2003. "Policies for Full Employment." London: London School of Economics, Center for Economic Performance, February 20, 2003.

Neumann, George, Peder J. Pedersen, and Niels Westergaard-Nielsen. 1991. "Long-Run International Trends in Aggregate Unionization." *European Journal of Political Economy* 7(3): 249–74.

Olsen, Karsten Bjerring, Rikke Ibsen, and Niels Westergaard-Nielsen. 2004. *Does Outsourcing Create Unemployment? The Case of the Danish Textile and*

Clothing Industry. Working paper 04-5. Aarhus, Denmark: Aarhus School of Business.

Organization for Economic Cooperation and Development (OECD). 1996. *Employment Outlook*. Paris: OECD.

————. 2001. *Employment Outlook*. Paris: OECD.

————. 2004. *Education at a Glance*. Paris: OECD.

————. 2005a. *Economic Outlook*. Paris: OECD.

————. 2005b. *Employment Outlook*. Paris: OECD.

————. 2006. *Productivity Database*. Paris: OECD.

Pedersen, Peder J., and Nina Smith. 2002. "Unemployment Traps and Financial Disincentives to Work." *European Sociological Review* 18(3): 271–88.

Rosholm, Michael, and Michael Svarer. 2004. "Estimating the Threat Effect of Active Labor Market Programs." Working paper 2004–06. Aarhus, Denmark: University of Aarhus, Department of Economics.

Smith, Nina. 1998. "Incentives to Work." in *Work, Incentives, and Unemployment*, edited by Nina Smith. Aarhus, Denmark: Aarhus University Press.

Westergaard-Nielsen, Niels. 1999. *Wage Dispersion, Employment, and Unemployment: Possible Trade-offs*. EC/DGV and OECD Seminar on Wages and Employment. European Commission.

CHAPTER 3

Feeling the Gale or Enjoying a Breeze in the Eye of the Storm? The Consequences of Globalization for Work and Workers in the Danish Food-Processing Industry

Lars Esbjerg and Klaus G. Grunert

Work in the Danish food industry is not low-wage work. Even though the globalization of the food industry has given food-processing companies strong reasons to focus on reducing costs (especially companies facing international competition), so far this has not led to strong downward pressure on wages. The production of some products for which price is the main competitive parameter has been offshored, but food companies have mainly responded to globalization by increasing capital intensity (through production automation and rationalization of production processes) and by focusing on quality and innovation.

Four major developments are currently influencing the Danish food industry—and the food industry in general. First, globalization and the liberalization of world markets have led to increased competition: Danish producers in world export markets (and at home) face competitors that have strengthened their competencies in areas in which the Danish industry has traditionally been strong, such as cost-effectiveness and efficient quality control. Second, because structural change in the retailing industry has led to changes in the power balance of food value chains, retailers are much stronger today (Dawson 2000; Grant 1987). Manufacturers have come under increased price pressure as retailers try to capture a larger part of the overall value creation in the chain by emphasizing private label programs. Third, consumer demands have become more fragmented and dynamic: the traditional demand for tasty and healthy foods is now supplemented by demands for varied, natural, and convenient products. Finally, developments in production technology and biotechnology have rapidly changed the whole production setup of the food industry. The industry's traditionally low R&D expenses may change given the new product development possibilities offered by biotechnology.

As companies have responded to these changes, workers in the Danish food-processing industry have experienced many changes in the nature and conditions of work. For many workers, the automation of labor-intensive work processes has changed the content of their jobs from manual labor to monitoring production processes and machinery. Workers are required to work faster. The increased work pace, the frequent changes of organizational structures and work processes, the introduction of new technology, and the uncertainty about the future of their workplaces have all caused many workers to experience work-related stress. Overall, however, job satisfaction appears to remain high. Changes in job content and work processes have largely been implemented without major conflict between workers and managers (although there have been exceptions). Workers and managers, in mutual recognition of the need for action and change, have generally worked together, although they have not always agreed about what changes should be made or how they could best be accomplished. At least part of the explanation can be found in the "Danish model" (see chapter 2), the associated trust between workers and managers, and the generally good labor market relations in Danish workplaces, as described in chapters 1 and 2.

In this chapter, we present the findings of a case study investigating how Danish food producers are coping with the changes in the food industry, particularly the pressures of globalization, and how these changes and food producers' responses are affecting pay and job quality for workers in the industry.

In the next section, we describe the methodology we used and discuss how we constructed and analyzed our empirical material. We then give an overview of the Danish food processing industry and various important institutions, focusing on the meat-processing and confectionary sectors. Next, we present the findings of our case studies. Finally, we provide conclusions and discuss our findings.

STUDY DESIGN AND METHODOLOGY

To study how companies in the Danish food-processing industry cope with globalization and the consequences of globalization for workers, we conducted seven case studies in two sectors, meat processing and confectionary. Meat processing has traditionally paid very high wages and been male-dominated, whereas more female workers have filled jobs in confectionary and the work has been less well paid.

We gained various degrees of access to the companies we studied, but our goal—not always realized—was to speak to top managers, human resource officials, frontline managers, employee representatives, and production workers at each of the companies (see the appendix for the main characteristics of the case companies). In total, we conducted thirty-four interviews with informants in the case companies and with two union representatives. The majority of the interviews were with individual informants, but in two companies we conducted focus groups with production workers.

We developed different interview protocols for managers, employee representatives, and production workers (for both individual and focus group interviews) that covered a number of topics, including the identity of the company, its economic context, its business strategy, its work organization, and the working conditions, wages and benefits, and training and career prospects for workers. Interviews were semistructured around these topics, but informants were given ample room to express their own thoughts and reflections and describe their experiences.

Interviews were tape-recorded and subsequently transcribed verbatim. To familiarize ourselves with the empirical material, we first read and coded interviews before we wrote up the individual case descriptions, focusing on the important themes that emerged from the empirical material. We then sent those write-ups to informants for their comments and clarifications.

THE DANISH FOOD INDUSTRY AND ITS INSTITUTIONS

The Danish food-processing industry is a broad industry covering subsectors such as the production, processing, and preserving of meat, fish, dairy products, fruits, vegetables, baked goods, oils, and beverages. The food industry is an important sector of the Danish economy: in 2005 it accounted for 22 percent of the total production of Danish industry, 16 percent of exported goods, and 18 percent of industrial employment.

Table 3.1 Danish Food Industry, by Sector, 2003

Sector	Number of Companies	Number of Full-Time Employees	Revenues (in Millions of Euros)
Slaughtering and meat processing	162	21,986	5,354
Dairies[a]	61	9,927	3,786
Bakeries	1,049	5,932	526
Beverages	38	5,431	1,692
Tobacco[a]	7	1,318	521
Other food industries[b]	443	26,431	8,272

Source: Statistics Denmark (2004); some of the data was drawn from the online database resources of Statistics Denmark, accessed at http://www.statistikbanken.dk.
[a] 2001.
[b] The "other" category includes companies producing fish, food ingredients, and processed foods such as cakes and cookies, confectionary, and processed fruits and vegetables.

The meat and dairy industries have traditionally been the dominant sectors of the Danish food industry (see table 3.1). Both sectors have been through a period of consolidation and are today dominated by Danish Crown and Arla Foods, respectively, both of which are farmer-owned cooperatives. Indeed, cooperative ownership has traditionally played a central role in the Danish food industry and continues to do so. The other dominant ownership form is private ownership; few food companies are listed on the stock exchange.

Generally, the highly concentrated Danish food industry is characterized by a small number of very large companies that tend to be among the world's largest in their sectors (see tables 3.2 and 3.3). Examples include Arla Foods in the dairy industry, Danish Crown in meat processing, Carlsberg in the brewery sector, and Danisco Cultor

Table 3.2 Danish Food Industry, by Number of Employees, 2003

	Zero to Nineteen Employees	Twenty to Forty-Nine Employees	Fifty Employees or More	Total
Number of companies	1,482	131	146	1,759
Number of full-time employees	7,287	4,116	59,719	71,122
Revenues (in millions of euros)	n.a.	n.a.	n.a.	20,429

Source: Statistics Denmark (2006).

Table 3.3 Industry Revenues and Concentration, by Subsector, 2003

	Total Revenues (in Millions of Euros)	Concentration	
		Top Three	Top Ten
Food, drink, and tobacco industry	18,244	35.6%	49.9%
Slaughtering and meat processing	5,234	73.2	89.4
Dairies	3,383	90.1	96.0
Other food industry[a]	7,592	14.4	31.2
Beverages	1,487	75.0	96.0
Tobacco	547	90.1	100.0

Source: Statistics Denmark (2006, 293).
[a] Includes companies producing fish, food ingredients, and procesed foods, such as cakes and cookies, confectionaries, and processed fruits and vegetables.

in the ingredients business. There are also many small companies (fewer than twenty employees), but relatively few medium-sized companies (between twenty and forty-nine employees).

Traditionally the Danish food industry has been export-oriented. Today more than two-thirds of total farm production is exported, and exports continue to grow in importance as international trade is liberalized and consumers across the world become more open to foreign food products. To continue to grow and to remain competitive in the face of trade liberalization and the expansion of the European Union, Danish food producers have begun to locate production and processing either close to the end users or where production and labor costs are lowest.

The Danish food industry is reacting in different ways to the four major developments outlined earlier. There has been a notable change away from producing commodities with an emphasis on cost-effectiveness and a move toward differentiated, value-added products. This change, in turn, has led to an emphasis on new product development and flexible production and consequently a reconfiguration of the value chain. Differentiated production not only requires changes in the production facilities of the processing plant but may also change the type of relationships to other value chain members, both upstream and downstream. Upstream, closer relationships to primary production are necessary if the product differentiation is rooted in differences in the raw material, as with organic milk or animal welfare pigs, and in this respect the traditional Danish cooperative form of organization, in which the farmers own the processors, may be an advantage compared to other forms of organization. Downstream, one way for food producers to counteract the increasing bargaining power of food retailers is to attempt to develop long-term relations in areas in which retailers rely on the competencies of food producers, like the development of their private label products.

These developments help explain why total food industry employment declined by 20 percent from 1997 to 2006. However, this decline is only slightly higher than the 17 percent decline in the total number of industrial employees during the same period.[1]

MEAT PROCESSING

Meat processing is the most important sector in the Danish food industry. It is a highly concentrated industry, with Danish Crown as the dominant firm. Pig production and the processing of pork are particularly important; the beef and poultry sectors are less significant. Given the importance of pig production in Denmark, the data available tend to concentrate on this sector. Although we focus on meat processing in the case studies, this section considers both slaughtering and meat processing.

The meat-processing industry has been through an intensive concentration process, as documented in table 3.4. In 1970 the Danish Meat and Bacon Council (DMBC), the meat industry's trade organization, had fifty-four members operating a total of sixty plants. At the end of 2003, the DMBC had only two members, Danish Crown and TiCan, with a total of sixteen slaughterhouses. In addition, there are ten private slaughterhouses that are not members of the DMBC. However, these slaughterhouses are of only marginal importance.

The majority of the pork produced in Denmark is exported. According to the Danish Meat and Bacon Council, about 85 percent of total Danish pork production is exported. In 2004 exports of pork totaled 1.75 million tons and earned €3.35 billion (US$4.57 billion) in foreign currency, making Denmark the world's largest exporter of pork. The majority of Danish pork is exported as chilled or frozen cuts to be used as raw materials for processing in importing countries. Most of the processed meat products produced by Danish meat processors, like pig liver paste, cold cuts, and sausage products, are not exported.

Table 3.4 The Number of DMBC Members and
          Slaughterhouses, 1970 to 2003

	1970	1980	1990	2002	2003
Companies					
Cooperatives	50	18	5	2	2
Private slaughterhouses	4	2	1	0	0
Total	54	20	6	2	2
Plants					
Cooperative	56	34	25	17	16
Private	4	2	2	0	0
Total	60	36	27	17	16
Non-DMBC member companies					
Private slaughterhouses[a]	n.a.	n.a.	7	10	10

Source: Danish Meat and Bacon Council accessed at http://www.danskeslagterier.dk.
[a] Only slaughterhouses that slaughter more than 10,000 pigs per year.

Whether the meat-processing industry can be considered innovative has been the subject of some public discussion, notably in industry journals. While the industry likes to think of itself as innovative, outside observers are not so certain and would probably consider many so-called innovations mere product improvements or adjustments.

Following a period of increasing concentration, the Danish poultry industry is dominated by two companies, which both focus on slaughtering and processing chicken. Denmark is the most important market, but more than half of Danish poultry production is exported to various European markets (primarily Sweden, Germany, and the United Kingdom) and Asian markets (Malaysia and South Korea), as well as to the Middle East (Dansk Slagtefjerkræ 2005).

CONFECTIONARY

The Danish confectionary industry is relatively small, with only a few important producers, several of which are subsidiaries of foreign companies. In this connection, it is noteworthy that several producers manufacture and sell products that have become integral parts of Danish culture.

The Danish confectionary industry produces both sugar-based

Table 3.5 Chocolate and Confectionary Production, 1988 to 2003

Year	Confectionary		Chocolate		Total	
	Tons	Revenues (in Millions of Euros)	Tons	Revenues (in Millions of Euros)	Tons	Revenues (in Millions of Euros)
1998	44,862	148.6	25,123	162.9	69,985	311.5
1999	49,913	169.1	23,933	157.4	73,846	326.5
2000	51,538	167.5	24,437	158.7	75,975	326.2
2001	52,290	168.5	27,512	174.2	79,802	342.7
2002	51,838	172.1	25,774	163.6	77,612	335.7
2003	52,509	167.9	25,677	164.4	78,186	332.3

Source: FødevareIndustrien (FI) (2004) (accessed at http://www.fi.di.dk).

confectionary (fruit gum, licorice) and chocolate (filled, bars). It is an industry that produces many products with short life cycles.

Confectionary is a mature industry. In recent years, production of both sugar-based confectionary and chocolate has been stagnant in terms of both volume and value (see table 3.5). Furthermore, there has been some discussion of the negative impact of candy consumption on public health, not least the health of children. In this business climate, companies have struggled to make a profit.

LABOR MARKET INSTITUTIONS IMPORTANT TO THE FOOD INDUSTRY

Chapter 2 outlined the general institutional framework surrounding low-wage work in Denmark. Here we discuss collective bargaining and industrial relations as they pertain to food processing, as well as the Innovation Act of 2001.

THE INNOVATION ACT OF 2001

In Denmark there is a long tradition of subsidizing research and development in the food sector in order to strengthen the sector's competitiveness. Most recently, the Innovation Act of 2001 provides a framework for supporting projects intended to further the innovation, research, and development efforts of the food, agricultural, and fisheries sector. Eligible projects include those that contribute to new products and production processes, those that build innovation competencies and train skilled workers, and those that seek to improve work conditions, traceability, and quality assurance. Companies can finance up to 50 percent of the expenses of such projects with Innovation Act funding.

The Danish Meat Association has its own research arm, the Danish Meat Research Institute (DMRI), which carries out projects on product quality, food safety, and automation of production processes. One source of funding for these projects is the Innovation Act.

That food processing is highly automated in Denmark, and meat processing in particular, can be attributed to a large extent to the Innovation Act (and similar previous acts) and the DMRI.

COLLECTIVE BARGAINING AND INDUSTRIAL RELATIONS

Formal or de facto closed-shop agreements have been common in the Danish food-processing industry, which is thus highly unionized.[2] Although closed-shop agreements have recently been ruled illegal by the European Court of Human Rights, it remains to be seen how this ruling will affect industrial relations in the industry. Nevertheless, the role played by unions appears to be dwindling. Some workers complain that the union has been too weak and unable to defend their interests. On the other hand, these same workers acknowledge that they could have been more supportive of the union and could thus have helped make it more powerful. The influence or importance of unions also depends on employee representatives being visible, vocal, and energetic. If they are not, the role of unions diminishes.

Food industry workers are mainly organized in the Danish Food and Allied Workers' Union (NNF) and United Federation of Danish Workers (3F) unions. Employers are also organized well. In the confectionary sector, most employers are members of the Association of Danish Chocolate and Confectionary Producers, which is a branch of the Confederation of Danish Industries (DI) and the Danish Employers' Federation (DA).

In the meat-processing industry, the DMBC represents the interests of the two big cooperative meat processors, Danish Crown and TiCan. Some of the small meat processors are members of FI (FødevareIndustrien), the food-sector branch of the Confederation of Danish Industries, which has a number of sector-specific branches, including the meat industry branch and a branch for the confectionary industry.

CASE STUDY FINDINGS

At the beginning of this chapter, we outlined four major developments that explain why the food industry is undergoing considerable change. In this section, we show that the companies affected respond to these developments in quite different ways. Our analysis suggests that the perception and response of Danish food companies to these developments depends on their outlook—that is, whether they see themselves as operating internationally or whether they focus on their domestic market.

Companies operating internationally are experiencing intense competition and have a strong cost focus. Managers in these companies stress the importance of lowering costs, especially labor costs, to being competitive. To keep costs down Danish food producers have not only automated production processes but also improved productivity through enhanced utilization of existing machinery. Internationally operating companies are either contemplating outsourcing or already doing so. Although these companies conceive of differentiation and innovation as means to avoid competing solely on costs, the emphasis in both words and deeds has so far been on reducing costs.

By contrast, companies that focus on the Danish market and have strong brands do not perceive cost pressures to be as immediate and central. The business strategies of these companies focus more on quality and freshness than on low costs.

Because Danish food producers are affected by and respond to globalization and other developments in different ways, we have chosen to divide our case study findings according to whether companies construe themselves as operating in the gale of globalization or, for different reasons, consider themselves to be insulated from its effects.

COMPANIES FEELING THE GALES OF GLOBALIZATION

Of the four developments that we outlined initially, globalization and liberalization of markets is the one that managers consider most important. It is interesting to note, however, that the companies we studied have responded to globalization and liberalization in different ways, with the common denominator being the objective of reducing costs.

The company PL Confectionary has changed its business strategy fundamentally, selling its brands, distribution companies, and a foreign factory in order to concentrate 100 percent on the production of private labels and private brands.[3] Having sold its brands, PL Confectionary has changed from being a market-oriented—even marketing-oriented—company to a production-oriented one. The company has a vision of being "the World's First Choice" in its narrow segment of the confectionary market. PL Confectionary wants to realize its vision through innovation and improved productivity. Since 2002, the company's focus has been on reducing costs in order to improve its competitiveness and achieve its vision. This has involved three rounds of mass layoffs of production workers, the number of whom has been cut by half since 2002, while production, as measured by volume, has remained constant. Informants from management describe the layoffs as "necessary" because highly inefficient production and unsatisfactory financial results threatened the long-term survival of the company. The layoffs have strained relations, however, between management and workers. In connection with the last round of layoffs, PL Confectionary tried to improve the laid-off workers' prospects of getting new jobs elsewhere by offering them retraining and up-skilling at an external training facility. Employees appreciated these efforts.

Although PL Confectionary has also contemplated moving production to countries with lower wage costs, it has chosen to keep production in Denmark for the time being because labor costs make up only a small percentage of total costs, owing to a very high degree of automation.

Multi-Food and JV-Food not only have contemplated moving production to other countries but have actually done so in order to lower labor costs and maintain their competitiveness. Multi-Food in particular views its competitiveness as under pressure from producers in the new EU member states. Multi-Food has several production facilities in Denmark and abroad. These compete against each other to maintain and attract production. Production facilities are benchmarked against each other, and top management threatens to move production from one facility to another if production costs grow too high. Several plant closures in recent years show that this is not an idle threat. The company cites international competition, lower

wages in other countries, unfavorable exchange rates, and historically high prices of production meat to justify the need for its organizational restructuring efforts. Employee representatives lament that
top management at Multi-Food is almost exclusively focused on cost
rather than being more open to working on innovation and producing higher-quality products.

Dane-Meat, the parent company of JV-Food, does not view globalization as a threat that will erode its competitiveness and threaten its
existence. Rather, it interprets globalization as presenting the company with new challenges and opportunities. JV-Food was thus explicitly established (as a joint venture with a Polish partner) in order
to gain a foothold in new EU member states and to exploit low Polish production costs.

The company Chicken is increasing the value it adds to its products by increasing the degree of processing in order to differentiate its
offerings and increase profits. At the same time, the company aims at
controlling costs and rationalizes production. As a consequence of
increasing the degree of processing, the number of production workers has increased despite ongoing rationalization. The company is extremely vulnerable to external conditions. On the one hand, Chicken
has benefited from fears about BSE and outbreaks of foot-and-mouth
disease in recent years. On the other hand, the company suffered
from an outbreak of Newcastle disease in 2002. Recently, the outbreak of bird flu and the "cartoon controversy" have had an adverse
impact on Chicken.[4]

Brand Confectionary is also under pressure to cut costs because of
slow growth in the confectionary market, competition from multinational confectionary producers, price competition in retailing, and its
own unsatisfactory financial results. The company wants to become
more flexible so that it can respond faster and adapt staffing levels to
changing seasons without having to hire seasonal workers, which top
management views as costly and as causing friction in the organization.

It is clear that keeping costs down, particularly labor costs, is an
important strategic issue for many Danish food producers striving to
maintain their international competitiveness. To improve their productivity and rationalize their production processes the companies
we studied have been downsizing their production facilities, going
through rounds of mass layoffs after plant closures, and introducing
new technology. As we show in the next section, this has had pro-

found consequences for employment and human resource management practices in these companies.

From Manual Labor to Monitoring

The nature of jobs in the food-processing industry is changing. In most companies the emphasis has shifted from doing manual, physically demanding tasks to monitoring increasingly automated production processes. The managers we interviewed were uncertain regarding the implications for employment, recruitment, and skill requirements in the future. One manager wanted to hire skilled machinists to operate technically complex packaging machines but had discarded the idea on the assumption that skilled workers do not consider such work challenging enough. The changing nature of jobs also poses a challenge to workers with poor Danish-language skills. As more tasks involve monitoring and controlling machines, the poor language skills of some workers limit the range of functions they can perform. They are stuck with traditional manual work and cannot use new machines and perform the more complicated tasks. This affects both non-native Danish speakers and dyslexic native Danish speakers.

Repetitive work used to be very common in the industry. Often workers had fixed workstations where they performed the same tasks day in and day out. To reduce health hazards and comply with tighter work environment regulations, companies now routinely implement job rotation schemes. According to informants at both the managerial and employee levels, some companies have had difficulty implementing job rotation schemes owing to resistance from employees who are more comfortable performing only a few tasks that they know well and are reluctant or even unwilling to perform other tasks. The Danish Working Environment Authority (WEA) has mandated frequent rotation in order to reduce the amount of repetitive work, but many workers find it a nuisance. On the other hand, several interviewees mentioned the benefits of job rotation schemes. Fatigue is reduced and internal flexibility is increased when workers are capable of performing more than one function.

Automation is important to Danish food producers as a means of reducing labor costs. Companies have invested heavily to automate production processes and thus have removed many manual tasks in favor of production monitoring.

Some companies have tried to implement self-governing teams. Very few of these efforts have been crowned with success. The main reason we were given for this is that managers only halfheartedly support the idea. At one company, workers were not involved in production planning, which one informant described as a prerequisite for successful self-governing teams. The company has now explicitly abandoned self-governing teams. Although companies have essentially abandoned self-governing teams, workers appear to have a large say in work organization and production planning. Indeed, some companies have workers make production plans (although sometimes they are overruled by management).

In several companies, workers can influence work routines and work organization if this improves efficiency, and work organization can differ between different plants within the same company.

COOPERATION AND STRAINS ON RELATIONS

In several cases, the good relations between companies and managers, on the one side, and unions, employee representatives, and workers, on the other, have been strained by company efforts to lower labor costs. It is not that employee representatives and workers have been unwilling to cooperate with management and work toward lowering labor costs, but rather that the change process has sometimes been dictated by management without consultation with employee representatives and workers.

Workers and employee representatives generally accept that work practices must be continually changed in order to improve efficiency and ensure that their employers are able to survive. They express willingness to contribute and make sacrifices, including reductions in the number of workers if this is considered to help the company and ensure its long-term survival. There are several examples in the case studies of this kind of worker cooperation. However, workers and employee representatives would generally like to have had a say in the changes that have been made already. They argue that managers fail to make use of their competencies and knowledge of production processes to the extent that is possible—and desirable—to avoid problems. Furthermore, by failing to involve workers in change projects, managers miss an opportunity to motivate workers and transfer "ownership" to workers. Furthermore, some informants complained that management does not learn from past mistakes. Although managers might promise to involve workers more when introducing new machines or IT systems, they often do not keep this promise.

Informants argued that it is in the interest of no one to harm the company. With a few notable exceptions, the often quite significant changes that were made to improve efficiency have led to no more than minor conflicts because of the overall acceptance of the need to change. In 2005 Chicken saw a "good old-fashioned conflict" over wages that resulted in a prolonged strike, and in the meat-processing industry Multi-Food and especially its parent company have been at the center of several conflicts in recent years. But at Multi-Food workers also collaborate with management.

In 2003 there were 137 work stoppages in the food industry, involving a total of 8,165 workers and resulting in 11,100 lost workdays. Recently there have been a number of high-profile work stoppages in the meat-processing industry, brought on by the ongoing restructuring of Danish Crown. For instance, there were work stoppages at Danish Crown's facility in Odense, where slaughterhouse workers agreed to new piece-rate contracts under the threat of the slaughterhouse closing because of excessive costs.

At one of the Multi-Food facilities studied, workers participated constructively in the rationalization process that reduced the number of positions. Relations between workers and plant managers are generally fine, whereas relations between workers and the top management of Multi-Food were described as strained because top management is constantly threatening to close factories and move production abroad. At Multi-Food, worker assistance plans are established in the event of plant closures. As far as possible, workers are offered jobs at other plants within the group, or they are invited to take part in training programs through which they can develop competencies that will qualify them for other jobs, perhaps in other industries.

Generally both managers and workers and employee representatives describe relations as positive and constructive. Sometimes managers and employee representatives have divergent interests or interpret issues differently. Managers may argue that employee representatives and workers are too slow to adapt to changing realities and that they cling too much to past practices. Overall, however, all parties recognize that they have complementary interests in the long-term survival of the company.

UNSKILLED WORKERS IN NEED OF FURTHER TRAINING?

Traditionally, the food-processing industry has required few formal skills of its workers. Companies have been able to hire unskilled laborers more or less off the street and relatively quickly provide them with the necessary skills through on-the-job training. This is reflected in the educational level of workers in the food-processing industry. Employees in food processing have either a vocational education or no education beyond primary school. This is true for both sectors covered by this study, although workers in meat processing are more likely than those in confectionary to have some form of vocational training.

Some of the companies studied used to be fairly generous in offering additional vocational training. The increased focus on costs, however, has put an end to such generosity. On the other hand, both companies and workers agree that some of the training that workers received was superfluous. Some criticize the supplementary vocational training offered by the Danish vocational education and training system (AMU) (see Søndergaard and Togo 2005) for being directed more at people outside the job market than people who already have a job.

A common complaint on the part of production workers is that they are not given sufficient instructions and training when new machines are introduced. Sometimes workers with limited pedagogical skills are assigned to train their colleagues. Moreover, if some workers have mediocre teaching skills, others have learning problems, and the combination can lead to problematic outcomes and high levels of frustration.

Increasing automation requires workers with IT skills. Many workers, however, especially older production workers, are IT-phobic. Also, it is becoming more important that workers be able to read (for example, instructions on computer monitors) and write (as documentation demands are increasing). Some workers are not willing to learn new skills or perform new tasks, while others have difficulties learning to perform new functions such as operating a different or new machine.

In recent years, the possibility for production workers to acquire additional skills has been limited as companies have tried to cut costs. Informants acknowledged that this can be a shortsighted strategy: the same companies expect their demand for skilled workers to increase in the future. Some companies are tentatively exploring the possibility of training some of their production workers to become machine, industry, or process operators (called "skilled unskilled" by one informant). Other companies, having no clearly identified need for such workers, are making no such efforts. Training industry operators has not been a success so far for any of the companies studied. Having completed their training, industry operators often returned to their previous position with only limited possibilities for further personal and professional development. Several companies have lost industry and process operators who were dissatisfied with not been given the new tasks and challenges that they expected and believed they could handle.

PL Confectionary is one company that has had negative experiences with training. Nevertheless, the vice president for human resources envisioned that within the near future up to 25 percent of production workers would have completed their process or industry operator training. Other companies also expect the number of process or industry operators to increase because many jobs are changing to focus more on monitoring production processes.

As jobs are changing and automation is increasing, it might be argued that companies have an incentive to strive to retain workers because stable, higher-skilled workers are needed to perform production works satisfactorily. Given the fact that most workers have little formal training and that companies have been offering little in the form of training in recent years, a question arises: where do workers acquire the skills necessary to cope with the changing nature of jobs, frequent restructurings, and changing work practices? Perhaps the Danish educational system, with its emphasis on group work and people skills, is one source. Moreover, the Danish social security system enables low-skilled individuals joining the Danish work force to cope better with changes in their job situation than is possible for low-skilled workers in many other countries, such as the United States.[5]

RECRUITMENT: ARE PROBLEMS EMERGING?

Generally speaking, food producers reported that they do not have problems recruiting unskilled workers. Companies tend to get so many unsolicited applications that they do not need to search actively for unskilled workers. When there are vacancies, word of mouth spreads the news quickly and results in workers telephoning to offer their services. One manager expressed his surprise at the number of phone calls he received when he posted a notice of a vacancy in the local paper. However, some companies have not hired significant numbers of new workers in recent years because of downsizing and restructuring.

Downsizing can have negative consequences for corporate reputation. Thus, both managers and workers in one of our cases believed that the company's reputation as a good workplace has suffered in recent years because the company's focus on increasing productivity has stepped up the work pace. Nevertheless, the company claims not to have had difficulties recruiting new workers.

Only one company reported that it was hard to recruit unskilled workers because of a tight local labor market and the higher pay offered to unskilled workers by other companies in the area. Having had to advertise for new workers for the first time in five years, the company found that its recruitment costs had risen recently. In this connection, it is important to note that this company was the last case studied. In the time since our interviews at our other case companies, they may also have experienced difficulties in recruiting unskilled workers. There are indications that labor supply in Denmark is becoming tight, and warnings that the Danish labor market might be overheating are frequent.

Generally, recruitment for production workers is not very formalized. Selection of new employees is mainly based on relatively informal criteria such as personal chemistry (with the line manager and prospective colleagues), employment history, personality traits, and the worker's sense of responsibility, motivation, stability, and reliability (as perceived by the recruiting manager).

Some companies explicitly require that workers be able to communicate in Danish. Immigrants form an important source of unskilled labor for food producers. The proportion of immigrants in the food industry workforce is about 10 percent—almost double what it is for the Danish economy as a whole (Landbrugsraadet 2005). Of the companies we studied, Chicken had the largest proportion of immigrants—about 30 percent of its production workers. Today the company has a policy of hiring only workers who can communicate in Danish. Chicken's past practice of hiring workers with insufficient language skills is still causing it problems, not only communication complications but potential safety risks. The company has offered language training to non-native Danish speakers, either during the day (paid) or after work, but the targeted workers have declined to participate in the program.

Some companies have formulated corporate values to guide all of their activities, including their human resource management policies. For instance, one company formulated these values: "We go forward, we create value, we take responsibility, and we show trust and respect." Another company defined a set of five values to guide all its activities (courage, networking, high performance, accountability, and persistence). From our cases, we gained the impression that company values serve mainly symbolic functions. They seem more like window dressing than concepts that have a real impact on human resource management practices, at least in relation to manual workers. In our interviews, only one informant explicitly referred to company values: PL Confectionary's vice president for human resources claimed to assess how well applicants for production work fit the company values. Furthermore, he said, PL Confectionary wants to hire production workers who can think for themselves, who can solve problems, and who believe in lifelong learning so that they are able to adapt.

While companies have few problems recruiting unskilled workers, it is more difficult to recruit skilled workers. As just pointed out, there are some positions that skilled workers are not interested in.

Some companies use various subsidized schemes to recruit workers. For instance, Chicken runs a job training program subsidized by local authorities at one of its facilities (not the one visited). During the six-week program, potential employees receive four weeks of basic education about poultry and two weeks of practical training; this program gives the company a chance to take a close look at potential workers before hiring them when they have completed the program. One informant characterized it as a six-week job interview. After workers complete the training program, the company can then hire the ones it is interested in keeping. The wages of these workers are subsidized for up to twenty-six weeks. The program is not an unconditional success, however, since some of the people eligible for the program are incapable of holding a normal job. Furthermore, employee representatives are skeptical about the program and want subsidized workers to be laid off first if production is scaled back.

Table 3.6 Minimum Wages for Adult Employees in Slaughterhouses (in Euros), 2006

	Euros per Week	Euros per Hour
Basic rate	302.73	8.18
Piece-rate deficiency payment[a]	39.24	1.06
Time rate bonus	224.25	6.06
Total	551.32	15.30
Piece-work basis (adults)		8.36
Overtime		8.77

Source: Danish Food and Allied Workers' Union (NNF) (2004b).
[a] Piece-rate deficiency rates are paid for all hours not worked on piece rates.

LOW-WAGE WORK: NOT AN ISSUE

There are only a few low-wage workers in the Danish meat-processing industry, as mentioned in chapter 2, and the percentage of low-wage workers has been more or less stable over the last ten years.

According to collective bargaining agreements, the minimum hourly wage for adult slaughterhouse workers is €15.30 (US$20.87) per hour (see table 3.6), while apprentices under age eighteen earn from €7.65 (US$10.43) per hour (see table 3.7). However, piece-rate agreements enable workers in the Danish pork industry to earn much more per hour in reality. Thus, in 2005, on average, a Danish slaughterhouse employee earned €30.05 (US$40.98) per hour (see table

Table 3.7 Hourly Wages of Apprentices in Slaughterhouses (in Euros), 2006

	Under Eighteen	Over Eighteen	Over Twenty
Basic rate	4.09	5.73	6.55
Piece-rate deficiency payment[a]	0.53	0.74	0.85
Time rate bonus	3.03	4.24	4.85
Total	7.65	10.71	12.25
Overtime		6.60	7.84

Source: Danish Food and Allied Workers' Union (NNF) (2004a).
[a] The piece-rate basis for apprentices is 75 percent of that for adult workers for the same performance after the first year of the apprenticeship.

Table 3.8 Average Hourly Wage for Slaughterhouse Workers (Current Prices), 1998 to 2005

Year	Euros per Hour[a]	Index 1980 = 100
1998	23.78	262
1999	24.51	271
2000	25.33	279
2001	26.55	293
2002	27.58	304
2003	28.63	316
2004	29.22	322
2005	30.05	331

Source: Danish Meat Association (2006).
[a] Includes holiday payment, public holiday payment, and social security.

3.8). This is a clear example of the power of local agreements, as described in chapter 1.

Fewer than 5 percent of workers in the Danish confectionary industry are classified as low-wage workers (see figure 2.15). According to the collective bargaining agreement between DI and NNF, adult workers earn a minimum of €12.40 (US$16.91) per hour, while workers under the age of eighteen earn at least €6.74 (US$9.19) per hour (see table 3.9). About 80 percent of low-wage workers in the confectionary subsector are female.

DI and NNF agree that it is appropriate to negotiate piece-rate agreements locally (Dansk Industri 2004) and that these should also

Table 3.9 Hourly Wages for Workers in the Confectionary Industry, 2006

	Adults (Euros)	Under 18 (Euros)
Time rate	12.40	6.74
Compensation rate (for work-time reduction from forty to thirty-seven hours per week)	0.71	0.71
Training allowance (for workers with more than twelve months' employment in the company)	0.16	0.16
Sector allowance	0.13	0.13

Source: Dansk Industri (2004).

cover work at production and packaging machinery. Piece rates are determined so that a work rate of 100 (according to the centi-minute system) results in adult workers earning at least 15 percent more than the hourly wage.

To improve productivity, one company set up a bonus system as an incentive for workers. In 2004 bonus payments were based on a single production indicator, kilograms per hour. That year production workers received bonus payments of between €4,000 and €5,300 (US$5,455.26 and US$7,288.99), depending on the production department they worked in. Several informants considered the bonus scheme highly effective in contributing to what they described as a "quantum leap" in productivity.

Several companies want to move away from paying all workers the same and to base pay instead on individual qualifications, skills, and productivity. However, this proposal has been met with resistance from workers.

RETENTION: SENIORITY IS INCREASING

Our interviews indicated that labor turnover is relatively low in all of the cases studied except at Chicken (although we did not manage to get reliable documentation supporting this). In meat processing, high wages contribute to low labor turnover. This is not the case, however, in the poultry sector. Chicken is experiencing problems with retention and increasing labor turnover because other employers of unskilled labor in the area offer substantially higher wages. Eighty to 85 percent of its workers have been with Chicken for more than a year, but labor turnover is 30 to 35 percent, which is slightly above the general turnover rate in Denmark (see chapter 2). This turnover rate reflects the fact that many workers work less than a year at Chicken. It also indicates that many workers try out a job at Chicken, but that those who stay more than a year tend to stay longer than employees at other firms.

Seniority is also high at several of the other companies we studied. Some of our informants had been with the same company for more than forty years. According to our informants, seniority has risen in recent years owing to the low number of new employees being hired. Some informants argued that an age gap is opening up, as many younger employees are leaving the industry. This represents a potential future problem for their company, they said. The very high seniority rates found in some companies are attributable to their excellent reputations as employers, although in some cases these have been tarnished by recent changes in practices.

Job satisfaction has suffered from the downsizing efforts at some companies. In one company, production workers claimed that the unique "spirit" and everything positive that used to distinguish their workplace had been lost.

Nevertheless, few production workers leave voluntarily. In our cases, the main reason given for leaving the company was being laid off, but sometimes it is a negative atmosphere among workers in a department that makes people quit their jobs.

There are few career prospects for unskilled workers, since companies rarely recruit line and production managers internally. Companies tend to hire line managers from outside the organization because they consider the transition from being a colleague to being the manager of one's former colleagues to be fraught with problems. The erosion of middle-management positions has also limited the possibilities for internal advancement. In this respect, food processing represents a contrast to food retailing, where there are still very good opportunities for advancement for people with few formal skills seeking a career in retailing (see chapter 4).

Internal and External Flexibility

The standard workweek in food processing is thirty-seven hours. Some companies have several work shifts depending on the demand situation. Day shifts tend to have the largest number of employees because companies have to pay workers extra on evening and night shifts. Companies' opinions on shift work differ, but most companies have fixed shifts. There is little actual shift work. Informants indicate only small differences in labor turnover between different shifts, with turnover apparently slightly higher for night shifts.

Agreements about working hours can be a source of internal flexibility. For instance, as one of the first companies in the Danish food industry, PL Confectionary has made an agreement with its production workers that they can work up to forty-two hours per week without being paid at overtime rates. The hours between thirty-seven and forty-two are "deposited" into an account, which workers then "draw on" during slow periods. Management expects that the agreement will help the company manage fluctuations in production volume better. Although it is possible to "hire and fire" workers according to the collective bargaining agreement, management does not consider it a sensible practice in light of how costly it is to recruit and train new employees. This is a different solution to the temporary layoff problem described in chapter 2.

During peak seasons, companies often hire people on short-term contracts, introduce extra shifts, or use overtime to increase production to meet demand. The use of temporary agencies as a source of flexibility is also increasing. One of the case companies uses temp agencies quite extensively. Managers are very positive, even surprised, about the quality of workers they can hire for a short period. Workers and employee representatives, on the other hand, bemoan the loss of "proper" jobs and the extra time it takes to instruct temps; they also complain that temps can perform only certain simple tasks. However, not all companies are interested in using temp agencies. Some prefer to recruit workers on temporary contracts.

WHAT IS IT LIKE TO WORK IN THE DANISH FOOD INDUSTRY?

Some aspects of work conditions in the Danish food-processing industry have improved substantially over the last ten to twenty years. On the one hand, investments in machinery and increased automation (partly to comply with tighter regulations, partly to lower labor costs) have eliminated many physically demanding tasks (see chapter 2). Many stressful and repetitive tasks remain, however, and the problem of worn-out workers still exists.

On the other hand, many workers complain about the high work pace, which in some cases is the result of efforts to improve productivity. Some informants complained that the increased work pace, the numerous rationalizations, the changes in work processes, and uncertainty about the future of their workplace caused them stress. These informants were uncertain whether management was aware of the extent of the problem; they believed that many workers are unwilling to inform managers about the true causes of sick days and resignations because succumbing to stress is a sensitive issue among workers.

Other common problems are poor work positions, repetitive and monotonous movements, having to lift heavy objects, stench, noise, dust, high and/or low temperatures, and drafts as well as poor ventilation.

Table 3.10 The Number and Incidence of Reported Work
           Accidents, 2004

	Number of Reported Work Accidents	Incidence of Reported Work Accidents per 10,000 Employees
Pig and cattle slaughterhouses	2,258	1,338
Poultry slaughterhouses, fish and fodder factories	637	557
Bread, tobacco, and confectionery	589	219
Total entire economy	41,943	155

Source: Arbejdstilsynet (2005).

Data from the Danish Working Environment Authority document
that working in food processing is dangerous work, especially in pig
and cattle slaughterhouses, where the rate of reported work accidents
is almost ten times the average for the Danish economy as a whole
(see table 3.10). Cutting and carving meat is inherently dangerous
work. The bread, tobacco, and confectionary sector is not nearly as
dangerous.

Although WEA works to improve working conditions, workers often consider WEA to be an "enemy" rather than an ally because some
WEA regulations are interpreted to make work processes more cum-
bersome and therefore sometimes have a negative impact on wages.
To increase output workers sometimes do not comply with working
environment regulations.

COMPARISON WITH THE UNITED STATES

Compared to the picture of meat processing in the United States
painted in a report by Human Rights Watch (2004), working conditions in the Danish food-processing industry are reasonably good.[6]

According to Human Rights Watch (2004, 11), "meatpacking
plants at the turn of the twentieth century were more than sweatshops. They were bloodshops, and not only for animal slaughter. The
industry operated with low wages, long hours, brutal treatment, and
sometimes deadly exploitation of mostly immigrant workers." Following large-scale trade union organization drives, the pay and conditions of workers in the United States' meatpacking industry improved from the 1930s to the 1970s. Wages rose to be substantially

higher than the average for the manufacturing sector (17 percent higher in 1980). During the 1980s, new companies became industry leaders by relocating plants from urban to rural areas, automating more of the production process, stepping up line speeds, squeezing skills out of jobs, and cutting wages (Human Rights Watch 2004). Companies that did not relocate often "shut down their plants, dismissed long-time organized workers, then reopened with a nonunion immigrant workforce" (Human Rights Watch 2004, 13). According to Human Rights Watch, employers have fiercely resisted efforts by workers to organize, firing key leaders and threatening to close plants where workers have tried to form new unions. As a consequence of these developments, good jobs in the meatpacking industry have been destroyed. By 2002, meatpacking workers' wages had fallen to 24 percent below the average American manufacturing wage, with simultaneous worsening of benefits and working conditions (Human Rights Watch 2004). At the turn of the twenty-first century, meatpacking in the United States in many ways resembled the situation one hundred years earlier.

Meat processing is inherently dirty and dangerous work. Human Rights Watch (2004, 33–47) identified a number of the dangers that give meat processing the highest rate of injury and illness in the manufacturing sector: line speed, close-quarters cutting, heavy lifting, sullied work conditions, and long hours, as well as inadequate training and equipment. Many of the injuries sustained in American meat processing, however, are preventable at reasonable cost, but because profit margins in early-stage meat-processing plants are very narrow, sacrificing worker safety and health is sometimes a conscious calculation (Human Rights Watch 2004).

Working in meat processing is also dangerous in Denmark, and companies have threatened to relocate or move production to other plants if workers do not cooperate in making production processes more efficient. Our informants also mentioned line speed and heavy lifting as concerns, but not to the extent documented by the American study.

In some ways, the developments in the United States' meatpacking industry over the last twenty years can perhaps be regarded as a precursor for how the Danish meat-processing industry will evolve. Certainly, our case studies indicate that line speeds are increasing and that companies actively use the threat of plant closure to change work processes and put pressure on wages. However, there are reasons for optimism on behalf of Danish workers (if not necessarily for workers in the countries to which production might be relocated). First of all, wages tend to be sticky in Denmark. It would be difficult to lower wages dramatically because of the high reservation wage that results from the Danish UI system (see chapter 2 for details). Second, unionization is generally higher (though declining) in Denmark (see chapter 2). Most meat processors have de facto closed-shop agreements and would find it very difficult to find non-unionized workers. Although closed-shop agreements have been ruled illegal by the European Court of Human Rights, newspaper reports indicate that they still exist in practice. Third, copying American practices might be most suitable for companies following a low-cost strategy. Although price considerations are important, most Danish food producers acknowledge that their focus in the future will have to be on product quality and innovation if they are to stay competitive. Finally, wholesale copying of American practices and militant anti-unionism run counter to the long Danish tradition of cooperation between companies and workers. Also, capital intensity is high in the Danish food industry, and labor costs therefore constitute a smaller share of total costs than in the United States.

DOMESTICALLY ORIENTED COMPANIES FEELING INSULATED FROM THE STORM

There are many similarities between the companies facing strong international competition and the food producers that consider themselves insulated from international competition in terms of who their workers are, what they do on the job, and what their working conditions are like. This section focuses on the differences between internationally and domestically oriented companies, some of which are due to the difference in outlook and some of which are explained by the peculiarities of the companies in question.

Some food producers operating domestically and with no international ambitions do not conceive of globalization as a major threat to their existence. They focus more on quality and less on price than their more internationally oriented counterparts.

Danish Liver produces a typical Danish product and sees itself as typically Danish. Although to some extent it experiences increasing competition and argues that it has to fight harder in order to maintain and defend its market position, nothing in the current competitive situation suggests that moving production is imminent. Danish Liver fears that moving production to, for instance, Poland would be detrimental to the brand equity of its strong national brand.

Like companies facing international competition, Danish Liver has abandoned self-governing teams in practice, but not explicitly, because managers perceived them to function inefficiently. At Danish Liver, some production workers are responsible for ordering the materials used in the production process, such as packaging materials and spices. According to the production manager, this is working very well. At Danish Liver, management and employee representatives agreed on a new wage scheme in which each employee's wage would depend on his or her flexibility, stability, and skills. However, this agreement was rejected by a majority of workers.

In a number of ways, Family Chocolate represents a very distinctive case. The company has its own retail outlets and is thus relatively isolated from the cost pressures experienced by manufacturers distributing through large retail chains. Family Chocolate considers itself a producer of premium-quality, handmade fine chocolates; to avoid sacrificing the positioning of the company's products, Family Chocolate interprets this role as limiting the scope for automation. Therefore, consistent with its positioning as a producer of handmade chocolates, there is still a high degree of manual work at Family Chocolate.

Furthermore, Family Chocolate interprets its external conditions as currently being very favorable because demand for premium-quality products has increased due to the buoyant Danish economy. The company has noticed that consumers have become more interested in the ingredients it uses. For instance, consumers are now interested in chocolate with a high cocoa content.

Moreover, Family Chocolate can offer skilled bakers and confectioners more attractive working hours and better working conditions than they can find in traditional bakeries. At Family Chocolate, the high work pace is a seasonal phenomenon. To cope with seasonal demand fluctuations, Family Chocolate has implemented flexible working hours, following a scheme similar to the one in place at PL Confectionary, but with important differences. In May and June, production is idle on Fridays. Workers are not paid for these days but may use their "paid personal days."[7] In November and December, scheduled overtime equals the number of hours off in May and June. Workers are paid overtime (time and a half) for these hours, although the company is not obliged to do so, as it could use hours saved in May and June to compensate.

Family Chocolate, which does not have a collective bargaining agreement, offers higher wages than stipulated in the collective bargaining agreement covering the confectionary industry. Unskilled workers start at €14.50 (US$19.76) per hour, and skilled workers at €16.11 (US$21.95) per hour.[8] One reason for the high wages is that the manager wants to avoid workplace conflicts.

We encountered high job satisfaction at both Family Chocolate and Danish Liver, and this is probably one reason for the high seniority rates we saw at both companies.

The Outlook for Domestically Oriented Companies

Globalization is an ongoing process. Companies are continuing the process of rationalization but are also looking to differentiate through innovation, production of high-quality products, and increases in the value added. Improved training of employees is also considered an option for development, although human resource managers are uncertain about how this should be accomplished.

Increased automation will entail less physical demands but will change the nature of jobs. Informants expected food industry jobs to involve more monitoring and less actual physical work. This will lead to more challenging and exciting jobs, some human resource managers argue. But it will also increase formal skill requirements. Traditional low-skilled jobs are disappearing, and the total number of unskilled workers is expected to decline.

Overall, our case companies and informants look toward the future with confidence. A company like PL Confectionary thinks that it will be able to sustain production in Denmark by focusing on innovation and differentiation. Other informants and companies express similar attitudes, namely, that companies in Denmark have to work smarter, not harder, to stay competitive.

DISCUSSION AND CONCLUSIONS

Based on case studies of seven Danish food producers in the meat-processing and confectionary sectors, we find that the globalization of the food industry has affected companies quite differently. Companies operating internationally are facing strong competition and have responded to the pressure to stay competitive by becoming highly cost-focused. They have rationalized production processes, increased automation, and contemplated moving production to countries with lower labor costs, if they have not already done so. In meat processing, however, although it is possible to move some processing of pork to other countries, most Danish-bred pigs are likely to be slaughtered and processed in Denmark for the foreseeable future. Meanwhile, companies that focus on the Danish market and have strong national brands have been relatively shielded from the gales of globalization, but they are not completely unaffected. These companies focus more on quality than on price, although they have also been working to improve efficiency.

To cope with the pressures of globalization, some of our case study companies have worked hard to rationalize production processes. In this connection, companies have been able to build on the good relations between employers and employees and their unions and have thus benefited from the Danish model (see chapter 2). Although rationalization has not been without conflict, managers and workers and their employee representatives have generally been able to maintain a constructive relationship based on a realization of interdependence. Certainly, the Danish food-processing sector has not seen a breakdown in relations between employers and employees, as has been the case in meatpacking in the United States. Also, work conditions and wages have not deteriorated, although line speed has increased and piece-rate agreements have been modified in order to cope with increased globalization and higher degrees of automation.

Flexibility in the sense of being able to adjust production to demand is regarded as an important issue in relation to maintaining and improving competitiveness. In this connection, the Danish labor market model makes it relatively easy for companies to hire and fire workers (see chapter 2). However, some of our case companies are trying to get away from the practice of hiring and firing employees according to the fluctuating demand for the company's products, because it is considered too costly. Instead, companies are attempting to develop various forms of internal and external flexibility. Internal flexibility is being developed through multiskilling and job rotation schemes that ensure that production workers are able to perform a number of different functions. Also, some case companies have implemented flexible working hour schemes, according to which employees work fewer hours during the slow season and more during the peak season without overtime payment. Another way of developing internal flexibility is to add extra shifts during peak seasons. Some companies are developing external flexibility through increased use of temps, although workers and employee representatives disapprove of this trend.

The nature of unskilled jobs is changing. As production processes are increasingly automated (to reduce labor costs), traditional manual tasks disappear. Increasingly, jobs in the food industry involve monitoring of the machinery that performs automated processes. This has important skill implications, since such jobs require less brawn and more intellect. Companies are still not certain how to handle this issue.

Table 3a.1 The Case Study Food-Processing Companies

	Brand Confectionary	Family Chocolate	PL Confectionary	Chicken	Danish Liver	Multi-Food	JV-Food
Sector	Confectionary	Confectionary	Confectionary	Meat processing	Meat processing	Meat processing	Meat processing
Ownership	Owned by foundation	Family-owned	Family-owned	Family-owned	Family-owned	Subsidiary of large meat company	Joint venture between Danish and Polish meat companies
Scope	MNC; three production facilities	Niche; one production facility	MNC; niche; one production facility	Denmark and export; three production facilities	Niche; practically no exports; two production facilities	MNC; eight production facilities in Denmark, two abroad	MNC; two production facilities (Denmark and abroad)
Competition	Slow, underlying growth of confectionary market; price competition in retailing	Market conditions favorable owing to consumer interest in quality products; strongest position in medium-size towns	Has gone through a turn-around process, cutting costs and improving efficiency, in order to become profitable again	Bird flu and the "cartoon controversy" have put pressure on entire industry, as has international sourcing by Danish retailers	Increasing competition, but company has strong brand, which makes it an attractive supplier for retailers	Intense competition	Strong international competition; company very influenced by international competition in the pork industry

Table 3a.1 (Continued)

	Brand Confectionary	Family Chocolate	PL Confectionary	Chicken	Danish Liver	Multi-Food	JV-Food
Business strategy	Sells mainly manufacturer brands, some PL (sold U.K. division that mainly made PL in 2005)	Two SBUs: production of coffee (mainly catering) and fine, hand-made chocolates (sold mainly through forty-three company-owned outlets); focus on high quality and freshness of products	Has sold all brands to international confectionary company; now manufactures only for B2B market; PL and OEM; the company vision is to become the world's preferred supplier in its category	Trend toward more value-added products has increased the number of employees (despite rationalization of production); strict cost management in order to stay competitive	Focus on quality and developing strong brands; diversification through purchase of sausage factory	Wants to produce tasty, safe, and high-quality food products (according to company vision) but also maintain cost focus; has moved some production away from Denmark to reduce labor costs; ongoing rationalization of production	Parent company has evolved from national slaughterer to international food company; JV-Food is one element in this strategy (also processing in Germany and United Kingdom); views globalization as a possibility for future growth; trend toward value-added products

Source: Authors' compilation.

Notes: All company names are pseudonyms.

Abbreviations: MNC—multinational company; PL—private label; SBU—strategic business unit; B2B—business to business; OEM—original equipment manufacturer.

NOTES

1. These numbers are based on data from the online statistical database of Statistics Denmark, accessed at http://www.statistikbanken.dk.
2. Under closed-shop agreements, employees are required to be members of a particular union (see chapter 2).
3. All company names are pseudonyms.
4. The "cartoon controversy" refers to the crisis between Denmark and large parts of the Muslim world that resulted from the publication of twelve cartoons depicting the Islamic prophet Muhammad in the Danish newspaper *Morgenavisen Jyllands-Posten* on September 30, 2005. The newspaper printed the cartoons to contribute to an ongoing debate on Islam and self-censorship. However, critics of the cartoons described them as Islamophobic and racist. In response to the publication of the cartoons, Danish Muslim organizations held public protests and spread information about the cartoons to the rest of the Muslim world, where protests in some countries escalated into violent riots and boycotts of Danish goods.
5. In Denmark, more than 30 percent of low-skilled individuals age twenty-five to fifty received public transfers as their only income in 2002 (Røed et al. forthcoming)
6. The chapter by Julia Lane and her colleagues in Eileen Appelbaum, Annette Bernhardt, and Richard Murnane (2003) is about the food service industry, and it is therefore difficult to draw comparisons with our case studies. Based on a suggestion from Rosemary Batt, we instead base our comparison between Denmark and the United States on *Blood, Sweat, and Fear*, a report published by Human Rights Watch in 2004 detailing work conditions and workers' rights in American meat and poultry plants. We have been unable to find similar material for the American confectionary sector, and our comparison thus solely focuses on meat processing.
7. There are two types of paid personal days in Denmark: those intended for oneself and those intended for taking care of one's children. The number of paid personal days is regulated in collective bargaining agreements, but typically full-time employees have five days a year for themselves and two to three days a year for taking care of each child under the age of fourteen.
8. A "skilled" worker is one who has served as an apprentice, but not necessarily within the confectionary industry.

REFERENCES

Appelbaum, Eileen, Annette Bernhardt, and Richard J. Murnane, eds. 2003. *Low-Wage America: How Employers Are Reshaping Opportunity in the Workplace*. New York: Russell Sage Foundation.

Arbejdstilsynet. 2005. *Anmeldte arbejdsulykker 1999–2004* [*Reported Work Accidents 1999–2004*]. Copenhagen: National Danish Work Environment Agency.

Danish Food and Alllied Workers' Union (NNF). 2004a. "Overenskomst mellem Dansk Industri for Foreningen af Danske Chokolade og Sukker-varefabrikaner og Nærings og Nydelsesmiddelarbejderforbrundet - Hand-værk/Industrigruppen, Sukkervare - og chokoladebranchen" ["Collective Bargaining Agreement Between the Confederation of Danish Industries for the Association of Danish Chocolate and Sugar Goods Manufacturers and the Danish Food and Allied Workers' Union, Craft/Industry Group, the Sugar Goods and Confectionary Industry"]. Fredriksberg, Denmark: The Danish Food and Allied Workers' Union.

————. 2004b. "Overenskomst og aftaler mellem Nærings - og Ny-delsesmiddelarbejderforbrundet Landbrugsgruppen og Dansk Industri gældende for slagteområdet 2004-2007" ["Collective Bargaining Agree-ment Between the Danish Food and Allied Workers' Union and the Con-federation of Danish Industries for Slaughterhouses for 2004-2007"]. Fredriksberg, Denmark: The Danish Food and Allied Workers' Union.

Danish Meat Association. 2006. *Statistik svin 2005* [*Statistics on Pigs 2005*]. Copenhagen: Danish Meat Association.

Dansk Industri. 2004. *Overenskomst mellem Dansk Industri for Foreningen af Danske Chokolade- og Sukkervarefabrikanter og Naederings- og Ny-delsesmiddelmedarbejder Forbundet, Haandvaerk/Industrigruppen, Sukker-vare- og Chokoladebranchen* [*Collective Bargaining Agreement 542290*]. Copenhagen: Confederation of Danish Industries.

Dansk Slagtefjerkræ. 2005. *Statistik: Slagtefjerkræ* [*Statistics on Poultry Slaughtering*]. Copenhagen: Dansk Slagtefjerkræ.

Dawson, John. 2000. "Viewpoint: Retailer Power, Manufacturer Power, Competition, and Some Questions of Economic Analysis." *International Journal of Retail and Distribution Management* 28(1): 5–8.

Fødevareindustrien (FI). 2004. "Branchestatistik for Chokolade og Konfek-tureindustrien" ["Industry Statistics for the Chocolate and Confectionary Industry"]. Copenhagen: Fødevareindustrien.

Grant, Robert M. 1987. "Manufacturer-Retailer Relations: The Shifting Bal-ance of Power." In *Business Strategy and Retailing*, edited by Gerry John-son. Chichester, England: John Wiley & Sons.

Human Rights Watch. 2004. *Blood, Sweat, and Fear: Workers' Rights in U.S. Meat and Poultry Plants*. New York: Human Rights Watch.

Landbrugsraadet. 2005. *Fødevarebranchen: Den farverige arbejdsplads* [*The Food Industry: The Colorful Workplace*]. Copenhagen: Landbrugsraadet.

Røed, Marianne, Iben Bolvig, Inés Hardoy, Merja Kauhanen, Reija Lilja and Nina Smith. Forthcoming. *The Labour Supply of Low-Skilled – Incentives in the Unemployment Insurance Systems. A Comparative Description Based on Nordic Countries.* NMR-report, Nordic Council of Ministers.

Søndergaard, Steffen R., and Finn Togo, editors. 2005. *The Danish Vocational Education and Training System*. Copenhagen: National Education Authority, Danish Ministry of Education.

Statistics Denmark. 2004. *Statistisk Aarbog 2004* [*Statistical Yearbook 2004*]. Copenhagen: Danmarks Statistik.

———. 2006. *Statistisk Aarbog 2006* [*Statistical Yearbook 2006*]. Copenhagen: Danmarks Statistik.

CHAPTER 4

Working in Danish Retailing: Transitional Workers Going Elsewhere, Core Employees Going Nowhere, and Career-Seekers Striving to Go Somewhere

Lars Esbjerg, Klaus G. Grunert, Nuka Buck, and Anne-Mette Sonne Andersen

Working in retailing is a low-status occupation in Denmark. Politicians and various members of the media routinely use supermarket checkout operators when illustrating how economic policies will affect "common people." Irregular working hours and mediocre pay are among the retail-related issues that crop up in the media regularly.

Danish retailers are acutely aware that retail establishments have a negative image as places to work and that this image has an impact on their ability to recruit and retain the workers they need now and will need in the future.

But what is it actually like to work in Danish retailing? In this chapter, we explore this question from the perspective of both managers and store workers. In eight Danish retailers, we investigated job quality, work organization, industrial relations, pay, training, and career prospects. We studied frontline workers who have a high degree of customer interaction: checkout operators and sales assistants in food retailing; and salespeople in electrical goods retailing.

One of our findings is that the stereotypical supermarket checkout operator is perhaps not so typical after all. Overall, it is possible to distinguish between three types of employees in Danish retailing: (1) transitional workers who are working in retailing either before or while they study; (2) core employees who have no career ambitions; and (3) career-seekers who want to make a career in retailing. The relative importance of the employee types differs between food retailers and specialty electrical goods retailers, which employ relatively fewer transitional workers and offer fewer opportunities for career-seekers than food retailers.

Retailers thus face the challenge of making retail work attractive and interesting for three types of employees with divergent interests and ambitions. So far they appear to have been successful. Despite (or because of?) very different goals and career plans, job satisfaction is high across the three employee types.

In this chapter, we begin by describing the overall design of our study and the methodology we used for the qualitative case studies. Next, a brief overview of Danish retailing describes the context of the case studies. Then, we present the findings of the qualitative case studies. We end with a conclusion and discussion of our findings.

STUDY DESIGN AND METHODOLOGY

The rationale for including retailing in a study of low-wage work in Denmark is straightforward: compared to other industries, a relatively high proportion of workers in retailing are classified as low-wage workers.

We designed the study based on the assumption that retail subsectors would differ with regard to human resource management strategies, employment structure, job quality, and job satisfaction. We thus studied two retail subsectors that we expected to differ, namely, electrical goods and food retailing. One important difference between these two retail subsectors is that the proportion of low-wage workers is almost twice as high in food retailing (28 percent) as in electrical goods retailing (15 percent).

The target occupations we were primarily interested in were checkout operators (the archetypical low-status retail job) and sales assistants (in the consumer electronics departments of supermarkets and hypermarkets) in food retailing and salespeople in consumer electronics specialty retailers. These are occupations with a large degree of direct customer interaction, but the content of these interactions differs significantly.

We conducted case studies of eight retail companies: five food retailers and three specialty electrical goods retailers. Three of the food retailers we studied also sell consumer electronics. In these three cases, we studied both checkout operators and sales assistants in the electronics departments. A brief summary of the cases is provided in the appendix.

We visited two or three stores per chain to gain a broader understanding of each chain. In all cases, we interviewed informants at several organizational levels. Typically, we interviewed human resource managers at the retail chain level, store managers, department managers, employee representatives, and checkout operators, sales assistants, or salespeople at the retail store level.

In total, we conducted more than 110 interviews. We recorded most of the interviews, but in a few cases where this was not possible—because the informant refused or because of technical difficulties—we took extensive notes, either during the interview or immediately afterwards. After transcribing and coding the interviews, we wrote up case descriptions for each retailer, using meaning condensation and narrative meaning structuring (Kvale 1996; Mishler 1986) to preserve the context of the empirical material (Mishler 1979). The next section provides a background for understanding our case study findings.

RETAILING IN DENMARK AND ITS INSTITUTIONAL CONTEXT

A characteristic feature of Danish retailing is that retail chains are becoming ever more important and have attained a dominant position in most retail sectors, including food retailing and electrical goods retailing (Bahr 2006). Increasing concentration and centralization thus characterize Danish retailing.

Food Retailing: Concentration and Centralization

Changing consumer behavior and economies of scale have set in motion a process of concentration in food retailing in western European countries (Colla 2004; Dawson 2000a). In Denmark this process has gone further than in most other countries: the three leading retail groups (Coop Danmark, Dansk Supermarked, and SuperGros) now have a combined market share of about 85 percent.[1] Each of these retail groups operates different types of stores under different store names (see table 4.1).

Table 4.1 Food Retailers in Denmark, 2006

Retailer	Retail Format	Number of Stores	Market Share
Coop Danmark[a]		1,150	36.3%
Kvickly Xtra	Superstore/hypermarket	14	3.1
Kvickly	Superstore	69	7.5
SuperBrugsen	Large supermarket	267	12.1
DagliBrugsen	Small supermarket	343	4.7
LokalBrugsen	Small supermarket	51	0.5
Irma	Supermarket	70	2.0
Fakta	Discounter	336	6.4
Dansk Supermarked		459	29.9
Netto	Discounter	375	11.8
Føtex	Superstore	70	5.1
Bilka	Hypermarket	14	12.9
SuperGros		881	20.6
SuperBest	Large supermarket	202	10.2
Spar	Small supermarket	270	3.0
Super Spar	Large supermarket	69	1.6
Edeka Danmark		232	3.9
Edeka Aktiv Super	Large supermarket	43	1.5
Edeka Merko	Small supermarket	90	1.1
Aldi Marked	Discounter	235	4.5
Rema 1000	Discounter	270	3.2
Lidl	Discounter	22	.5
Others	Various	63	1.5
Total		3,312	100

Sources: Bahr (2006), Dansk Handelsblad (2006), company websites.
[a] Includes both centrally owned stores and stores run by independent consumer cooperatives.

Coop Danmark has its origin in the Danish cooperative movement. It is part of Coop Norden, a pan-Nordic retail group created through the merger of Coop Danmark, Coop Norge, and KF (a Swedish cooperative) in 2002. Dansk Supermarked is a privately owned retail group. For many years, Dansk Supermarked has been the most profitable and expansive Danish retail group. Finally, SuperGros is a wholesaler-sponsored buying group. It is the result of a merger between Dagrofa, a wholesaler, and Samkøb and Centralkøb, two voluntary buying groups. The objective of the SuperGros merger was for independent retailers to regain competitiveness relative to Coop Danmark and Dansk Supermarked, to whom independent retailers had lost market share.

Danish food retailing is dominated by the modern retail formats (discounters, supermarkets, hypermarkets) that enable concentrated and planned purchasing of groceries (Colla 2004). Traditional grocery stores are disappearing, and other marketing channels for food and groceries are of only marginal importance. For many years, the supermarket has been the most important retail format in Denmark, but discount stores are growing in importance; they currently account for about 30 percent of food retailing. Aldi introduced the discount format to the Danish market in 1977. A number of Danish imitators quickly followed, including current market leaders Netto (owned by Dansk Supermarked) and Fakta (acquired by Coop Danmark in 1987). Planning restrictions, which aim to protect city-center retailing and smaller independent retailers, make it virtually impossible to open new hypermarkets, thus limiting the market share of this format.

Danish food retailing is characterized by intense competition. Several factors contribute to this, among them the growth of the discount sector, as existing discount chains continue to open new stores and new chains enter the market, and the large weekly circulars crammed full of special offers distributed to consumers by all food retailers. Nevertheless, Denmark has the highest consumer prices in the EU (Eurostat 2005).

Decisionmaking is increasingly centralized with regard to buying, marketing, and human resource management, among other issues. This is particular true for Coop Danmark and Dansk Supermarked. The high degree of centralization facilitates the implementation of coordinated initiatives related to these areas.

Although Coop Danmark is a division of Coop Norden, foreign retailers have traditionally played only a limited role in Danish grocery retailing. Aldi (Germany), Edeka (Germany), and Rema 1000 (Norway) have been active in Denmark for a long time but continue to be of marginal importance. Lidl (Germany) made a much-publicized entry into the Danish market in 2005 but has yet to establish a strong position. Entry barriers are quite low, but economies of scale are a prerequisite for being competitive (Dawson 2000a).

Internet retailing is still in its infancy in Denmark with regard to food products. All food retailers have an Internet presence, but none are selling food on the Internet (Bahr 2006). In Denmark food retailing on the Internet is the domain of small, specialized Internet retailers, which typically offer consumers a subscription service and deliver foods on a weekly or biweekly basis.

ELECTRICAL GOODS RETAILING: A FOREIGN AFFAIR

Electrical goods retailing is also characterized by price competition, especially due to the significance of large chains (Bahr 2006). "Brown goods" (hi-fis, televisions, and so on) are sold through both large electrical goods "supermarkets" and small specialty stores, as well as through many food retail outlets. Independent retailers own many electrical goods stores (see table 4.2). However, most have joined some kind of chain. There are thus several voluntary chains, most notably Expert/2Tal and Panasonic, which have about one-third of the market for brown goods. Centrally owned chains such as F-Group, El-Giganten, Merlin, and Hi-Fi Klubben have a combined market share of about 50 percent. Compared to food retailing, more electrical goods chains are voluntary or based on franchising. As a consequence, decisionmaking is less centralized than it is in food retailing with regard to buying decisions, marketing, and human resource management practices.

"White goods" (large household appliances) are sold through specialty retailers, typically franchise-based voluntary chains such as Punkt1 or Skousen, and large electrical goods supermarkets such as El-Giganten or Electric City. In recent years, the industry has become more consolidated, and there have been a number of foreign takeovers. Foreign retailers thus play a larger role in electrical goods retailing than in food retailing.

Internet sales are more important to consumer electronics than to food products. According to a recent study, 31 percent of consumers who had bought products and services via the Internet during the previous year bought consumer electronics (Statistics Denmark 2006). This compares to 8 percent for food products.

Table 4.2 Major Electrical Goods Retailers in Denmark, 2003

Retailer (parent)	Operations	Ownership	Number of Stores	Revenues (in Millions of Euros)
F-Group[a]	Brown goods	Centrally owned chain	84	311
Fona Gruppen[b]	Brown goods	Centrally owned chain	79	
Electric City	Brown goods	Centrally owned chain	5	
Punkt1[c] (Expert, Norway)	White goods	Voluntary chain	115	161[f]
Merlin (Wizard Holding, Iceland)[d]	White and brown goods	Centrally owned chain	54	144
Electronic World	White and brown goods	Centrally owned chain	5	
Merlin	White and brown goods	Centrally owned chain	49	
El-Giganten (Elkjøp/ Dixons)	White and brown goods	Centrally owned chain	22	118[f]
Expert[e]	Brown goods	Buying group	100	107[f]
2Tal[e]	Brown goods	Voluntary chain	138	107[f]
Skousen	White goods	Combination of corporate chain and franchise	62	64
Panasonic Technics	Brown goods	Voluntary chain	50	27
Hi-Fi Klubben	Brown goods	Corporate chain	22	24[f]

Sources: Mintel (2003, 124) and company websites.
[a] F-Group has about 1,400 employees, of which Fona accounts for about 900.
[b] Fona was merged with Fredgaard in 2003.
[c] Punkt1 was established in 2003.
[d] Merlin was a fully owned subsidiary of FDB until 2005, when it was acquired by an Icelandic consortium. It has around 700 employees.
[e] Expert and 2Tal merged on January 1, 2004.
[f] Estimated.

INSTITUTIONAL FRAMEWORK OF DANISH RETAILING

Danish retailing operates within the overall institutional framework outlined in the first two chapters of this volume, but there are also a few institutions that are important specifically to retailing.

UNIONIZATION AND COLLECTIVE BARGAINING

In retailing, the main collective bargaining parties on the employers' side are HTS (Handel, Transport, Service), the employer association for commerce, transportation, and service, and DH&S (Dansk Handel & Service), an employer association for the retail and services industries. On the employee side, most workers are organized in HK Handel, the union representing white-collar workers in retailing. HK Handel represents the interests of about 100,000 members and is one of five sectors represented by HK (Union of Commercial and Clerical Employees in Denmark).

The collective bargaining agreements between HTS or DH&S and HK Handel regulate issues such as wages, benefits, working hours, pension schemes, education, and sickness. As of March 1, 2006, the minimum monthly wage for an unskilled worker was €2,021 (US$2,759.36), according to the collective agreement between DH&S and HK, and €2,222 (US$3,033.18) for a skilled worker. A special feature of the agreement is that it can be in force only if at least 50 percent of the workers at a workplace are members of HK Handel. Another important feature of the agreement is that the employer must present every employee with a schedule for his or her working hours sixteen weeks in advance. However, it is possible to change the work schedule with four weeks' notice.

In January 2006, the European Court of Human Rights ruled that forcing workers to be members of a particular union is in violation of human rights, thus making closed-shop agreements illegal. Some retailers have had closed-shop agreements with certain unions that require workers to be members of those unions. For instance, Coop Danmark has had a closed-shop agreement with HK. Those retailers that do not have a collective agreement with HK—such as Fakta (the only chain belonging to Coop Danmark not to have had a closed-shop agreement with HK)—just adhere to the collective agreement between HTS or DH&S and HK Handel.

Planning Regulations and Restrictions on Opening Hours

Stores are permitted to stay open from 6:00 AM on Mondays to 5:00 PM on Saturdays, with no requirement that they close in between. However, in practice the possibility of being open around the clock is not exploited. On weekdays, food retailers typically are open from 9:00 AM to around 7:00 or 8:00 PM. Sunday opening has traditionally been prohibited (with the exception of small food stores with an annual turnover below €3 million (US$4.09 million), along with outlets at train and bus stations, harbors, airports, and gas stations), but recent legislative changes allow stores to be open twenty Sundays a year. Food stores are not allowed to sell alcohol, beer, or wine between 8 PM and 6 AM.

Finally, planning regulations are very strict. There is a general ban on the establishment of new food stores over 3,000 square meters and nonfood stores over 1,000 square meters. Negotiations regarding planning regulations are ongoing, but it is unlikely that they will be abolished completely.

Developments That May Change the Nature of Retail Jobs

Before presenting our case study findings, we briefly discuss a number of interrelated developments that may influence, or at least have the potential to influence, the nature of retail jobs, including lean retailing (Abernathy et al. 2000; Wright and Lund 2006), the emergence of new information technologies, the deskilling of many retail jobs, the internationalization of retail chains, the growth of discounting and category killers, the increasing concentration of retail markets (Dawson, 2000a, 2000b), and the emergence of Internet-based retailers.

Lean thinking, which originated as "lean production" in car manufacturing, has in recent years become a general philosophy of operational innovation (see, for example, Hammer 2004; Womack and Jones 1994). Common themes in lean production are a focus on eliminating waste and reducing inventory and buffer stocks; moving production systems from a "push" to a "pull" approach, based on customer demands and requirements; developing closer relationships with suppliers; and the continuous improvement of work processes (Wright and Lund 2006). Furthermore, proponents argue that lean production entails the development of a multiskilled, flexible, and team-based workforce. Critics have questioned this, however, arguing instead that lean production results in significant work intensification and a system of "management by stress" (Parker and Slaughter 1988).

In the retailing context, lean thinking is encapsulated in industry terms such as "efficient consumer response" (Joint Industry Project on Efficient Consumer Response 1995), "lean logistics" (Wright and Lund 2006) or, simply, "lean retailing" (Abernathy et al. 2000; Christopherson 2001). Through improved category management (CM), continuous product replenishment, and the use of enabling technologies (primarily electronic data interchange [EDI] and electronic payments), efficient consumer response (ECR) is intended to meet consumer needs better, faster, and cheaper (Joint Industry Project on Efficient Consumer Response 1995). ECR or lean retailing, like the lean movement in general, is thus based on innovations in information and communication technology. Implementation of lean retailing requires large investments by retailers and their suppliers and rests upon four building blocks: bar codes, electronic data interchange, modern distribution centers, and the promulgation of standards across firms (Abernathy et al. 2000).

The emergence of *new information technologies* such as standard bar codes, scanning technologies, computerized inventory control and replenishment systems, and electronic data interchange has eliminated some manual tasks within stores and contributed to an increase in retail productivity (Davis et al. 2006; Sieling, Friedman, and Dumas 2001). Technological innovations such as computerized warehouses and checkout scanners are often associated with the *deskilling of retail jobs* and thus are seen as responses to retailers' perceived need for driving down labor costs (Carré, Holgate, and Tilly 2005). However, the introduction of new technologies has also resulted in the up-skilling of some tasks, owing to higher requirements for computer literacy and technical knowledge.

A number of factors contribute to the cost focus inherent in lean retailing. As retailing has become increasingly *international*, retailers have been able to transfer techniques and concepts that are successful in one market to other markets (Schurr and Fischer 1996). For instance, German discount retailers such as Aldi, Lidl, Penny, and

Plus have been relatively successful in transferring their basic concepts to other markets. The *growth of discounting*, with its focus on low prices, in itself contributes to a focus on reducing costs, as does the *increasing concentration of retail markets*. As has already been discussed, these developments are also evident in the Danish retail sector.

Finally, the emergence of *Internet-based retailers* may have an impact on human resource management practices in the future and may result in a decrease in retail employment. As mentioned, Internet-based retailers have had little impact thus far on Danish food retailing. With regard to electrical goods retailing, different Internet sites enable customers to make easier price comparisons, and it is possible to buy products on most brick-and-mortar electrical goods retailers' websites.

CASE STUDY FINDINGS

Efficient and effective human resource management practices can be a significant determinant of business success for retailers of any size (Arrowsmith and McGoldrick 1996; Miller 2006). As pointed out by Dale Miller (2006), the multifaceted nature of large-scale retailing presents human resource managers with special challenges. For instance, staff are often spread across many retail roles and functions as well as physical locations. Nevertheless, the human resource management practices of retailers have not been the subject of extensive academic study (Marchington 1996; Miller 2006).

Food Retailing: Dead-end Jobs or Opportunities Galore?

There are striking similarities in the intended business strategies of the various food retailers we studied. They all want to offer high-quality food products and other groceries at low prices. Nevertheless, the differences in business strategy across these companies can be discerned and are related to the store format (discounter, superstore, or hypermarket) which they operate—and hence to service quality.

The two discount chains we studied both want to be the preferred neighborhood food store. Both carry a fixed, narrow assortment of groceries and an ever-changing assortment of weekly special offers. Disc prides itself on being more innovative than other discounters, whereas Fast wants consumers to perceive its stores as easy, fast, and cheap places to buy groceries.[2]

Supermarket and hypermarket chains emphasize breadth of assortment and product quality in addition to price, as they conceive consumers to be very price-focused. The growth of the discount sector has thus put traditional retail formats under pressure. Particularly small supermarkets and independent retailers are struggling, as are some supermarket chains. Intense competition and poor results have led one supermarket chain to focus on cutting costs in recent years by, for instance, reducing the quality of the service offered to consumers. Thus, manned delicatessen counters have been closed in several stores, and the number of employees working in stores has been reduced significantly. These efforts are regarded as successful: the company posted its best-ever financial results last year. According to our informants, the reduction in the number of store workers has not had negative consequences for the remaining employees' job satisfaction.

The food retailers we studied are all characterized by a high degree of centralization of decisionmaking in relation to buying, marketing, and HRM practices and by a formalization of work routines. Of special interest for the present study is that the chains we studied all have central human resource management departments. Perhaps not surprisingly, central human resource managers argue that human resource management is important for the successful implementation of business strategies. Several managers stressed the importance of employees for the differentiation of retail chains. To operate efficiently and effectively retail chains have to recruit, retain, and develop good employees at all levels. Ensuring that this happens is the task of the central human resource department working with managers throughout the chain.

The central human resource manager from Fast realized that all companies claim that their employees are "our most important asset." It is important to back such claims by action, he argued. To attract and retain workers this discounter wants to be the preferred employer in grocery retailing, and to achieve this ambition it claims to focus on workers and has defined a number of corporate values (sense of humor, responsibility, trust, consistency, and pride) that are posted in all staff rooms. Another initiative reflecting the importance attributed to employees is that this discounter has developed a new marketing platform that focuses on employees, with individual employees being identified as the senders of specific marketing communication messages.

The Nature of Jobs: Multiskilling or Deskilling?

We have studied checkout operators and sales assistants in food retailing. We now discuss the content of these jobs, how the work is organized, and by whom.

With regard to the content of jobs, it is possible to draw a distinction between discounters, on the one hand, and supermarkets and hypermarkets, on the other. In discount stores, employees typically do a little bit of everything (stocking shelves, checkout work, sweeping floors, and so on) rather than performing only one specific task. The responsibility of store managers for day-to-day operations requires that they be involved in all aspects of the store. In discount stores, even store managers will sometimes, for instance, clean toilets. Because of their small size and limited number of employees, work organization is very decentralized in the discount chains and is often negotiated in discussions between store managers and their employees. Administrative tasks are primarily the responsibility of store managers, but typically some tasks are delegated to assistant managers and other full-time employees. For instance, responsibility for the day-to-day operation of departments (such as fruits and vegetables or dairy products) is typically divided among full-time employees.

Because supermarkets and hypermarkets are larger, a greater degree of job specialization is possible. In these stores, checkout operators tend to work almost exclusively at checkouts. Checkout operators thus have a narrowly defined job focused on scanning products, receiving payment, and giving change. Sales assistants in the electrical goods departments of supermarket and hypermarket food retailers stack shelves, assist customers, and order goods. In one of the supermarket chains, there used to be very clear demarcations between departments. These demarcations are not so clear anymore, and there is increasing emphasis among the departments on helping each other, thus increasing internal flexibility.

One of the chains has experimented with a job rotation scheme in one of its outlets because managers expected that working only at checkouts was boring for employees. According to the job rotation scheme, checkout operators worked three weeks at checkouts and one week on the shop floor. This experiment was a complete disaster, however, according to the central human resource manager of the chain, because checkout operators actually preferred "just" sitting at checkouts and interacting with customers.

Specialization and automation have changed the nature of jobs in food retailing, with consequences for the skill requirements and training of entry-level employees. Very few formal skills are required to work as a checkout operator in supermarkets and hypermarkets or as sales assistants in a discount store. Through the specialization, routinization, and formalization of work processes, many retail jobs have been deskilled. For instance, the centralization of buying functions has reduced or eliminated the discretion that individual stores and employees can exercise over assortments of stock.

The application of modern information technology supports efforts to improve efficiency and effectiveness through the automation of some tasks. For instance, the introduction of new hand-held scanners in one discount chain was construed as very important in relation to the ordering of goods and registration of damaged goods. Managers at different organizational levels regarded the latter in particular as an important element of cutting costs. The planned introduction of automatic reordering of goods was expected to reduce the time required to order goods from one hour to fifteen minutes a day.

Who performs the tasks just described? To illustrate, we provide three typical tales of fictional employees working in Danish retailing, followed by a more detailed discussion of who works in Danish food retailing.

Tales of Three Types of Retail Workers

Monday, 9:00 AM   Susanne is on her way to university and this week's first lecture. But that is not what's on her mind. Her head is full of memories of Saturday night's get-together with some colleagues from the discount store where she works two or three shifts each week. They had met at her place for dinner and later gone to a pub. As always, they'd had lots of fun. She'll see a couple of them this afternoon when she goes to work, and she hopes they'll have time to talk. However, Monday afternoon is normally very busy, and she'll probably be sitting at the checkout all the time. Still, it's not a bad job. She doesn't have to invest too much of herself in it, and it's nice to have the extra money on top of her student allowance to spend on new clothes and stuff.

Monday, 9:00 AM   Anne is sitting at the checkout waiting for the first customers of the day. She has worked at Super Too for nine years. She likes her job, especially interacting with customers and training new checkout operators. Sometimes customers are grumpy, but some people are just never satisfied, right? The money isn't great, but she can make ends meet, and her fixed schedule gives her time to be with her two young children and pursue her other interests.

Monday, 9:00 AM   Michael is rounding up his coworkers in the fruit and vegetables department of Hyper to discuss the day and week ahead of them. Since becoming head of the department six months ago, he has been very busy, but he likes the opportunities presented to him, the ability to make changes to the department in order to improve sales, and the instant feedback he gets from seeing how customers respond. He also likes to work with people and is looking forward to next week's training session at Hyper's training facility. The topic will be interviewing, and from experience he knows that he will learn new techniques that he will be able to put into practice immediately. He is only twenty-two years old, but he has already accomplished more than most of his friends going to college. He sometimes teases them about how long it will be before they are managers.

WHO WORKS IN DANISH FOOD RETAILING?

These short vignettes represent the three types of employees working in Danish grocery retailing whom we found in our study: (1) transitional workers who do not envision a career in retailing (Susanne); (2) core employees who have no ambitions of promotion to managerial positions (Anne); and (3) career-seekers who want a career in retailing (Michael). In this section, we discuss these three types of retail employers and food retail employment more generally.

Transitional Workers   The first type of employee, the transitional worker, is typical of Danish retailing. It has been noted that the large number of students and people under the age of eighteen working in retail jobs for a short period of time is a special feature of the Danish labor market (see chapter 2, this volume; Böll 2001). Transitional work-ers make up more than one-quarter of the workforce in retailing. Typi-cally they work only part-time and thus are a source of time flexibility for Danish retailers. According to Joachim Böll (2001), five factors ap-pear to explain the large number of transitional workers in retailing:

1. Increased price competition provides an incentive to keep wage costs down.

2. Extended opening hours create a need for flexibility.

3. Working time clauses in collective agreements limit the flexibility of full-time employees.

4. Other sources of part-time workers are not available.

5. Retailing faces a general recruitment problem because of a tight labor market combined with low wages, unattractive working hours, and a general reputation for offering unattractive work conditions.

Similar arguments were used by the human resource managers and store managers in our cases. Transitional workers are particularly prevalent in food retailing and especially in the target occupations of interest in this study, checkout operators and sales assistants. All five food retail chains we studied employ a large number of transitional workers as checkout operators in supermarkets and hypermarkets and as sales assistants in discount stores.

There are only a few full-time checkout operators in supermarkets and hypermarkets. Many of these full-time checkout operators are young people taking a year off after high school before beginning their formal education, and they too can be classified as transitional workers.

In the cases we studied, checkout operators are predominantly students (high school or college level) working part-time. Typically, fewer than 10 to 15 percent of checkout operators in supermarkets and hypermarkets are full-time workers. For instance, in one of the supermarket outlets we visited, one-quarter of the checkout opera-tors were age sixteen or seventeen. Of these youths, about 50 percent were retained once they turned eighteen.[3] The checkout manager preferred to recruit students as checkout operators early in their (high school or college) studies so that they could stay with the retailer for some years. Furthermore, this manager preferred to hire students for a maximum of eight hours per week, because the store then did not have to pay sickness benefits when they fell ill.

A major reason given for employing part-time transitional workers is that they provide numerical flexibility. Thus, it becomes relatively easy to increase staffing levels during peak periods. Students are often interested in working extra hours if the need arises—for instance, when a coworker is sick.

Similarly, discount stores often have very few full-time employees and rely to a large extent on a large number of part-timers, who are typically students working a limited number of hours per week. Because they employ fewer people per store, it can sometimes be difficult for discounters to call in extra people, although stores sometimes "borrow" employees from other stores belonging to the same chain. If they do not succeed in finding workers to cover all shifts, assistant managers and especially store managers have to step up and cover the holes in the schedule themselves and everyone has to work faster.

The two discount chains in particular are very cost-focused, and store managers have to work with very tight wage budgets. One way to manage this is to hire people under the age of eighteen. More than 13,300 persons between the ages of fifteen and seventeen work in the Danish food retail sector. This compares with a little over 34,000 adults working in this sector.

Out of the 34,000 adults working in food retailing, roughly 12,000 are classified as checkout operators or sales assistants. The typical checkout operator or sales assistant is female, of Danish ethnicity, and between the ages of eighteen and thirty (see table 4.3). About 29 percent are low-wage workers. In food retailing, almost 80 percent of low-wage workers in the target occupations are women, compared to 66 percent of non-low-wage workers, making women slightly overrepresented among low-wage workers. It is thus not coincidental that the first two persons in the stories told earlier are female and the aspiring manager is male. This gender breakdown characterizes grocery retailing in other countries as well (Maxwell and Ogden 2006).

The retailers we studied strive to have workforces that reflect the communities in which their stores are located in terms of ethnic composition; thus, there are large geographic variations in the proportion of immigrants working in stores.

Table 4.3 Number of Checkout Operators and Sales Assistants in the Food Retailing Industry

| | Employees (Excluding Students) | | Students | | |
	Low-Wage	Not Low-Wage	Low-Wage	Not Low-Wage	Total
Gender					
Men	592	2,592	282	408	3,874
Women	2,170	5,139	415	483	8,207
Age					
Eighteen to thirty	1,459	4,054	695	888	7,096
Thirty-one to forty	412	1,504	n.a.	n.a.	1,921
Forty-one to fifty	350	1,075			1,425
Fifty-one to sixty	541	1,118			1,659
Ethnicity					
Danish	2,630	7,447	663	855	11,595
Foreign	132	304	34	36	506
Education					
Secondary	1,789	2,127	468	545	4,929
Upper secondary	1,519	5,439	205	320	7,483
Postsecondary	54	185	24	26	289
Total	2,762	7,751	697	891	12,101

Source: Authors' calculations from Center for Corporate Performance (CCP) data.
Note: "Low-wage" is defined as two-thirds of the median hourly wage of the entire economy.

Core Employees In addition to transitional workers, retailers employ a second type of employee as checkout operators and sales assistants: stable, core employees who have often worked in retailing for many years but have no ambition of rising to a management position. They do a good job and often train new recruits. Several human resource managers and store managers we interviewed stressed the importance of having some stable employees of this type. They provide continuity and make up the backbone of the store. Sometimes they are referred to as "core workers."

According to several human resource managers, food retailing is a place where many people like to shop but few people like to work. Although, generally speaking, none of the retailers studied had experienced problems in recruiting entry-level checkout operators and sales assistants, informants expected that in the future organizational reputation would be of critical importance in attracting employees.

Career-Seekers   The third type of food retail employee is the career-seeker, who often starts his or her career as an apprentice or trainee. Both training and recruitment are important with these employees, but only supermarkets and hypermarkets take in apprentices and trainees. Apprentices get sales assistant training, while trainees get more management training and are given greater responsibilities during the trainee period. Recruitment drives take place twice a year. Human resource managers argue that these recruitment campaigns are necessary because few young people enter the workforce each year and food retailers face strong competition for them from other industries, such as banking, insurance, and shipping. Food retailers recruit apprentices and trainees in part by stressing that they offer employees the possibility of pursuing a career and that their large internal training departments can assist the personal and professional development of these employees.

For aspiring managers, there are numerous opportunities for training. Retailers have designed comprehensive training programs that contain several modules covering topics such as how to conduct interviews. Training is very practically oriented and focuses on teaching skills that are immediately transferable to the workplace.

An important driving force behind these training programs is the need to recruit future managers (at different organizational levels, such as store, region, or corporate). Many of the participants in retailer training programs, especially those in courses for aspiring store managers, are very ambitious and highly committed. These workers continuously have to be presented with challenges, need to experience personal and professional development, and must be given new tasks if the retailer is going to be able to hold on to them. One human resource manager viewed the training of workers as an investment for the retailer. He believed that the people who had gone through the company's training scheme would remember where they had been taught their skills and would spread the word.

Employee turnover is significant in food retailing, particularly among transitional workers, who switch jobs frequently. Although transitional workers are a potential recruitment pool for permanent positions (Böll 2001), the majority of the transitional workers we spoke to regarded employment in retailing as attractive only in the short run. They planned to work in retailing only during after-school hours or before moving on to study or travel. Retailers would like to change this pattern. One human resource manager acknowledged

that employees often start working in retailing by chance. It is up to
the retailer, he argued, to ensure that the employee considers work
for the retailer to be interesting and that employees are socialized
into the corporate culture.

Because human resource managers realize that retailing is not seen
as an attractive industry to work in by many in the target group they
want to attract, it is important for them to inform their current employees, including apprentices and transitional workers working
only a few hours a week, about the opportunities that work with the
retailer can offer them. Some chains evaluate workers who are com-
pleting their apprenticeship in order to identify those with "development potential"; these apprentices are then invited to participate in a
three-day training program. As early as possible, these chains want to
inform apprentices about what they can offer in terms of training, development, and career opportunities. In this way, they are able to recruit a large share of their future middle managers. One chain has
even established a working group in order to share information
among outlets on how to retain store workers.

Recruiting managers from within is a priority for all the food retailers we studied. One chain has set a goal of recruiting 80 percent of
its managers from within, but is not achieving this goal yet.

Because of low unemployment, employee loyalty is perceived to
have declined. This underscores the importance of offering workers
challenges, personal and professional development, and career opportunities, several of our informants argued. In general, employee
turnover is perceived to be highest in the greater Copenhagen area
and other major urban areas, but it is also seen to be increasing in rural areas.[4]

In food retailing, sales assistants have good prospects for career advancement, especially in the discount sector, where many store manager positions are filled by internal applications, typically from assistant managers. The assistant manager position is also fairly easy to
obtain for sales assistants who are interested in career advancement
and have the requisite skills (being able to read, write, and do arith-
metic, being a bit of a computer freak, and knowing the industry). If
sales assistants have the right skills and the drive, there are good career opportunities for them in both supermarkets and hypermarkets.

However, not all of our informants were interested in being promoted to a management position. They gave various explanations.
One informant had been a manager earlier in her career and was not

interested in a management position because of the many hours she would have to put in and because she feared she would suffer from stress. Others were only interested in a steady income. The main reason cited by some informants, however, was that they planned to work only temporarily in food retailing until, for example, they began studying at university, completed their university degree, had saved enough money to travel around the world, or got the opportunity to fulfill their dream of working in specialty retailing.

The Training and Recruitment of Checkout Operators and Sales Assistants

Retail chains use their websites to explain the job and career opportunities they offer. The food retailers we studied rarely use ads in newspapers to recruit checkout operators because they receive many unsolicited applications; instead, many current workers recommend friends and acquaintances.

Training happens mainly on the job. An experienced colleague typically shows new recruits what to do and then observes and gives instructions as appropriate when the new recruits are let loose. Sometimes a specific worker has been assigned the task of providing initial on-the-job training because management trusts that person to pass on the "right" attitudes and values to new recruits.

The two discount chains both have introductory programs for new employees. In one chain, new employees are introduced to the company through e-learning modules on the internet before they can begin working in stores. The first module is a cash register training module that has to be completed immediately; a second module can be completed within a month. If an employee does not complete the training modules on time, headquarters closes his or her staff card, indicating that that employee cannot work checkouts.

Besides introductory training, checkout operators and sales assistants working in food retailing have very limited access to training. This is particularly true for part-time transitional workers.

What Is It Like to Work in Food Retailing?

It is noteworthy that, across the three employee types, our informants generally expressed high job satisfaction. When discussing job satisfaction, it is relevant to consider several different issues, includ-

Table 4.4 Pay and Compensation for Workers in Danish Retail Stores, 2006

	Euros per Month	Euros per Hour
Minimum wage[a]		
Unskilled workers	2,021	12.61
Skilled workers	2,222	13.86
Under age eighteen		
Normal	1,057	6.59
Doing skilled work	1,278	7.97
Apprentices		
First year	1,167	7.28
Second year	1,311	8.18
Third year	1,384	8.63
Fourth year	1,456	9.08
Unsocial hours compensation (extra pay)		
Weekdays, 6:00 PM to 6:00 AM		2.65
Saturdays, 3:00 PM to 12:00 AM		5.00
Sundays, 12:00 AM, to Monday, 12:00 AM		5.70
Overtime		
First three hours on weekdays		+50%
More than three hours and Sundays		+100%

Source: Wages stipulated by the collective bargaining agreement between DH&S and HK Handel for 2004 to 2006 (DHS 2004).
Note: Pay and compensation figures exclude the 15 percent vacation pay.
[a] The minimum wage is stipulated in the collective bargaining agreement. Employees can earn more than this minimum wage depending on firm-level or establishment-level agreements. The minimum wage is not politically determined.

ing wages, working hours, working conditions, and the social aspects of work.

Although it is possible in Denmark to earn a living as a checkout operator or sales assistant (despite media coverage sometimes suggesting the opposite), pay is low for these positions, as indicated by the high proportion of low-wage workers in food retailing. To a large extent, wages are regulated through the various collective agreements (see table 4.4 and chapter 2 for a discussion of how these agreements work). Generally speaking, food retailers pay checkout operators and sales assistants according to the relevant collective bargaining agreement.

Retailing is a "minimum-wage" area, meaning that collective agreements set a lowest wage. The retailer can choose to add a certain amount to that through local agreements. However, the wage budgets of retail stores and departments are usually tight, and store managers often feel that they have little room to maneuver for individual agreements or wage increases.[5] Store managers in discount stores operate with particularly tight monthly wage budgets. Wages are an important cost factor for discount retailers, and it is therefore essential that actual wages be within budgets. If a store manager exceeds his wage budget in one period, the store has to save on its wage budget in the coming period. Supermarkets also try to keep down labor costs. Managers at one of the supermarkets we visited were proud of having one of the lowest "wage percentages" among stores in the chain.

Most transitional workers earn the minimum tariff stipulated in collective bargaining agreements (see chapter 2), while most core employees earn personal allowances based on, for example, seniority or qualifications. Managers and aspiring managers earn higher wages. As an incentive for managers, retailers have developed bonus schemes tied to different indicators such as store profitability and whether managers meet their wage budgets. Managers thus have an incentive for not giving personal allowances to sales assistants and checkout operators.

While getting paid is an important motivation for working in the first place, wages are not the main reason for the high job satisfaction reported. On the other hand, neither were wages a major cause of complaint in our interviews. It is common knowledge that food retailing is a low-wage area. Therefore, transitional workers and steady full-timers have relatively low expectations with regard to their wages.

A majority of our informants working for food retailers were union members, but they expressed only limited interest in unions and saw no reason for unions to play a more significant role in their workplace. Informants contacted their employee representative when they had a problem or called the union directly. Similarly, most employees at specialty retailers join the union so as to have backup if they need assistance in the future, but they are not interested in union matters as such.

Human resource managers and store-level managers generally express satisfaction with the working relationship they have with the main union that organizes store workers. This reflects the generally good relations between employers and unions in Denmark (see chapter 2).

Another issue that gives retailing a poor image as an area of employment is the likelihood of working irregular hours. However, our case studies suggest that we should be careful not to simplify the issue of working hours. First of all, relatively few employees in our target occupations (checkout operators and sales assistants) work full-time (thirty-seven hours per week). Most transitional workers work only one or two shifts a week, and many steady employees work less than thirty-seven hours.

Anecdotal evidence and media reports (see, for example, Krogsgaard and Olsen 2007) suggest that store workers are often pressured by superiors to put in "interest hours" in addition to their scheduled working hours—that is, to stay on after their shift has ended or to arrive ahead of schedule. However, the notion of workers being required to put in interest hours was regarded as a myth by some of the human resource managers we interviewed. They stressed that the explicit policies of their companies was that workers should be compensated for the hours worked. Only workers in managerial positions were expected to work more than full-time; many of them reported working forty-five to fifty hours a week.

Intensifying competition and longer opening hours increase demands for flexibility and internal efficiency and require that workers develop new competences. Workers often have irregular working hours, working evenings, Saturdays, Sundays, or, for discounters, very early mornings (in order to receive goods), and some informants reported long days. In addition to being compensated for displaced working time, informants often mentioned having a specific day off during the week in return. Several human resource managers and store-level managers argued that it is important for a store's internal flexibility to have a large number of workers who work only limited hours in order to take into account fluctuating customer streams. However, flexibility is not a one-way street where only retailers can demand flexibility from employees. Flexibility is also imposed on retailers by workers who strive to combine their private life with their working life or who look for work that will not interfere with their studies, as is the case for many transitional workers. Retailers acknowledge that in the current job market they have to accommodate the wishes of workers and that being flexible contributes to having satisfied employees. Both transitional workers and steady employees therefore have considerable influence over their own work schedule.

According to collective bargaining agreements, store workers are entitled to get their work schedule sixteen weeks in advance. However, coworkers are able to swap shifts, with the approval of their superior or manager, and part-time workers are often willing to take extra shifts when asked. The managers and employees we interviewed all regarded the practice of swapping shifts as a very positive contribution to flexibility for both employers and employees.

Workers in discount food retailing chains can have particularly tough working conditions characterized by a very fast work pace. In one chain, some informants reported that they had shed considerable weight after starting work for one of the discounters. Nevertheless, the work is not as physically hard as it used to be because a new central warehouse has made it possible to stack pallets more efficiently and many package sizes have been reduced. Psychologically, however, working in retailing can be very stressful. Informants mentioned several examples of customers who were physically and especially verbally abusive and even described store managers receiving death threats. If necessary, employees were entitled to psychological counseling to help them handle these situations, but most often such incidents were something that they simply tried to "shrug off" or that they talked to superiors or coworkers about.

In supermarkets, work can also be physically demanding, particularly shelf stacking. Here as well, however, several informants said that the physical strain of work has decreased because goods are increasingly delivered in packaging that can be placed directly on shelves or because clothing is delivered on hangers, for instance. Some goods, such as tinned goods and pasta, are increasingly displayed in crates, thus reducing time-consuming and tiring shelf-stacking tasks. In one of the supermarket chains, the work pace increased following downsizing. However, informants considered it a positive development that there are fewer idle moments during their workday, since they preferred to have a busy day (though not too busy).

Some informants indicated that stress is a serious problem, particularly for middle managers such as department managers and assistant store managers. Some informants who had witnessed colleagues succumb to stress and not return to work used this to explain their own lack of ambition. Even very young workers, according to a middle manager, suffer from stress—and report in sick—because of the many conflicting demands and expectations they face and attempt to meet and reconcile (work, friends, studies, family, and so on). However, because our informants always referred to others when talking about stress, this did not seem to be a factor that influenced their own job satisfaction.

Several other factors contribute to the generally high job satisfaction of all three types of employees. Career-seekers appreciate having many career and training opportunities, and many informants derived satisfaction from working for what they considered to be well-run and successful retailers. Informants generally appreciated interacting with customers, but not the hassle they sometimes get from disgruntled or dissatisfied ones. Previous research has shown that workers develop strategies for coping with such customers (see, for example, Rafaelli 1989). Among the other negative aspects of retail work our informants bemoaned were a lack of appreciation from superiors and the disruptiveness of frequent management changes (as career-seekers move from one position to another or to another store) (Broadbridge, Swanson, and Taylor 2000).

When discussing what they liked about their jobs, our informants repeatedly stressed the importance of having good colleagues. This is consistent with previous studies that have found that the companionship of fellow workers is a major aspect of job satisfaction in retailing (see, for example, Broadbridge, Swanson, and Taylor 2000). On the one hand, it is important that workers can function together socially on the job. For instance, several informants emphasized that it is important for coworkers to share a similar sense of humor, as this contributes to a positive atmosphere among them and enables them to cope with an often hectic and busy workday. On the other hand, it is important to many workers that they can meet with colleagues outside of work. Transitional workers in particular often meet socially outside of work, and in supermarkets and hypermarkets there are often very active staff clubs. Informants frequently mentioned the importance of their workplace as a way to build a social network after having moved to a new city.

Retailers realize the importance of these social aspects of work for the functioning of stores and often provide financial support for the social initiatives of staff clubs or other such initiatives (such as company picnics and bowling nights). Retailers also organize events such as large company parties and sporting events in order to promote a sense of belonging and togetherness among employees across stores. Many of our informants identified quite strongly with their workplace or employer, especially if they considered their employer a successful and well-run retailer.

SPECIALTY ELECTRICAL GOODS RETAILERS: WE ARE SALESPEOPLE!

We now turn to specialty electrical goods retailers, in particular focusing on what distinguishes these retailers from our food retailer.

The business strategies of the three specialty electrical goods retailers we studied all focus on offering high-quality service, although price is also important. However, there are differences between them in emphasis. The business strategy of White One is focused on creating economies of scale in purchasing and marketing, based on its position as market leader. After going through a process of transition and professionalization, The Goods regards its core strength as service and wants to avoid competing only on price. Finally, Music strives to clearly differentiate its product line from that of the companies it considers its main competitors (a number of centrally owned brown goods retailers). The chain aims to offer consumers the best value-for-money and excellent customer service. It is very open about its strategy and tries to involve salespeople in strategic decisionmaking. Our informants perceived the high degree of decentralization and openness at Music as very positive.

The specialty electrical goods retail chains comprise both centrally owned stores and stores operated by franchisees. The relative importance of company-owned stores and franchise stores differs among chains. One central human resource manager argued that local ownership of franchise stores contributes to greater commitment on behalf of the owner-manager. Stores belonging to these chains are small and typically employ four to ten employees.

In the specialty electrical goods chains, central human resource managers serve in the role of consultant to the managers of franchise stores. Because these stores are not centrally owned, human resource managers cannot impose human resource management policies on the stores, even though they would like to influence their practices in this area. It is a different matter at the centrally owned stores: at two of the chains, the central human resource managers are directly involved in managing human resources, although store managers are in charge of day-to-day operations.

The Nature of Work: Selling!

All employees in the specialty electrical goods stores we visited considered themselves salespeople. Their primary task is to sell goods, but of course there are other tasks that have to be taken care of, such as sweeping floors, ordering goods, stocking shelves, and displaying goods. Managers also have administrative tasks. Specialty electrical goods retailers thus resemble food discount chains in their work organization: salespeople typically perform all kinds of functions, although there can be some specialization, often depending on the knowledge and interests of the salespeople working in a particular store. There can also be a more formalized specialization if an employee is responsible for a particular product group, section, or department of the store. However, because specialty retail stores typically have few employees, it is important that they help each other in order for the store to function properly.

Who Works for Specialty Electrical Goods Retailers?

Compared to food retailing, a larger proportion of workers in specialty electrical goods retailers have completed vocational training. Also, electrical goods retailing continues to be male-dominated, whereas food retail employment has become feminized (see table 4.5). In fact, at one chain, Music, there are no female employees in the stores.

The three types of workers identified in food retailing can also be found working for specialty electrical goods retailers. However, there are relatively few transitional workers and more limited prospects for career seekers due to the small unit size and limited staff turnover. In electrical goods retailing the majority of workers belong to our second type, steady full-timers.

Among full-time employees, labor turnover is low at specialty retailers. This can be a problem for retailers, because there are few

Table 4.5 Number of Salespeople in the Specialty Electrical Goods Industry

| | Employees (Excluding Students) | | Students | | |
	Low-Wage	Not Low-Wage	Low-Wage	Not Low-Wage	Total
Gender					
Men	162	1,011	12	21	1,206
Women	41	184	7	8	240
Age					
Eighteen to thirty	193	697	19	29	938
Thirty-one to forty	7	293			300
Forty-one to fifty	2	129			131
Fifty-one to sixty	n.a.	76	n.a.	n.a.	77
Ethnicity					
Danish	194	1,178	19	29	1,420
Foreign	9	17			26
Education					
Secondary	75	169	10	8	262
Upper secondary	127	980	9	16	1,132
Postsecondary	n.a.	46	n.a.	5	52
Total	203	1,195	19	29	1,446

Source: Authors' calculations from Center for Corporate Performance (CCP) data.
Note: "Low-wage" is defined as two-thirds of the median hourly wage of the entire economy.

openings for store managers and thus limited career prospects for salespeople, who consequently may start to look elsewhere. Typically, the only possibility to advance is to become a store manager in a centrally owned store or perhaps a franchisee. The Goods is expanding rapidly and therefore needs to hire new store managers on an ongoing basis, but in a chain like Music, which expands only slowly, there are limited career prospects. Therefore, holding on to good store workers who wish to advance can be problematic.

Of the specialty retailers studied, only Music employs part-time salespeople. Part-time salespeople are important to the chain because they enable the company to adjust staffing levels to peak periods (afternoons, Saturdays, and the periods following the distribution of circulars to households). In the other specialty chains, full-time workers have to fill all shifts and handle peak periods.

RECRUITMENT AND TRAINING

Among specialty electrical goods retailers, recruitment practices differ in the degree of formalization. On the one hand, the recruitment process used by Music is quite informal. The chain used to do a lot of tests and use professional recruiters, but it has abandoned this practice. Music is not so concerned about whether new recruits have a background in retailing or have completed an apprenticeship. The chain is more interested in people who have an interest in the products it sells and have the "right" attitude. Music gets many unsolicited applications from enthusiasts who would like to work for the chain. Some applicants are too "geeky," however, to be hired.

The Goods, on the other hand, has a very formalized recruitment process. In the first step, the central human resource manager and the regional manager formulate a job description and test applicants. Job descriptions are formulated centrally and differ depending on the store location, since the profile needed to perform well in rural Jutland is assumed to be different from what is required in a store in Copenhagen. All new employees are tested for their understanding of the service concepts and their ability to handle customer complaints. Only then does the store manager or franchisee interview the applicant to test the personal chemistry between them. Recruitment is primarily based on recommendations from current workers, but recently the chain has tried to work with an external recruitment agency, the advantage being that this company has a substantial database of prospects upon which to draw. Using an external agency, however, is a costly way to recruit: the agency charges 12.5 percent of the yearly wage for its services.

Whereas skill requirements are quite low in food retailing, both of the specialty white goods retailers in our study preferred to hire skilled employees, that is, people who had completed vocational training in the white goods sector. However, such applicants are hard to come by. Informants argued that the shortage of skilled applicants is due to there being too few apprentices in this retail sector. Because electrical goods stores tend to be quite small, it is considered too demanding to train apprentices who alternate between working in the store and attending school. Therefore, retailers often try to lure good workers away from each other in order to attract the most talented employees and cope with labor shortages.

Music does not place great emphasis on formal qualifications. It is more important to this chain that salespeople have a keen interest in the products it sells and that they are genuine hi-fi enthusiasts without being too "geeky." An important aspect of working in a Music store is being able to analyze the needs of customers. The chain is considering developing a training course that will help an employee uncover the needs of customers so that he or she can sell them the stereo or TV set that exactly satisfies their needs (the conception of service quality).

At the specialty retailers, the emphasis is on teaching employees "product knowledge"—the salespeople have to know a lot about the products they sell in order to provide high-quality service. Sometimes suppliers conduct product seminars. The salespeople we interviewed generally valued supplier-run seminars, although they felt these sessions could sometimes be too one-sided.

What Is It Like to Work for a Specialty Electrical Good Retailer?

Employee satisfaction is generally high in electrical goods retailing. At specialty retailers, wages typically (but not necessarily) are higher than in the electronics departments of supermarkets and hypermarkets. Salespeople typically earn a basic wage and commission based on actual sales or a bonus based on meeting sales targets or budgets. Some Music informants complained that sales budgets were set unrealistically high following several good years of strong growth, thus making their ability to exceed sales targets nearly impossible; wages had subsequently declined even though the chain and the store were performing well. It is important to note that salespeople in franchise stores are better paid than those in centrally owned stores. At Music, wages for full-time employees vary from €2,214 per month to €3,354 per month (US$3,022.67 to US$4,579.06). At one of the specialty electrical goods retailers we studied, one employee expressed frustration over the high work pressure and low pay (due to a sales budget that was very difficult to meet and surpass). This employee's store was centrally owned; by contrast, satisfaction was high at the two franchise stores belonging to the same chain that we visited.

At specialty retailers, employees often lift heavy objects such as loudspeakers, washing machines, and dishwashers, but our informants did not consider the work to be too physically demanding.

The importance of having good colleagues was also stressed repeatedly in our electrical goods retail cases.

Stress was mentioned as a problem at Music and attributed to a large increase in sales without a corresponding increase in staff levels. Some Music informants complained that their work schedule was changed frequently and with short notice.

SIMILARITIES AND DIFFERENCES BETWEEN FOOD AND ELECTRICAL GOODS RETAILING

In our study, we have compared the nature of retail jobs across different retail sectors (food retailing and electrical goods retailing) and different occupations (checkout operators and sales assistants in food retailing and salespeople in specialty electrical goods retailing).

In some ways, our case companies are very similar. In all cases, human resource managers stress the importance of human resource management policies as a means to realizing overall business strategies. None of our cases report general recruitment problems, although electrical goods retailers experience some difficulties finding skilled salespeople.

Differences between sectors are found in terms of employment structure. In electrical goods retailing, the majority of salespeople are male, whereas females are in the majority among checkout operators and sales assistants in food retailing. Furthermore, the use of transitional workers is more prevalent in food retailing.

Work organization differs depending on the size of retail outlets. Thus, discount stores and specialty electrical goods retailers are similar in how they organize work. Because these outlets tend to be small, employees often perform many different tasks. In contrast, job specialization is higher in supermarkets and hypermarkets, where checkout operators typically only work checkouts.

Differences exist across retail sectors in terms of skill requirements, training, and development. Skill requirements are generally low for the target occupations in food retailing (checkout operators and sales assistants), whereas the specialty electrical goods retailers prefer skilled employees.

Our food retail cases have all developed extensive training schemes. These are mainly directed toward employees who want a career in retailing, and the training is intended to provide them with the formal skills they need to perform management functions. Such training schemes are not found in the three specialty electrical goods cases, in part because the degree of central control is lower; many of these stores are operated by franchisees and are thus not under the direct control of the chain. In addition, the career prospects in these stores are much lower.

The three supermarket and hypermarket chains we studied have extensive apprentice programs. Such programs were not found in discount stores, and only a few of the specialty electrical goods re-tailers have them. According to our informants, the electrical goods sector trains too few apprentices, making it difficult to recruit enough skilled salespeople.

Wages are higher in electrical goods retailing than in food retail-ing, and this is one potential explanation for lower labor turnover in the former. Different human capital requirements—specialty electri-cal goods retailing calls for a higher degree of specialist knowledge than food retailing—is another. The high labor turnover in food re-tailing also reflects the fact that many employees regard their work in food retailing as temporary.

There are good career prospects for interested (and talented) em-ployees in food retailing. It is relatively easy to rise to middle man-agement positions, particularly at discount stores. On the other hand, working conditions appear to be poorest in discount stores ow-ing to the high work pace and more physically demanding jobs.

Relations between retailers at the chain level and unions are good and based on trust, as is typical for the Danish labor market (see chapter 1). The same goes for relations between managers and em-ployees in the stores we visited. Union membership is high, but em-ployees see it mainly as an insurance policy in case they encounter problems. Not all retailers have formal collective bargaining agree-ments, but they follow them anyway to avoid problems.

Many store workers identify quite strongly with their workplace, particularly those who work for discount chains and for Music. These chains appear to have developed strong corporate cultures and identities.

DISCUSSION AND CONCLUSIONS

In this chapter, we have explored the conditions of low-wage work in Danish retailing, which, together with hotels, is the sector studied in this book with the highest proportion of low-wage workers. We have studied what frontline workers (checkout operators and sales assistant in food retailing and salespeople in specialty electrical goods retailers) do, who they are, and what they think about the conditions of their jobs. Furthermore, we have examined the business strategies and human resource management practices of retailers and the impact that strategies and practices have on low-wage work.

The nature of entry-level retail jobs such as checkout operator or sales assistant is changing as new information technologies facilitate the deskilling of these jobs. The deskilling of jobs makes it possible for retailers to employ lower-skilled (and lower-paid) employees. In our study, we have encountered three types of retail employees: transitional workers, steady core employees, and career-seekers. Most low-wage earners in food retailing are transitional workers who will leave the low-wage group as they graduate from high school or university and go on to formal jobs and careers. Because they do not expect a career in retailing, these employees have modest pay demands. They want work to be fun, which they mainly associate with good companionship with fellow workers, both on and off the job.

Core employees constitute the backbone of retail employment, as they often work in one job for a long time. Unlike transitional workers, they are in it for the long haul, but they have only modest career ambitions (as opposed to career-seekers, who often switch positions within and between stores). Typically, core employees are not low-wage workers because they earn above the minimum wages stipulated in collective bargaining agreements owing to personal allowances.

Especially in food retailing, the many promotion opportunities for motivated and qualified workers create a high degree of internal mobility. Retailers strive to develop future managers in-house and have comprehensive training schemes and career programs for talented employees seeking a career in retailing.

To sum up, and as discussed more generally in chapter 2, low-wage workers in Denmark do not stay in low-wage work but move up in the income distribution. In retailing, workers move out of low-wage work because they work in such jobs for only a short period of time before moving on to other types of higher-paid jobs (transitional workers), because they form the backbone of employment and earn more than minimum wage (core employees), or because they move up the internal career ladder (career-seekers).

A Comparison of Retailing in Denmark and the United States

In the United States, increased competition from large-scale formats (such as warehouse clubs, mass merchandisers, and supercenters) has combined with substantial technological change and declining unionization to transform food retailing (Davis et al. 2006). Partly because of union protection, supermarket jobs have traditionally been among the most highly paid and coveted retail jobs in the United States. As unions have become less important, however, owing to increased competition from non-union retailers, two-tier wage agreements have proliferated since the 1980s, and as a consequence new hires are usually paid much less than tenured workers (Hughes 1999). In the United States, most retail jobs offer low wages, few benefits, and limited formal training (Carré, Holgate, and Tilly 2005). Since the 1970s, nonsupervisory retail employees have experienced overall wage loss in both absolute and relative terms compared to all private-sector employees in the United States. Retail employees also fare worse than the American workforce as a whole with regard to employer-sponsored benefits, partly because part-time employment, which often precludes fringe benefits (Tilly 1996), is more common in the retail sector than in the American economy as a whole. This is not an issue in Denmark, since benefits such as health care are not tied to employers (see chapter 2).

Olive Robinson (1993, 3–4) has argued that in the United States part-time work in retailing does not afford "an equitable or mutually beneficiary reconciliation of the interests of workers and their employers." In Denmark, part-time work reflects the interests of both workers and their employers. Part-time employees are often transitional workers who, as students working part-time to supplement their student allowance, are interested in working afternoons and weekends, when customer streams are large and retailers have to adjust staffing levels, and less often single mothers, who are much more dependent on structured working hours and clearly prefer daytime work.

Some prominent American retail chains are strongly anti-union and work actively to prevent employees from joining unions. Such a stance would be unacceptable in a Danish context—even unthinkable given the Danish labor market model and the tradition of cooperation between employers and workers (see chapter 2). Instead, most Danish retailers have realized that it is an advantage to work with unions to secure good conditions and thus attract the best workers. Unionization remains high in Denmark but is declining because young people tend to postpone membership. This decline might gain momentum following the recent ruling by the European Court for Human Rights against closed-shop agreements. The effects of this ruling on Danish retailing, however, have yet to be seen.

APPENDIX

Table 4A.1 The Case Study Food Retailers and Specialty Electrical Goods Retailers

	Disc	Fast	Super One	Super Too
Store type	Soft discounter	Soft discounter	Super stores	Super stores
Business strategy	Used to be Aldiclone. Now has a more innovative concept.	Founded in response to Aldi's market entrance. Has decentralized decision-making competence to store managers. Wants to turn the chain into a brand in its own right and focus on retailer brands. Wants to be the preferred store for groceries in the neighborhood.	On average opens three new stores every year.	Has had to focus on cutting costs in recent years, closing some manned counters (for example, fish and meat) and reducing the number of workers. Last year reported best results ever.
Concept	Neighborhood stores with products of high quality at the lowest prices on the market.	Fast and convenient grocery shopping at low prices.	Primarily quality food products and clothing, but also consumer electronics and hardware.	Broad range of food and non-food products.
Product range	Food and other groceries as well as weekly offers. Relatively narrow assortment.	Primarily food products and other groceries along with an ever-changing assortment of weekly	Broad and deep food assortment and significant nonfood assortment.	Broad and deep range of grocery products and broad range of electrical goods.

Service quality	Low	Low	Medium	Medium
Human resource management	Central HRM department	Central HRM department	Central HRM department	Central HRM department
Recruitment	Two issues considered essential for recruitment, retention, and development: company culture and reputation. Active effort to recruit older employees (age 50 and older).	The chain receives more than 5,000 unsolicited applications annually and is not experiencing any recruitment problems. Hires 16-year-olds as "service workers" for menial chores (cleaning and so on). Sales assistants hired by store manager. Flexibility is important.	Large, yearly apprentice and trainee recruitment campaign. Necessary because of competition for young people from banks and shipping. Large number of applicants. Generally no recruitment problems.	No recruitment problems. Receives many unsolicited applications (particularly from students). Focus on commitment. Tries to hire students early in their studies. In one store, 25 percent of cashiers are age sixteen to seventeen, of whom half are retained after they turn eighteen.
Retention	Owing to low unemployment, employees are not as loyal as they used to be. Therefore important to offer employees challenges, personal development, and career prospects. Employee turnover highest in Copenhagen and other large cities.	High labor turnover, although declining.	Upon completion of apprenticeship, sales assistants are introduced to career possibilities/training program. Many 25-year anniversaries.	Large turnover owing to many part-timers (typically students). Not regarded as problematic.

Table 4A.1 (*continued*)

	Disc	Fast	Super One	Super Too
Training	On-the-job training and introductory training at company HQ for new employees. Significant training program for budding store managers.	Mainly on-the-job training and e-learning modules for new sales assistants. Comprehensive training scheme for budding managers.	Large in-house training program (for future managers in particular). Own training facility.	Mainly on-the-job training. No additional training for cashiers. Offers a comprehensive training program for budding managers.
Working conditions	Fast work pace. Some physically demanding work.	Fast work pace. Some physically demanding tasks. Several informants had experiences with drunk, abusive, or violent customers. Even several cases of death threats were mentioned.	Generally described as good, but at times work pace high (although this is not necessarily regarded as bad). Some problems with repetitive work, heavy lifts, and cold. Frequent changes of managers disruptive, as new routines have to be learned, and workers have to make good impression on new boss.	Generally described as good. Some physically demanding tasks, but large improvements have been made. Work can be stressful (especially for middle managers), but employees prefer to be busy. Some problems with workers succumbing to stress. Manager in Copenhagen store had been very understanding in relation to two workers who were sick for prolonged periods.

	Hyper	Music	White One	The Goods
Number of stores visited	Three	Three	Three	Two
Informants	HR manager (chain), three district managers, three store managers, eleven sales assistants.	HR manager (chain), one district manager, two store managers, four assistant managers, one sales assistant.	HR manager (chain), three store managers, employee representative, three middle managers, eight cashiers/sales assistants.	HR manager (chain), two store managers, two managers responsible for cashiers/checkout, two employee representatives, five cashiers/sales assistants.
Store type	Hypermarket	Brown goods specialty store	White goods specialty store	White goods specialty store
Business strategy	Not possible to grow within Denmark owing to planning restrictions.	Company turned around from loss to profit in last couple of years. Wants to expand, but only moderately. Imports several brands that are sold exclusively by this chain. Has vertically integrated into production and bought suppliers.	Economies of scale in purchasing (volume discounts because largest buyer).	Has gone through a process of transition and professionalization. Expanding. Has worked to improve competitiveness in relation to core strength: service. Not only competing on price. Wants to be the neighborhood store (not located in shopping centers).

Table 4A.1 (continued)

	Hyper	Music	White One	The Goods
Product range	Quality products at discount prices. One-stop shopping. Focus also on shopping experience and good customer service.	Only brown goods (hi-fi and TV). Medium- to high-end. Typically sells own brands or brands sold exclusively by chain.	White goods, lighting, and consumer electronics.	Predominantly white goods.
Service quality	Medium	Very high	High	High
Human resource management	Central HR manager and HR manager in each store	Central HR manager	Central HR manager; can only act as consultant to stores, as he has no direct authority.	Central HR manager (relatively)
Recruitment	Large, yearly apprentice and trainee recruitment campaign. Necessary because of competition for young people from banks and shipping. Large number of applicants. Generally no recruitment problems.	Unsolicited applications. Or post job opening on own website. Often applicants are customers and therefore know the chain.	Difficult to hire skilled personnel, therefore often have to hire workers without experience in the white goods sector	Prefers to hire skilled salespeople (vocational training) from local community. Age or nationality not important, but whether applicant is a good salesperson. Internal recruitment and word of mouth. Many applications for apprenticeships.
Retention	Upon completion of apprenticeship, sales	Low turnover among full-timers, including	Some employee turnover.	Average seniority around five to seven years in

	assistants are introduced to career possibilities/training program	store managers. Hence few opportunities for career advancement.		Jutland, four to five years on Seeland. Large number of new openings lower average. Many employees in older stores have celebrated ten- or even twenty-five-year anniversaries.
Training	Large in-house training program (for future managers in particular). Own training facility.	No tradition for paid training and education, although country manager says all have access to this.		Introductory program for new employees and catalog of different courses. Internal training program for store managers/franchisees.
Working conditions	Generally described as good. Informants stress good social relations among employees.	Large differences in work pace between stores; in one of the three stores, significant problems with staffing and high work pace were reported. Some heavy lifting, but not considered to be problematic.	Some heavy lifts, but work not considered hard physically. Interviewees stress that they have good colleagues.	Many heavy lifts, but working conditions generally described in positive terms.

Table 4A.1 (continued)

	Hyper	Music	Whtie One	The Goods
Number of stores visited	Two	Three	Three	Three
Informants	HR manager (chain), one district manager, two store managers, four assistant managers, one sales assistant.	Country manager (responsible for marketing and HRM), three store managers, six full-time salespeople, one part-time sales-man.	HRM manager, two store managers, six sales people.	HRM manager, two store managers, one assistant manager, two salespeople.

Source: Authors' compilation.
Note: The names of all chains are pseudonyms.

NOTES

1. The top-three concentration ratios for the other countries covered in this series are as follows: France, 81 percent; Germany, 65 percent; the Netherlands, 64 percent; the United Kingdom, 65 percent; and the United States, 36 percent (A.C. Nielsen 2005).
2. Disc, Fast, and other names used here for the retail chains we studied are pseudonyms.
3. Workers below age eighteen earn significantly lower wages, even where there is a union contract (see table 4.4).
4. We have no statistical material from our cases confirming this assertion.
5. In this connection, it is interesting to note that, in order to attract good employees, IKEA has recently increased wages for checkout operators across the board.

REFERENCES

A.C. Nielsen. 2005. *The Power of Private Label 2005: A Review of Growth Trends Around the World.* New York: A.C. Nielsen Global Services.

Abernathy, Frederick H., John T. Dunlop, Janice H. Hammond, and David Weil. 2000. "Retailing and Supply Chains in the Information Age." *Technology in Society* 22(1): 5–31.

Arrowsmith, James, and Ann E. McGoldrick. 1996. "HRM Services Practice: Flexibility, Quality, and Employee Strategy." *International Journal of Service Industry Management* 7(3): 46–62.

Bahr, Henning. 2006. *Kaeder i dansk detailhandel 2006* [*Chains in Danish Retailing 2006*]. Frederiksberg, Denmark: Stockmann-Gruppen.

Böll, Joachim L. 2001. "The 'Transitional Workforce': A Source of Time Flexibility in Danish Retail Trade." Paper presented to the eighth "Symposium on Working Time." Amsterdam, March 14–16, 2001.

Broadbridge, Adelina, Vivien Swanson, and Christine Taylor. 2000. "Retail Change: Effects on Employees' Job Demands and Home Life." *International Review of Retail, Distribution, and Consumer Research* 10(4): 417–32.

Carré, Françoise, Brandynn Holgate, and Chris Tilly. 2005. "What's Happening to Retail Jobs? Wages, Gender, and Corporate Strategy." Paper presented to the annual meeting of the International Association for Feminist Economics and the Labor and Employment Relations Association. Boston, Mass., January 5–8, 2005.

Christopherson, Susan. 2001. "Lean retailing in marktliberalen und koordinierten Wirtschaften" ["Lean Retailing in Liberal Market Economies and Coordinated Economies"]. In *Aldi oder Arkaden? Unternehmen und Arbeit im europäischen Einzelhandel* [*Aldi or Arcases? Firms and Work in European Retailing*], edited by Hedwig Rudolph. Berlin: Edition Sigma.

Colla, Enrico. 2004. "The Outlook for European Grocery Retailing: Competition and Format Development." *International Review of Retail, Distribution, and Consumer Research* 15(1): 47–69.

Dansk Handel & Service. 2004. *Landsoverenskomst for butikker mellem Dansk Handel & Service- og HK Handel [National Collective Bargaining Agreement for Stores Between Dansk Handel & Service and HK Handel]*. Copenhagen: DH&S.

Dansk Handelsblad. 2006. *Hvem er hvem: Dansk dagligvarehandel [Who Is Who: Danish Grocery Retailing]*. Aarhus, Denmark: Dansk Handelsblad.

Davis, Elizabeth E., Matthew Freedman, Julia Lane, Brian P. McCall, Nicole Nestoriak, and Timothy A. Park. 2006. "Product Market Competition and Human Resource Practices: An Analysis of the Retail Food Sector." Accessed at SSRN, http://ssrn.com/abstract=717403.

Dawson, John. 2000a. "Retailing at Century End: Some Challenges for Management and Research." *International Review of Retail, Distribution, and Consumer Research* 10(2): 119–48.

———. 2000b. "Viewpoint: Retailer Power, Manufacturer Power, Competition, and Some Questions of Economic Analysis." *International Journal of Retail and Distribution Management* 28(1): 5–8.

Eurostat. 2005. *Europe in Figures: Eurostat Yearbook 2005*. Luxembourg: Office for Official Publications of the European Communities.

Hammer, Michael. 2004. "Deep Change: How Operational Innovation Can Transform Your Company." *Harvard Business Review* (April): 84–93.

Hughes, Katherine L. 1999. *Supermarket Employment: Good Jobs at Good Wages?* Working paper 11. New York: Columbia University, Institute on Education and the Economy (April).

Joint Industry Project on Efficient Consumer Response. 1995. *Category Management Report*. Washington: Grocery Manufacturers of America.

Krogsgaard, Niels, and Michael Olsen. 2007. "Butikkernes ansatte arbejder for egen regning" ["Retail Employees Work for Free"]. *Politikken*, January 8.

Kvale, Steinar. 1996. *Interviews: An Introduction to Qualitative Research Interviewing*. Thousand Oaks, Calif.: Sage Publications.

Marchington, Mick. 1996. "Shopping Down Different Aisles: A Review of the Literature on Human Resource Management in Food Retailing." *Journal of Retailing and Consumer Services* 3(1): 21–32.

Maxwell, G., and Ogden, S. M. 2006. "Career Development of Female Managers in Retailing: Inhibitors and Enablers." *Journal of Retailing and Consumer Services* 13 (2): 111–20.

Miller, Dale. 2006. "Strategic Human Resource Management in Department Stores: A Historical Perspective." *Journal of Retailing and Consumer Services* 13(2): 99–109.

Mintel. 2003. *European Retail Handbook 2003–2004*. London: Mintel.

Mishler, Elliot G. 1979. "Meaning in Context: Is There Any Other Kind?" *Harvard Educational Review* 49(1): 1–19.

———. 1986. "Research Interviewing: Context and Narrative." Cambridge, Mass.: Harvard University Press.

Parker, Mike, and Jane Slaughter. 1988. "Management by Stress." *Technology Review* 91(7): 36–44.

Rafaelli, Anat. 1989. "When Cashiers Meet Customers: An Analysis of the Role of Supermarket Cashiers." *Academy of Management Journal* 32(2): 245–73.

Robinson, Olive. 1993. "Employment in Services: Perspectives on Part-time Employment Growth in North America." *Service Industries Journal* 13(3): 1–18.

Schurr, Paul H., and Heiko R. Fischer. 1996. "Marketing as Technology Transfer in Developing European Markets." *Journal of Euromarketing* 5(1): 83–98.

Sieling, Mark, Brian Friedman, and Mark Dumas. 2001. "Labor Productivity in the Retail Trade Industry, 1987–1999." *Monthly Labor Review* 124(12): 3–14.

Statistics Denmark. 2006. "Befolkningens brug af internet 2006" ["The Use of the Internet by the Population 2006"]. *Statistiske Efterretninger* 35.

Tilly, Chris. 1996. *Half a Job: Bad and Good Part-time Jobs in a Changing Labor Market.* Philadelphia, Penn.: Temple University Press.

Womack, James P., and Daniel T. Jones. 1994. "From Lean Production to the Lean Enterprise." *Harvard Business Review* (March–April): 93–103.

Wright, Christopher, and John Lund. 2006. "Variations on a Lean Theme: Work Restructuring in Retail Distribution." *New Technology, Work, and Employment* 21(1): 59–75.

CHAPTER 5

Restructuring Meets Flexicurity: Housekeeping Work in Danish Hotels

Tor Eriksson and Jingkun Li

D anish hotels do not differ much from hotels in other parts of the world. Big hotels and hotels in the major cities are typically operated by international chains, whereas other Danish hotels are considerably smaller and scattered around the country. Customers include business travelers and tourists. Approximately half of overnight stays in Danish hotels are by foreigners. The tendency toward larger units and chains in particular is a fairly recent phenomenon in Denmark as well as in the rest of Scandinavia. There are two main reasons for this late entry into the market: the international chains have predominantly been interested in the capital areas only, and they also prefer so-called management contracts, a contract form that is largely unknown in Scandinavia.

Hotels, restaurants, and the tourism industry make up the third-largest one-digit industry in the Danish economy in terms of sales. As a proportion of total employment, the industry's share is about 16 percent, of which hotels account for one-fourth. During the last five years, the industry turnover has grown on average 2.6 percent per year, which is in line with the average growth rate of the economy.

The first years of the new millennium were difficult for the hotel industry worldwide. The international economic downturn and the decline in international tourism as a consequence of the SARS outbreak, the war in Iraq, and international terrorism had a clearly adverse impact on the global hotel industry, including the Danish hotel sector. The negative consequences were particularly significant in the Copenhagen area. Since 2004, however, there has been a turn, and growth has picked up quite rapidly.[1]

What has been said so far could have been said about hotels in many other European countries. Denmark is somewhat different, however—at least different enough to warrant a study of its hotels sector. Wages are higher than in most other countries, particularly for unskilled labor, which makes up a considerable portion of the sector's employment. As we will see later, hotel employees are in general satisfied with their jobs despite the work being as strenuous and the work pace as high as elsewhere. In contrast to the United States, the hotel industry in Denmark does not stand out as a sector with significantly higher labor turnover than average (see Bernhardt, Dresser, and Hatton 2003). How can that be? In this chapter, we aim at providing some answers to this question.

STUDY DESIGN AND METHODOLOGY

Although a fairly large literature exploiting detailed microdata analyses of low income, low pay, and poverty has built up in Denmark in the recent decade, studies focusing on specific sectors are thin on the ground. Moreover, analyses of specific occupations are nonexistent, probably owing to the lack of reliable detailed data at the occupation level. For the purpose of the present chapter, where the focus is on housekeepers within the hotel industry, especially room attendants, this implies that there is no earlier evidence on which to build. Of course, we also face the problem of a dearth of adequate data sources. As a consequence, at times we have to use data that describes the hotel industry while recognizing that these may not paint an entirely accurate picture of developments in housekeeping. The absence of microdata is partly compensated for by the use of information collected through the project's case studies.

The case studies detailed in this chapter include eight hotels from the capital area and a number of provincial cities (see table 5.1). All eight hotels have more than fifty bedrooms. Two are members of multinational hotel chains that have operations in all five European countries included in the low-wage project, and two belong to a Nordic hotel chain.[2] As in the other countries studied, we wanted to contrast four hotels in the capital area (Copenhagen) with hotels in a number of provincial cities—Aalborg, Aarhus, and Kolding.

The country-specific contrast chosen for this study is between in-house and outsourced housekeeping. This was motivated by the fact that outsourcing has been quite common in Danish hotels and by our interest in examining differences in job quality according to contract type. As can be seen from table 5.1, three of the case hotels had outsourced their housekeeping at the time of our interviews.

The interviews at the case hotels were typically organized as fol-

Table 5.1 Service Quality and Housekeeping at the
Case Hotels

	Housekeeping Arrangement			
Service Quality	Copenhagen		Provincial Cities	
Luxury hotel (four to	Hotel 1	Outsourced	Hotel 5	In-house
five stars)	Hotel 2	In-house	Hotel 6	Outsourced
Budget hotel (two to	Hotel 3	In-house	Hotel 7	Outsourced
three stars)	Hotel 4	In-house	Hotel 8	In-house

Source: Authors' compilation from HORESTA data.

lows. First we interviewed the hotel's general manager, followed by
another interview with the operations manager or, alternatively, the
head (or assistant head) housekeeper. Next we interviewed a sample
of room attendants. These interviews were organized with groups of
three to five room attendants. We began the interviews with the room
attendants by asking them to fill out a brief, two-page questionnaire
about themselves, economic issues, and job and employment satisfaction. The length of the interviews varied from thirty to sixty minutes. In the hotels where housekeeping was outsourced, we interviewed the person in charge from the external cleaning company as
well as groups of room attendants from the company working at the
hotel. The format of these interviews was the same as for those with
in-house housekeeping. In addition to the hotel cases, we also interviewed an industrial relations specialist at HORESTA, the employers'
organization of the hotel, restaurant, and tourism industry. A more
detailed summary of the case hotels is provided in the appendix.

HOTEL INDUSTRY PERFORMANCE

The competitive position of Danish hotels is negatively affected by
two structural factors. First, owing to the compressed Danish wage
structure, wages in the lower end of the wage distribution are high by
international standards. Since hotels are a typical low-wage industry—only the food retail sector has a higher portion of low-paid employees—this wage structure affects labor demand and staffing in
Danish hotels. Second, the Danish value-added tax is the highest in
Europe—25 percent—and Denmark is one of only three European
countries that have not introduced a lower VAT on hotel and restau-

Figure 5.1 Number of Hotels, 1995 to 2005

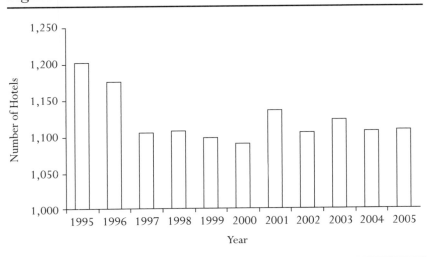

Source: Authors' calculations from Statistics Denmark and HORESTA data.

rant services.[3] According to a comparison of hotel prices in twenty-nine major European cities carried out in 2002, Copenhagen ranked twenty-fifth (HORESTA 2004). But since the comparison looked at prices before the VAT, Copenhagen's low rank does not imply that hotel prices there are relatively low. On the other hand, they are not at the higher end of the price distribution either. A consequence of the high costs is that price differences between quality categories are smaller than in many other countries. This is likely to have an impact on the demand of the more price-elastic hotel guest segment (that is, nonbusiness travelers) for hotel services in Denmark.

During the ten-year period from 1995 to 2005, the number of hotels in Denmark fell considerably, from 1,201 to 1,107 (see figure 5.1). Although the number of hotels has declined, total hotel capacity has increased, owing to the strong increase in the size of the hotel units. Total revenue in the hotel sector increased by 15 percent recently, from DKK 8.0 million (US$1.46 million) in 2001 to DKK 9.2 million (US$1.68 million) in 2005. Occupancy rates have fallen, and in 2005 they were still below those in the late 1990s, despite a considerable increase compared to 2004.[4] Despite the tendency toward larger units, the hotel industry in Denmark is still characterized by a

Figure 5.2 Hotel Size Distribution, 1998 and 2004

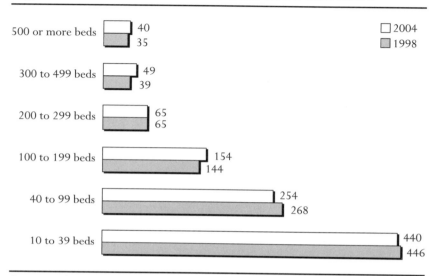

Source: Authors' calculations from Statistics Denmark and HORESTA data.

large number of small hotels. Thus, in 2005 ninety of the hotels that were members of HORESTA had more than three hundred guest-room beds. At the same time, slightly fewer than 40 percent of the hotels had between ten and forty beds (see figure 5.2). Of course, the size distribution also reflects the fact that Denmark is a relatively small country, with respect to both its population and geographical area; therefore, there is less demand for hotel services outside the major cities.

The high number of small hotels also reflects the fact that many of them—50 percent in 1999—are privately owned. However, the number of privately owned hotels has declined somewhat (see figure 5.3). The rest of the hotels are distributed evenly among three ownership types: two limited liability companies (aktieselskab and anpartsselskab, respectively), which differ regarding the minimum capital requirement in the firm, and limited and unlimited partnerships. The big hotels are typically stock companies (aktieselskab).

About 16 percent of Danish hotels are organized in chains. A little over half of these are members of chains with common owners. The other half includes members in chains that cooperate on marketing, sales, and purchases, illustrating that branding is becoming an in-

Figure 5.3 Ownership of Hotels in Denmark, 1993 and 1999

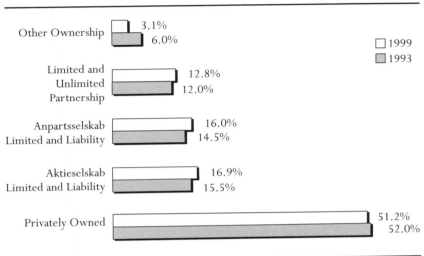

Other Ownership 3.1% 6.0%

Limited and Unlimited Partnership 12.8% 12.0%

Anpartsselskab Limited and Liability 16.0% 14.5%

Aktieselskab Limited and Liability 16.9% 15.5%

Privately Owned 51.2% 52.0%

☐ 1999
▣ 1993

Source: Authors' calculations from HORESTA data.

creasingly important element in hotels' competitive strategy. The hotels in chains with common owners have a 55 percent market share, and on average they are large hotels. The "voluntary" chain members' market share is about 18 percent. Consequently, while the nonchain hotels make up a clear majority of all hotels (and, despite being smaller, also have 55 percent of the stock of hotel rooms), their market share is only 25 percent.

Although a large share of small firms continues to be a characteristic feature of the Danish hotel industry, there is a clear tendency toward more mergers and acquisitions, especially among the larger players. Because the hospitality industry is very sensitive to business cycle conditions, political crises, and other events, the turnover of firms in the industry is rather high: the annual rate of bankruptcies in recent years has varied between 8 and 12 percent.

The proportions of Danes and foreigners staying in Danish hotels are about the same: during the years 2001 to 2003, Danes spent about 4.6 million nights per year in hotels in Denmark, whereas foreigners (the vast majority of whom came from neighboring countries), spent 4.5 million nights per year in Danish hotels. During this period, there was only a tiny growth in the overall number of overnight stays in

Figure 5.4 Profitability of Hotels from 1994 to 2002

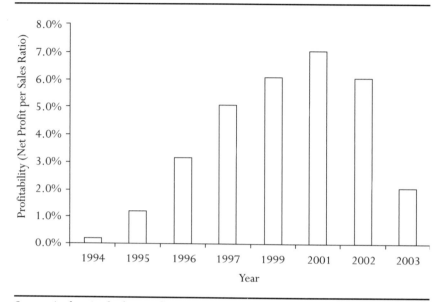

Source: Authors' calculations from HORESTA data.

hotels. Going a little bit further back in time to the early 1990s, however, we note that there has been a strong increase in demand for hotel beds, and in recent years the demand has increased again. Thus, in
2005 the increase in the number of hotel nights per year as compared
to 2004 was 4.7 percent. To a great extent, the growth is due to increasing numbers of international guests, and growth has therefore
been concentrated in the Copenhagen area.

As in other countries, the Danish hotel sector was adversely affected in the years 2001 to 2003 by the international economic
downturn in conjunction with SARS, the war in Iraq, and threats of
international terrorism. As can be seen from figure 5.4, profitability
(measured as the net profits per sales ratio), which had been increasing for seven years in a row, declined a little in 2002 and then
plunged to 2 percent in 2003. The capital area was hit especially hard,
partly because Copenhagen is more dependent on international
travel than other regions of Denmark, and partly because of the expansion of capacity in recent years.

As the hotel industry has been growing during the last decade, the

Figure 5.5 Employee-per-Room Ratios in Selected Cities, 2004

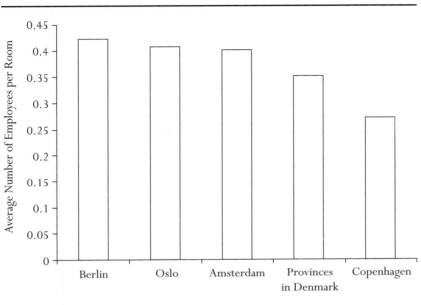

Source: Authors' calculations from HORESTA data.

overcapacity problem has also increased, resulting in stronger competition as prices have been pressed to the bottom. According to HORESTA (2004), the hotels reacted by cutting costs without decreasing productivity, in particular by lowering the employee-per-room ratio. This was achieved by improving productivity, but also at the cost of lower quality of service. The employee-per-room ratio was low to begin with, reflecting the relatively high wage levels among especially low-paid employees, and it fell even further from 1998 (0.41) to 2003 (0.22 in Copenhagen. Corresponding ratios for other capitals like Oslo, Berlin, and Amsterdam are about 0.4 (see figure 5.5).

To cope with the competitive pressure and maintain an internationally comparable service quality, hotel employers are under significant pressure to restructure their business. The possibilities for restructuring the jobs of the group of employees studied here, the room attendants, through improving technology or substituting labor with capital are very limited, and hence, hotel employers' high and increasing costs have to be matched by higher labor productivity. As employers have reached the upper limits on increasing the pace of work, they have increasingly shifted their focus to more flexible utilization of the workforce. In some cases, employers have resorted to outsourcing housekeeping tasks as a means of solving these problems.

As a consequence of the strong growth of the Danish economy in recent years, the hotel industry has begun to experience increasing difficulties in recruiting personnel. Thus, while employment in hotels remained constant from 2000 to 2004, in 2005 employment grew by 1.7 percent. In conditions characterized by a general shortage of labor, the retail sector has proven to be the main competitor in the hotel sector's labor market.

LABOR MARKET INSTITUTIONS AND LABOR RELATIONS

Given the short-term nature of many employment relationships in the hotel industry, it is natural that industrial relations are less developed here than in many other sectors. It should first of all be noted that Danish trade unions typically are organized according to crafts, not by industry. Hence, in some firms, workers may be represented by many different unions. The main union in the hotel sector is RBF (Restaurationsbranchens Forbund), which has about 22,000 members.[5] Since the total number of employees in hotels and restaurants is about 80,000, the union density in this industry is clearly much lower than in most other sectors in Denmark, where it is close to 80 percent (see chapter 2). On the employer side, the main organization is HORESTA (the nationwide employers' and industry organization of the hotel, restaurant, and tourism industry), the coverage of which is 85 and 50 percent of the turnover in hotels and restaurants, respectively. In terms of the number of hotels and restaurants, the coverage is considerably lower, since the large firms are more likely to be members.

However, the coverage of the collective agreements extends considerably beyond what is indicated by the union density and the rate of organized employers, since these agreements set a norm for the vast majority of hotels in the industry. This wide coverage is not the result, as in many other EU member states, of "erga omnes" legislation but rather reflects the representativeness of the organizations. According to an industrial relations expert at HORESTA whom we interviewed, the hotels that diverge from the collective agreement by offering their employees inferior pay and working conditions pay a price for this policy by attracting personnel of a considerably lower quality. Consequently, hotel employers do not in general strongly oppose their employees being union members.

A distinguishing feature of industrial relations in the hotel industry is the trade-off between employers' desire for more flexibility and employees' desire for increased job security. These two issues are discussed in the negotiations under the headings of "demarcation flexibility" and "working hours." Flexibility discussions center on the question of which tasks employees may perform outside their normal set of tasks and how they are to be compensated. Another key issue is how much should be agreed on locally or at the industry level. Striking a balance between flexibility and security is the key, said the employers' representative whom we interviewed; on the one hand, too much flexibility has adverse effects on worker quality, and on the other, too much security is bad for profitability.

Since the late 1980s, collective bargaining has become successively less centralized as wage setting first moved down from the national to the industry level and then, during the 1990s, further down to the company level (see chapter 2). A key characteristic of Danish industrial relations is the "Danish model" (described in chapter 2), according to which many issues related to the labor market are regulated by agreements between employers and their employees, not by legislation. These agreements regulate not only wages but also working time, employment protection, notification of layoffs, and so on. The Danish model does not, however, completely exclude regulation. For instance, legislation regulates holidays and work environment and safety, but these are exceptions. In recent years, the Liberal-Conservative government has tried to introduce more legislation of the EU variety, but these attempts have been met with opposition from both employers' organizations and trade unions.

EMPLOYMENT AND HUMAN RESOURCE MANAGEMENT

Two key features of the hotel industry are the seasonality and cyclicality of demand. Both have a notable influence on the labor market within the industry. A considerable fraction of employees are young or casual workers, and a large portion of them work part-time. Relying on part-time workers helps hotels meet short- as well as medium-

Table 5.2 Unemployment Insurance Coverage in the
Hotel Industry, 2002

Employees	Low-Wage Employees	Non-Low-Wage Employees
Full-time workers (thirty hours a week or more)		
Full-time insured	27.1%	82.8%
Not insured	72.9	17.2
Part-time workers (excluding students)		
Insured	17.4	56.0
Not insured	82.6	44.0

Source: Authors' calculations from Center for Corporate Performance (CCP) data.
Note: "Low-wage" is defined as two-thirds of the median hourly wage of the entire economy.

term fluctuations in demand. The Danish unemployment insurance system, which is characterized by generous replacement ratios (about 90 percent for low-paid workers), absence of experience rating, and no waiting periods before entitlement, acts as an important subsidy to seasonal industries like hotels because it lowers the (explicit as well as implicit) costs of temporary layoffs for both employers and employees (see Jensen and Westergaard-Nielsen 1990). The extent of the subsidy should not be overstated, however, since the proportion of employees insured is much lower than in other industries and roughly the same as the share of unionized workers; in fact, unemployment insurance and trade union membership largely coincide (see Neumann, Pedersen, and Westergaard-Nielsen 1991).

As can be seen from table 5.2, the fraction insured in the hotel industry is generally lower than the national average for low-wage workers.[6] It is particularly low among low-paid employees. This is partly because many hotel employees are students, but it is also partly due to the fact that the workers either intend to hold their jobs for only a short period or have been working in the industry for a short period and therefore are not entitled to unemployment insurance benefits. Only 27 percent of full-time low-wage workers are covered by unemployment insurance. Part-time workers are also covered by unemployment insurance to a significantly lower extent than full-time workers. The majority of part-time low-wage workers are not covered by the system. The main explanation is that it is relatively expensive to be a member of an unemployment fund, especially for those who work only part-time. The monthly unemployment insurance fee is approximately €60 and €110 (US$81.63 and US$149.68) if it includes earlier retirement benefits. For someone who works, for example, twenty hours per week, the unemployment insurance fee would be 5 to 10 percent of their total income. Moreover, he or she would have to work for a certain number of hours equivalent to one year for full-time insurance and thirty-four weeks for part-time insurance in order to be able to receive unemployment benefits. Thus, paying the unemployment insurance fee is not financially worthwhile for those who plan to work in the industry for only a short period.

Cleaning work is characterized by certain increased health risks. One risk is the likelihood of skin disease that can result from frequent exposure to harmful substances; strenuous working positions can also lead to back problems. Physical working conditions are regulated in Denmark by fairly general working environment legislation and monitored by the national Working Environment Authority (WEA). In recent years, the Liberal-Conservative government has made several attempts to simplify legislation and reduce the influence of the WEA. Only a few of these proposals, however, have been implemented. Both employers' and workers' organizations have been critical of state intervention in the area of work environment and have tried to reach industry-level agreements among themselves.

We should not, however, exaggerate the importance of regulations and legislation in the housekeeping area. In several interviews with the room attendants, it was obvious that these workers, especially the immigrant workers, were rather ignorant of the rules—as well as ignorant of their rights. Thus, for example, in some hotels the room attendants did not make use of their right to be absent from work owing to illness and to have this time off paid for by the sickness insurance system; instead, they were substituting for each other when one of them fell ill. One of the interviewed workers told us with considerable pride that during all her years in the industry she had never been absent from work because of illness. She was not exceptional: we encountered several other employees who were equally proud of being able to make this claim. This is quite remarkable in a country like Denmark, where economic disincentives from short-term absence because of illness are virtually nonexistent.

Figure 5.6 Employment and Average Nominal Hourly Wages in the Hotel Industry

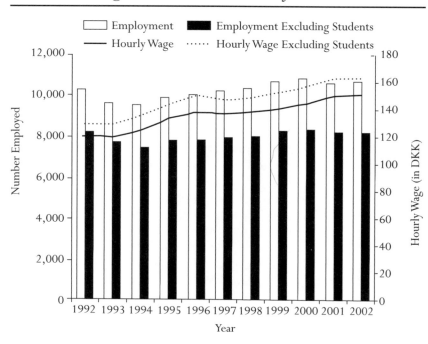

Source: Authors' calculations from Center for Corporate Performance (CCP) data.

In figure 5.6, we show the development of employment and average wages for the hotel industry. Since students make up about 20 percent of hotel employees, we also present corresponding numbers with students excluded. We may start by noting that from 1994 onwards, there has been an increase in hotel employment and that this has been slower for nonstudent employees. Second, the business cycle influence on employment is clearly visible, and this is more profound for student employees. Students and other casual workers are thus used as a buffer to meet cyclical changes in demand. We believe that this is the case even more with respect to seasonal changes, although we cannot provide numbers in support of our conjecture.

Wages have increased almost uninterruptedly. Student workers get a lower hourly wage than regular employees. A full-time student at a

higher education institution in Denmark is entitled to a state education grant at an amount approximately equal to one-third of the average low-wage income, but he or she cannot as a full-time student
become a member of an unemployment insurance fund. Besides this
requirement, students are allowed to earn up to an amount equivalent to twice the size of the grant before the grant is deducted. Consequently, many students work part-time to earn extra money, and
they account for a relatively large proportion of low-wage workers, as
was demonstrated in chapter 2. This is obviously a key subsidy to
employers in low-wage industries. The differential in average wages
for including and excluding student employees has remained fairly
constant during the period.

The proportion of low-wage workers in the hotel sector is now
around 20 percent, using the definition of low-paid work as two-
thirds of the median hourly wage. This is the second-highest share
among the six industries studied in this book (see chapter 2). The
hotel industry differs from most of the other industries in that the
portion of low-paid employees has been very stable, whereas in the
other industries the share of low-wage workers has declined somewhat since the early 1990s. To some extent, this stability is due to the
fact that low-wage jobs in hotels cannot be outsourced to other countries and are rather unaffected by technological innovations. Nevertheless, the constancy of the share is remarkable.

Table 5.3 describes the composition of the nonstudent low-paid
workforce in the hotel industry. It is noteworthy that students make
up about 50 percent of all low-wage workers in hotels; since most of
them are employed on a part-time basis, the numbers in the table
mainly pertain to full-time employees. Still, even after excluding students, the portion of low-paid employees under the age of thirty
never falls below 50 percent. Another characteristic feature of the industry is the high proportion of female low-wage employees, which
varies around 70 percent. The educational level of these hotel employees is rather low: only about one-third have some vocational or
postsecondary level of education.

THE EMPLOYMENT OF HOUSEKEEPERS IN THE HOTEL INDUSTRY

Room attendants, including assistant head housekeepers and head
housekeepers, constitute the target occupational group in this study.

Table 5.3 Distribution of Hotel Industry Low-Wage Employment (Excluding Students), by Gender, Age, and Education

Year	Gender		Age					Education					
	Men	Women	Nineteen to Thirty	Thirty-one to Forty	Forty-one to Fifty	Fifty-one to Sixty-five	Sixty-six and Above	1	2	3	4	5	6
1992	27.6%	72.4%	59.9%	11.0%	12.0%	13.9%	3.1%	48.2%	18.1%	29.9%	1.7%	1.8%	0.4%
1993	26.3	73.7	57.4	13.5	14.4	11.9	2.9	46.3	23.9	26.2	1.5	1.5	0.5
1994	28.8	71.2	59.1	10.8	14.1	12.2	3.7	48.7	22.5	24.3	2.1	1.9	0.5
1995	29.2	70.8	61.7	14.0	10.4	11.1	2.8	43.2	26.7	25.7	1.3	2.5	0.5
1996	28.7	71.3	61.4	14.6	11.5	10.3	2.2	40.0	30.3	23.1	2.6	2.7	1.2
1997	30.7	69.3	58.8	13.4	10.4	13.8	3.7	40.3	25.3	28.6	1.6	3.4	0.8
1998	27.6	72.4	55.0	16.0	13.1	12.5	3.4	37.6	27.5	30.1	2.0	2.4	0.3
1999	30.7	69.3	53.5	16.1	12.3	13.7	4.4	41.2	24.9	27.8	2.3	3.1	0.8
2000	29.2	70.8	50.5	18.0	12.0	14.4	5.2	42.2	22.4	27.9	2.8	4.0	0.7
2001	30.0	70.0	54.5	16.2	10.8	14.2	4.2	43.7	24.5	26.4	1.7	3.1	0.7
2002	29.7	70.3	51.7	16.4	12.6	15.0	4.3	45.0	22.6	26.5	2.3	3.1	0.6

Source: Authors' calculations from Center for Corporate Performance (CCP) data.
Note: "Low-wage" is defined as two-thirds of the median hourly wage of the entire economy.
Education: 1 = primary school; 2 = high school; 3 = vocational education; 4 = short college degree; 5 = college degree; 6 = master's or higher degree.

The vast majority of room attendants are women. In fact, we met only one male assistant head housekeeper out of the two hundred housekeepers we interviewed at the eight case hotels. Most room attendants have a low level of education, typically compulsory education only. The exceptions are employees on temporary contracts, who are mostly students. A few immigrant workers have a relatively high educational background and work in the industry because lack of language skills make it difficult for them to gain other employment or recognition of their vocational education.

The employment of immigrants in the hotel sector has increased in recent years, especially in the 1990s, owing to the overall increasing flow of immigrants to Denmark during the period. Fourteen percent of the hotel industry's labor force were immigrants in 2003; this figure had increased from 8 percent in 1992. Still, compared to the other four European countries in the project (France, Germany, the Netherlands, and United Kingdom), the proportion of immigrant labor is lower in the Danish hotel sector. It should be noted that immigrant workers have access to the Danish social security system on an equal footing with native Danes. In the case hotels located in Copenhagen, about 80 percent of the room attendants were of non-Danish origin. The share was lower in the cities outside the capital area (about 60 percent). Most of the head housekeepers were native-born; we met only one head housekeeper of non-Danish origin. An important reason why immigrants are overrepresented in the housekeeping industry is that the need for Danish-language skills is relatively low. More than half of the case hotels require only very little or even no proficiency in Danish of their room attendants. In addition, many immigrants, typically housewives, prefer to work part-time, which is commonplace in the hotel industry.

Only a small share of the room attendants work full-time. The majority are employed on part-time contracts and work twenty to thirty hours a week. Almost all of the case hotels and the external cleaning companies hire temporary contract workers, who usually work weekend shifts, weekday shifts in peak periods, and as substitutes for sick absentees. Only one hotel does not make use of temporary contracts but uses a temporary work agency instead.

Unemployment among hotel personnel, in particular receptionists, kitchen staff, and waiters, is higher than for all wage earners on average. Among UI fund members (in the RBF), the annual unemployment rate during the previous eight years varied between 22 and

Table 5.4   Unemployment Experience Among Hotel
Employees (Excluding Students), 2003

	Low-Wage Employees	Non-Low-Wage Employees
Experienced unemployment during 2003	13.8%	27.6%
Experienced unemployment:		
Less than 10 percent of the year	34.0	38.4
10 to 30 percent of the year	30.2	33.9
30 to 50 percent of the year	20.6	17.5
50 to 80 percent of the year	13.1	9.5
More than 80 percent of the year	2.1	0.7

Source: Authors' calculations from Center for Corporate Performance (CCP) data.

10 percent. As show in table 5.4, the high unemployment rates are due to a high unemployment inflow, and unemployment spells are typically of short duration. The overwhelming majority of employees were out of work for less than 30 percent of the year, in the industry's worst period in a long time. Notably, low-wage employees experience less unemployment than non-low-wage workers, because their ineligibility for unemployment insurance benefits gives them little incentive to register as unemployed. Moreover, many of them work only part of the year.

Worker turnover in the industry is relatively high but does not differ from turnover in many other sectors of the Danish economy (Bingley and Westergaard-Nielsen 2003).[7] In 2003—which, it should be remembered, was a particularly bad year for the hotel industry—21 percent of hotel employees left the employer they had been working for in the previous year.[8]

ROOM ATTENDANTS AT THE CASE HOTELS

PAY AND BENEFITS

The wages of room attendants are clearly in the lower tail of the wage distribution in the hotel industry.[9] In general, room attendants are paid on an hourly basis, except when they are full-time employees. But the full-time workers' "hourly wage" is higher than that of housekeeping employees on other types of contracts. Room attendants usually get paid for extra hours when these are considered reasonable (this is decided by the head housekeeper). This practice, however, is less prevalent in external cleaning companies. Other employee benefits are minimal and mainly are confined to access to social activities and discounts when using the chain's hotels. Of our case firms, the four-star hotels pay on average slightly higher wages, but the difference is not big.

All of the case hotels pay at least the minimum hourly tariff wage according to the collective agreement, even when they have no collective agreement themselves. The wage rates for room attendants in the case hotels vary from €13.00 to €14.70 (US$17.69 to US$20.00).[10] Extra payment for working on weekends is commonly paid by the hotels following the rules in the collective agreements and typically amounts to €1 to €3 (US$1.36 to US$4.08) per hour. When hotels outsource their housekeeping, overtime premiums are paid either by the hotels or by the external cleaning companies. From our interviews with the employees, it was clear that external cleaning companies are more reluctant to compensate their employees for extra hours.

Although housekeeping staff clearly are at the lower end of the labor market wage distribution, Danish room attendants' wages are relatively high from an international perspective, owing to the very compressed Danish wage structure.[11] Since a considerable number of hotel guests are international travelers (especially in the Copenhagen area), and since hotel prices (net of VAT) are not significantly higher in Denmark than in other comparable European countries, this naturally begs the question: how can Danish hotels afford to pay these high wages without radically lowering the quality of services?

There are several interrelated reasons why Danish hotels have been able to stay afloat despite their high labor costs, and we discuss some of them later in the chapter. Here we would like to point out that for the same reason that room attendants' wages are relatively high—the compressed wage structure—the wage costs for other groups of employees (especially managerial jobs) are relatively cheaper. This cannot, however, be the sole explanation.

Employee Turnover and Recruitment

Housekeeping is unskilled work in the sense that no special skills are required. Reasonably good physical health and trustworthiness are the two main qualifications that employers commonly look for when hiring room attendants. Only one of the case hotels holds it as a condition for employment that the room attendant should be able to speak and understand (some) Danish. When a hotel contracts with an external cleaning company to undertake its housekeeping, the external firm is usually responsible for recruiting the staff needed. Hotels and cleaning companies recruit room attendants through several channels: job ads, word of mouth, walk-ins, and job centers. In the multinational chain case hotels, the room attendants can apply for housekeeping positions in the other hotels in the chain.

The duration of jobs for room attendants varies a lot, but the bulk of them are of short duration. For those working on temporary contracts, the duration is typically about six months, whereas those on more permanent-type contracts stay for about two years. However, we also found examples of employees who have stayed with the same hotel for ten to twenty years. This is more common in the smaller cities.

Work Patterns

Working hours are typically about five or six hours per day. A typical working day commences between 6:00 and 9:00 AM and stops between 1:00 PM and 4:00 PM. It is commonplace in most case hotels that room attendants have some flexibility to start working one hour earlier or later in the morning. Usually they work alone, but in many of the hotels they also work in teams to help each other get all the rooms completed by the end of the workday. Job tasks are relatively broad. Besides cleaning rooms, housekeepers often clean the common areas and the reception area. In one of the case hotels, room attendants also cleaned the restaurant and the bars.

Most of the room attendants on permanent contracts work five days per week. Some of them have weekend shifts every second week. However, it is more common for weekend shifts to be filled by temporary contract workers. Overtime occurs only in peak periods. Working hours are usually based on the number of rooms that have to be cleaned. Most hotels have maximum requirements for how much time room attendants should use per room. The norm is fifteen to twenty minutes for the external cleaning companies and twenty to twenty-five minutes for in-house cleaning. Rooms in high-quality hotels take somewhat longer to clean. On average, therefore, the number of rooms to be cleaned per day is in the neighborhood of twenty rooms. Thus, there is substantial difference in work pace. Working hours are monitored by the head housekeeper. Many hotels guarantee their room attendants a certain number of weekly paid working hours, irrespective of how many rooms there are that have to be cleaned. This reduces the variation in pay. In return, employees are expected to be flexible with respect to variations in the workload, job tasks, and so on.

We would expect that faced with growing competitive pressure, hotel employers would put more pressure on their employees. Do we see signs of this in the Danish hotel sector? We certainly do. For all employees in our case hotels, there has been a significant fall in the employee-per-room ratio (almost 50 percent since the late 1990s). Unfortunately, we do not have access to similar statistics for different groups of employees, and for room attendants in particular, but our impression from the interviews at the case hotels is that the change in the ratio for our target group has been considerably less significant. The decline in the employee-per-room ratio is therefore more likely to be the outcome of the tendency toward larger hotels and ensuing reductions in jobs as a result of economies of scale.

During our interviews, we rarely heard room attendants working in-house complain about an increasing pace of work or saying that they felt pressured by their bosses to make an extra effort. This was less true for the outside cleaning firms, whose work pace is higher, but even here complaints were rare. Consequently, we can conclude that there has indeed been strong pressure on increasing labor productivity in the industry, but that this has affected the target group under study to a much lesser extent than the other categories of hotel employees.

TRAINING AND DEVELOPMENT

Almost all room attendants are trained on the job. They usually start by getting a short introduction from the (assistant) head housekeeper and then work together with them or experienced housekeepers. It normally takes one to two weeks before the new employee can work unmonitored.

Figure 5.7 Career Advancement Opportunities for Room Attendants

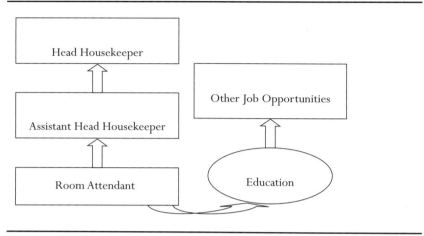

Source: Authors' compilation.

Job careers for room attendants are limited, and training beyond the initial session is very rare.[12] Thus, unless room attendants take some training outside work for other jobs in the industry, careers for them do not exist. The only exception is promotion to assistant head housekeeper or head housekeeper. Once individuals have attained these positions, however, there are no further job opportunities for them within their workplaces.

With the increasing shortage of labor and the increasing competition for unskilled labor from the retail sector, the hotel sector has recently been considering possibilities to enhance certain elements of its internal labor markets, including further on-the-job training. These plans, however, are still very much in their infancy; for room attendants, they will in all likelihood be of marginal, if any, importance.

IN-HOUSE OR OUTSOURCING?

There are no particular regulations of subcontracting cleaning services in the Danish hotel industry. Thus, hotels are free to choose to outsource housekeeping or not.

Of the eight case hotels visited, three had outsourced housekeeping to an outside cleaning company at the time of the interview. Four additional hotels, however, had outsourced cleaning work at some point during the previous ten-year period and had subsequently returned to in-house housekeeping. Thus, only one of the case hotels had had no outsourcing experience.

The main motivation for contracting room attendants' work is to save on the recruitment and administration costs associated with a category of employees characterized by high turnover. Contracting costs basically include two kinds. First, since the quality of housekeeping is important in the hotel industry, there has to be one employee—typically the operations manager or head housekeeper—who is in regular contact with the outside contractor and is responsible for maintaining a satisfactory level of quality. Thus, not all administrative costs can be avoided. A second source of costs mentioned by the managerial employees is the inflexibility that arises, for example, from the narrowly defined job tasks for outsourced room attendants. This may at first sound surprising, since one of the frequently mentioned aims of outsourcing is to obtain more flexibility. It should be noted, however, that most of the same rules and legislation that apply to in-house employees also apply to employees from outside contractors. Moreover, outsourced employees were said to have less of the workplace "spirit" that characterizes in-house employees and contributes to their greater willingness to be flexible.

The hotels that had outsourcing experience and had abandoned the arrangement pointed out that savings from outsourcing were limited and to a large extent outweighed by the additional costs just mentioned. Also, differences in wage rates between in-house and outside housekeepers are small and actually work to the advantage of employees in the outside firms.[13] To some extent, this wage differential could reflect compensation for the considerably higher work pace at outside contractors, which would be consistent with the fact that in-house employees said they were "very satisfied" with their jobs whereas housekeepers from outside firms stated that they were "satisfied."[14] As far as we can tell based on the interviews, there were no differences in labor turnover (which is high) between the satisfied group and the very satisfied group.

Thus, the gains from outsourcing housekeeping seem to be limited, and recently the trend appears to have been away from rather than toward outsourcing room attendants' services.

Why So Satisfied?

A quite remarkable finding from our case studies is the high level of job satisfaction reported by room attendants. It is a well-known fact that numerous happiness and satisfaction studies have shown that Danes are among the happiest and most satisfied people in the world (see, for example, Johansson and Kristensen 2006). However, a large majority of room attendants generally in Denmark and of those we interviewed are not of Danish origin, and so cultural differences in reporting are unlikely to provide an explanation. Two other possibilities seem to be more promising. The first is that in Denmark, unlike in many other countries, the negative associations with housekeeping are compensated for by higher wages, both relative to other groups of employees and in absolute terms. We cannot test this conjecture, however. The second explanation is that a large proportion of Danish room attendants work relatively short hours; given the high wage rate in Denmark for unskilled work, these employees can thus spend more time with their families or on their studies. The work is daytime work, and the hours more or less coincide with children's school hours. Moreover, in Denmark low-paid employees remain eligible for several income transfers. Consequently, there is no one-to-one correspondence between low pay and low income.

It should also be noted that many room attendants are from countries where women spend considerably more time with their children and families than western European females do. Most of the employees we interviewed, in particular those with family responsibilities, had only one job. But we also met employees who had two cleaning jobs, which shows that this is indeed possible if the worker is interested in earning more money. Again, we cannot provide direct evidence in favor of this family and work hypothesis, but we think that the international patterns lend some support.

But money is not everything. The room attendants frequently mentioned the friendly colleagues, good atmosphere, and strong cohesion within the team as equally important sources of satisfaction. Surprisingly enough, we found that satisfaction was greater in the budget hotels, where work is often harder because there is much more cleaning to do than in the luxury hotels, whose guests mainly sleep and work during their stay. This could reflect smaller differences in status between categories of employees in two- or three-star hotels than in the four- or five-star ones.

As mentioned earlier, we also observed a difference in the satisfaction levels of housekeepers employed in-house, who said they were "very satisfied" with their jobs, and those working for outside contractors, who were "satisfied," despite the fact that wages among in-house employees on average are smaller than wages for outside employed housekeepers.

Few room attendants remain in that occupation for their entire lives. Most of the employees we interviewed had fairly short tenure at their current employer.[15] Several—but far from all of them—had had similar jobs before. Many of them recognized the fact that there were few career prospects in their current jobs and said that they had the job "for now." We repeatedly heard that "to move up, you have to do something else than this." For many unskilled immigrants, however, a room attendant's job is a stepping-stone to the labor market that can be combined with looking after young children and other family responsibilities.

Tracking room attendants over time in Statistics Denmark's register data is not possible, mainly because occupation is partly self-reported in connection with the filing of tax reports and people tend not to report occupations that they conceive of as transitory. Hence, there is a huge underreporting of occupations like room attendant. However, we do know from research on low-paid workers in general (OECD 1997) that mobility out of low-paid work in Denmark is quite high. A recent careful analysis of low-paid private-sector employees (excluding students) by Iben Bolvig (2005) demonstrates that the large majority of low-wage jobs are transitory and that there is considerable upward mobility, primarily by changes to higher-wage jobs at the same employer, but also by switches to other jobs at other employers.[16] Of course, we do not know the extent to which these findings also apply to the target group of this study. But it is important to emphasize that for a considerable share of employees in housekeeping it would be very misleading to characterize them as persistently low-paid or poor.

Is "Flexicurity" at the Hotel Level the Secret?

The employers we talked with told us that there are two groups of employees in the hotel industry: those who want to have a full-time job with more or less fixed time schedules, and those who are looking for a secondary job and are fairly flexible about scheduling and who in fact may prefer flexible work hours. Clearly, setting up work arrangements that satisfy both groups is quite difficult and therefore by necessity a compromise. The employers' problem is deciding how to use flexible staffing to respond to variability of demand even though the work of the more flexible secondary workers is of a lower quality.

A distinguishing characteristic of the Danish labor market is what has frequently been labeled "flexicurity": a high degree of flexibility of workers in terms of job mobility combined with the strong income security created by the social insurance system (see chapter 2 for details). Unlike most other EU countries, Denmark has not used legislation very much to guarantee job security, thus imposing costs on employers in cases of high worker turnover. High income security in Denmark is the result of a generous unemployment benefit insurance system, membership in which is generally expensive, coupled with the fact that most social benefits, vacation rights, and pensions are transferable across employers.

As we have seen in the previous sections, however, a substantial fraction of hotel industry employees lack the income security that comes from membership in UI funds. For some employees, it could be that their demand for such security is lower because they are interested in only a short-term employment relationship or are considering working in the industry for only a relatively short period. Other employees lack unemployment insurance, however, because they are ignorant about the Danish social security system. This is often the case with immigrant workers. It is important to note that immigrants and students do not lack access to the Danish social security system. In any event, the outcome is that the hotel sector is one in which the Danish flexicurity system is not fully operative.

Nevertheless, our interviews with case hotel employees reveal proof that the combination of flexibility and security is indeed present in the hotel sector, not chiefly through the social security system but within the hotels, which give employees a guaranteed number of paid weekly hours. Like several automatic stabilizers in the Danish social policy system, this guarantee protects employees against changes in demand. In exchange for this insurance, employees are expected to demonstrate some flexibility regarding workloads. Other forms of flexibility are also common. In particular, jobs are defined broadly in terms of tasks—that is, there are broad areas, the boundaries of which are respected, but in many situations a task can be performed by several different employees irrespective of their exact job titles. This flexibility is mainly an outcome of an implicit contract. To be sure, some rules and demarcations have been agreed upon with the unions, but both parties recognize that for practical purposes the contracts must be flexible. This flexibility is not something that the employers have unilaterally imposed on employees because, with relatively low proportions of unionized labor, because unions are weak in the hotel sector.

Both hotel employers and the unions recognize the trade-off between flexibility and security and between flexibility and quality of work, and in negotiations they aim at striking a balance. The recent difficulties in recruiting staff have led both parties to look for ways to increase on-the-job training and develop internal labor market careers, as in the retail industry, which is the hotel sector's main competitor for unskilled labor. This is an example of a step toward more employment security, but it is unlikely to have much of an effect on the jobs within housekeeping.

DISCUSSION AND CONCLUSIONS

As elsewhere, increasing competition in the Danish hotel industry has forced employers to look for new ways to restructure their business. However, the possibilities for restructuring housekeeping jobs by means of new technologies are of only marginal importance. A room attendant's job has not, and in all likelihood cannot, change much. Reorganizing work and increasing work intensity are other possible routes. Labor productivity in hotels has increased considerably, but this growth has affected housekeeping employees only marginally in recent years.

Hotels began some years ago to try to restructure by subcontracting services, but outsourcing turned out not to be advantageous for housekeeping services, and the expected economic gains did not materialize. The current trend seems to be toward maintaining in-house housekeeping.

Flexible staffing seems to be a more promising avenue and has been chosen by many employers. This restructuring strategy depends, however, on recognizing the limits set by employees and their organizations. The price of increased flexibility is more security (of income or employment). Flexibility is facilitated by several Danish

212 of Low-Wage Work in Denmark

labor market institutions, such as internationally low hiring and firing costs, generous unemployment insurance and other social benefits, and government-provided (that is, not linked to employers) social insurance benefits. These are all features of so-called flexicurity, which has had a prominent place in recent discussion and has become one of the EU's latest fads. Flexibility in the hotel industry goes beyond staffing and applies to job content as well—that is, Danish hotels can manage with fewer employees than, for instance, hotels in the United States. However, the flexicurity system should not be given too much weight, since it has not been fully operative in the Danish hotel sector. The security aspect of the high job mobility and low variance in individuals' incomes that characterize most Danish employment is weaker in the hotel sector, chiefly because a considerably lower portion of the employees are covered by unemployment insurance than workers in other sectors. Thus, there is a kind of dual system in the industry: one largely within the traditional Danish model, and another at least partly outside of it. But even when employee security is absent, owing to lack of coverage by legislation or bargains between the labor market parties, many Danish employers in the hotel industry still provide some elements of security. For room attendants, security comes in the form of a guaranteed number of weekly hours.

With the recent enlargement of the European Union and increases in access to the Danish labor market for unskilled workers from central and eastern Europe, Danish hotels can soon expect further increases in the number of immigrant workers from these countries. Clearly, this could put additional pressure on the sector's current dual system and the social norms by which hotels do not deviate significantly from firms in other industries with respect to providing secure and flexible work for their employees.

We are deeply grateful to Lene Enevoldsen for helping us find the cases used in this study and for superb handling of communication with the hotels. Lene also took part in several of the interviews and has contributed many useful comments on the work reported here. We are also grateful to two referees and to Rosemary Batt, Annette D. Bernhardt, Françoise Carré, Sheldon H. Danziger, and other participants in the Amsterdam meeting in September 2006 for valuable comments and suggestions. Thanks also go to Morten Brustad and Benedikte Rosenbrinck at HORESTA for providing us with data and useful information about the hotel industry. Last but not least, we are of course extremely grateful to the case hotels and their staffs, who gave their valuable time to help us. Needless to say, without their often cheerful cooperation, we would not have been able to make this report.

APPENDIX

Table 5A.1 The Case Study Hotels

	Hotel 1	Hotel 2	Hotel 3	Hotel 4
Interviewed	Operations manager, responsible person from external cleaning company, assistant head housekeeper, two room attendants	Operations manager, head housekeeper, four room attendants	Administration manager, head housekeeper, assistant head housekeeper and three room attendants	General manager (in charge of two chain hotels), assistant head housekeeper supervisor, three room attendants
Hotel status	Independent	Independently owned group	International chain	International chain
Star rating	Four stars	Four stars	Four stars	Three stars
Location	Copenhagen	Aalborg	Copenhagen	Copenhagen
Number of rooms	366	210	93	80
Market segmentation	Many business guests. Targets its customers broadly, from business travelers to leisure guests.	Both business and leisure guests mainly from Denmark, Norway, and Sweden.	Mainly business clients. Some leisure guests at weekends.	60 percent leisure guests, 40 percent business guests.
Occupancy (2005)	70 to 80 percent	45 to 50 percent	68 percent in 2005	80 percent
Rack rate	€162 to €335	€107 to €242	€201 to €429	€74
Number of staff	100	n.a.	117 (three chain hotels)	100 (three chain hotels)
Number of room attendants	One person responsible from cleaning company; three housekeeper supervisors; three thirty-hour fixed contract workers; forty part-time and casual workers	Seven room attendants: permanent contracts (one full-time, six fixed-hour contract); twenty to thirty room attendants; casual contracts	Two to five full-time room attendants; four to six fixed-hour contract room attendants; two to four casual contract room attendants	Four full-time; three to four fixed-hour contract room attendants; nine to fifteen casual contract
Contract cleaning?	Yes	No	No	No

Hotel 5	Hotel 6	Hotel 7	Hotel 8
Operations manager, head housekeeper from external cleaning company, three room attendants	Head housekeeper, three room attendants	Operations manager, head housekeeper, five room attendants	General manager, head housekeeper, three room attendants
National chain	International chain	Independent	National chain (Scandinavian)
Two to three stars	Four stars	Three stars	Three stars
Aarhus	Copenhagen	Aarhus	Kolding
92	201	108	180
Leisure guests and business guests (craftsmen, etc.). Good location. Cheap and clean.	Leisure guests and business guests.	Mainly business guests. Leisure guests are also important for the hotel.	Mainly business and conference guests. Leisure guests in summer.
0 percent	80 percent	45 to 50 percent	72 percent
€71 to €119	€166 to €225	€73 to €170	€156 to €197
Approximately thirty-five	Approximately eighty	Approximately. forty-one (thirty full-time)	Approximately ninety
One full-time; twelve fixed-hour (fifteen hours) contract	No full-time room attendants; fixed-hour contract, typically 27.5 hours per week (three room attendants work fifteen hours per week)	One head housekeeper (twenty-five hours per week); three full-time room attendants; three casual contract room attendants	One head housekeeper (fifteen to thirty-seven-hour contract); sixteen fixed-hour contract; four casual contracts (students) when busy
es	No	No	Yes

Source: Authors' compilation from HORESTA data.

NOTES

1. Thus, in 2005 revenues of the hotel industry increased by 13.5 percent as compared to the year before.
2. One of the multinational chains is a high-service-quality chain, whereas the service at the other is rated at the three-star level.
3. The VAT in the hotel sector is 5.5 percent in France, 16 percent in Germany, 6 percent in Holland, and 17.5 percent in the United Kingdom.
4. The numbers for the first half of 2006 show a further increase; thus, revenue grew by 6 percent compared to the first half of the previous year.
5. Some room attendants are also organized in other unions, such as 3F (Fagligt, Faelles, Forbund). Their share is considerably smaller than RBF's.
6. An employee is defined as low-paid if his or her pay is lower than two-thirds of the median pay. This is a frequently used definition of low pay (see, for example, OECD 1997).
7. As a matter of fact, turnover in the hotel industry is lower than the average for the private sector.
8. Note that these figures refer to the workforce in the hotel industry from which we have deducted student employees. We cannot provide precise information about the turnover rate among room attendants because the register data are not good at accurately capturing employment relationships shorter than one year. Moreover, many holders of these jobs do not report the job title to the sources on which the registers build.
9. For reference, the average wage rate in the whole economy in 2005 was €29.70 (US$40.42) and in manufacturing the same year €27.70 (US$37.69); for room attendants in the case hotels the average wage rate varied between €13.00 and €14.70 (US$17.69 and US$20.00).
10. These wage rates do not include vacation pay, which is 12.5 percent of the previous (vacation) year's earnings.
11. For example, wages for Danish room attendants are about twice as high as their counterparts in the United Kingdom earn (in euros), even controlling for purchasing power parity.
12. Some of the bigger chains offer courses whose main purpose seems to be creating company spirit. There is little emphasis on actually improving the skills of employees.
13. The hourly wage rate in the outside companies varied between €14.60 and €14.90 (US$19.87 and US$20.27), whereas the in-house wage rates were between €13.00 and €14.30 (US$17.69 to US$19.46).
14. Some of the employees we interviewed had experience working both

in-house and for external contractors. They clearly preferred the working conditions in the former.

15.	And yet we suspect there was an upward bias in tenure among those we interviewed.

16.	This is the opposite of what has been found to occur in the United States (see Andersson, Holtzer, and Lane 2005).

REFERENCES

Andersson, Fredrik, Harry J. Holtzer, and Julia I. Lane. 2005. *Moving Up or Moving On: Workers, Firms, and Advancement in the Low-Wage Labor Market*. New York: Russell Sage Foundation.

Bernhardt, Annette, Laura Dresser, and Erin Hatton. 2003. "The Coffee Pot Wars: Unions and Firm Restructuring in the Hotel Industry." In *Low-Wage America*, edited by Eileen Appelbaum, Annette Bernhardt, and Richard J. Murnane. New York: Russell Sage Foundation.

Bingley, Paul, and Niels Westergaard-Nielsen. 2003. "Returns to Tenure, Firm-Specific Human Capital, and Worker Heterogeneity." *International Journal of Manpower* (24): 774–88.

Bolvig, Iben. 2005. "Within- and Between-Firm Mobility in the Low-Wage Labor Market." In *Job Quality and Employer Behavior*, edited by Stephen Bazen, Claudio Lucifora, and Wiemer Salverda. New York: Palgrave Macmillan.

HORESTA. 2004. *tendens* (March).

———. 2006. *tendens* (July).

Jensen, Peter, and Niels Westergaard-Nielsen. 1990. "Temporary Layoffs." In *Panel Data and Labor Market Studies*, edited by Joop Hartog, Gert Ridder, and Jules Theeuwes. Amsterdam: North-Holland.

Johansson, Edvard, and Nicolai Kristensen. 2006. "New Evidence on Cross-Country Differences in Job Satisfaction Using Anchoring Vignettes." Working paper 06-1. Aarhus, Denmark: Aarhus School of Business, Department of Economics.

Neumann, George, Peder J. Pedersen, and Niels Westergaard-Nielsen. 1991. "Long-Run International Trends in Aggregate Unionization." *European Journal of Political Economy* (7): 249–74.

Organization for Economic Cooperation and Development (OECD). 1997. "Low-Wage Jobs: Stepping-stones to a Better Future or Traps?" *Employment Outlook*. Paris: OECD.

CHAPTER 6

The Upgrading of the Skills of Nursing Assistants and Cleaning Staff in the Danish Public-Sector Hospitals

Jacob K. Eskildsen and Ann-Kristina Løkke Nielsen

In this chapter, we present the results from the study of low-wage workers in Danish health care. The target occupations are the nursing assistants, cleaners, and hospital service assistants who perform basic nursing tasks, clean wards, and serve meals in hospital departments.

Danish hospital services are concentrated in public establishments, which, until January 1, 2007, were administered by fourteen different county administrations. The sector employed close to 100,000 people in 2004 (approximately 87,000 of them full-time), the equivalent of 3.5 percent of the Danish labor force. Out of these 100,000 employees, approximately 10,000 are nursing assistants and 5,000 are cleaners and hospital service assistants.

Since 1980, health care employment has been on the rise, and the increase was roughly equal between men and women throughout the period. The workforce is dominated by women, who accounted for 81 percent of total health care employment in 2004. This rather high fraction of women has been virtually constant since 1986.

Over the last decade, all elements of the Danish health care industry, but especially hospitals, have experienced fundamental and rapid changes, owing to a political focus on higher productivity and quality. Traditionally, Danish hospitals have had a highly hierarchical structure. Because the hospital management paradigm has been centered on employees' professional competencies within their field of expertise, hospitals have long been departmentalized, with relatively little cross-functional cooperation. Today's political focus on productivity and quality, however, is changing the management paradigm. More and more, hospitals are restructuring to reflect the process flow that the patients follow through the hospital, thus abandoning the highly departmentalized organizational structure. These changes have involved restructuring individual work groups' job functions as well as reorganizing these work groups. To facilitate such changes top management is relying on management philosophies such as business process reengineering, total quality management (TQM), lean manufacturing, and knowledge management. In other words, management no longer focuses solely on employees' professional competencies but also takes their personal competencies into account. The political focus on productivity and quality has also reduced the number of public hospitals, from seventy-six in 1998 to fifty-two in 2004.[1]

The purpose of this chapter is to give an overview of the industry and to examine how these changes have influenced the current jobs of the workers in Danish hospitals employed in cleaning, food service, and patient care as nursing assistants.

The research presented here was conducted in 2005–2006 in Danish hospitals. A total of nine case studies were completed. The main findings are:

To not only increase efficiency but improve quality in patient care, the hospitals have focused on upgrading the skills of the cleaning assistants and integrating the functions of cleaning, food service, and hospital porters into the new "hospital service assistant" occupation.

A general task slide is taking place among the occupational groups involved in treating and caring for patients. This is similar to the adoption of multiskilled or enhanced positions at some of the hospitals in the United States hospital study. The motivation for this task slide is twofold. First, it offsets the shortage of doctors and nurses in Denmark (more than 20 percent of doctor positions were vacant in December 2006). Second, the task slide improves jobs, improves quality, and reduces costs through increased employee flexibility, as was also the case in the American study.

At some of the case study hospitals, there has been a task slide from nursing assistants to hospital service assistants, who have taken over some of the routine nursing assistant tasks, such as replenishing supplies and handing out food.

At some of these hospitals, there has also been a task slide from nurses to nursing assistants, who have received additional training to enable them to hand out prescription drugs, perform catheterization, and carry out other nursing-related tasks such as doing rounds with the doctors.

The number of nursing assistants in the somatic hospital sector has been declining since 2002, probably in large part because of the trend toward fewer bed days for many treatments. Another contributing factor is probably the growing complexity of care, due to an increasing technification of treatments and equipment.

Hospitals with relatively high productivity appear to be more on the forefront in work organization than the less-productive hospitals.

STUDY DESIGN AND METHODOLOGY

In 2005 and 2006, we completed a total of nine case studies focusing on the medical departments at Danish hospitals.[2] At each hospital, we interviewed executive-level managers, human resource managers, and managers of cleaning and nursing assistants. In these interviews with managers, we gathered information on the pressures facing their hospitals and asked them to describe their strategies for increasing efficiency.

In addition, we conducted two focus group interviews with the target groups at each hospital. Each focus group interview involved five or six cleaning and nursing assistant representatives. We asked these employees about their job function, training possibilities, work conditions, and general job satisfaction. Besides the field research, we used various register data sources, both internal (from the hospitals' own systems) and external.

We selected our case hospitals with an eye to contrasting hospitals with relatively high and low productivity. A recent study (Olesen 2004; Olesen and Petersen 2002) revealed distinctive differences in productivity across Danish hospitals.[3] The analytical technique applied in the study is called data envelopment analysis (DEA), also referred to as "frontier analysis." DEA can be used to evaluate the relative efficiency of a number of decisionmaking units—in this context, hospitals. It is an extreme-point technique that compares each hospi-

Table 6.1 Case Study Hospitals, by Productivity

Low Productivity	High Productivity
Horsens (Hospital 1)	Randers (Hospital 2)
Hjørring (Hospital 6)	Holstebro (Hospital 3)
Brønderslev (Hospital 7)	Herning (Hospital 4)
Nykøbing (Hospital 8)	Ringkøbing (Hospital 5)
Thisted (Hospital 9)	

Source: Olesen (2004).

tal with an efficient frontier estimated as a linear combination of the decisionmaking units that perform best in turning input into output.

Another study, this one conducted by the Ministry of the Interior and Health (2003), showed that to a large extent these productivity differences are due to county-specific differences, which raises the question as to whether the cross-hospital differences are due to differences in the political governance of the counties and are therefore to some extent outside the control of hospital managements. Table 6.1 shows the case study hospitals split according to this contrast.

We allocated each of the hospitals to one of the two groups based on whether their productivity was relatively high or low compared to the other hospitals in the study. Their categorization does not say anything about the actual differences in productivity—only about their relative standing in the Olesen study. The nine case study hospitals are quite different with respect to size and the number of specialties they offer. A brief overview of these differences is given in table 6.2.

About fifteen years ago, the first step was taken to expand the scope of the cleaning function to include a service function, which was to include cleaners, nursing assistants, and porters. At present, only case hospitals 1 and 2 have fully implemented the hospital service assistance concept. Case hospitals 3, 4, and 5 are implementing the concept. Case hospitals 6 and 7 have reeducated some cleaners to become hospital service assistants, but put the implementation of the concept on hold as of January 1, 2007, pending a centralized implementation strategy in the new regional organization. Case hospitals 8 and 9 have decided to await the centralized regional decision before taking any reeducation initiatives.

Those hospitals that have not yet introduced the hospital service concept have avoided it thus far for reasons that are mainly physical and cultural in nature, as one of the managers expressed it. The phys-

Table 6.2 Statistics for the Case Study Hospitals

County	Hospital 1 Vejle	Hospital 2 Aarhus	Hospital 3 Ring-Købing	Hospital 4 Ring-Købing	Hospital 5 Ring-Købing	Hospitals 6 and 7 Northern Jutland	Hospitals 8 and 9 Viborg
Beds (2001)	251	315	299	280	65	360	201
Bed days (2004)	67,922	121,568	97,746	93,544	15,870	117,623	47,150
Occupancy rate (2003)	78%	89%	85%	86%	85%	79%	90%
Dismissed patients (2004)	16,535	30,269	21,410	20,928	3721	24,881	10,630
Ambulatory treatments (2004)	24,143	40,637	37,116	26,015	3,801	28,150	18,390

Source: National Board of Health (2006), Amtsraadsforeningen (2001).
Note: Patients treated at the emergency room are excluded from the ambulatory treatments.

ical challenge is the reluctance of some female cleaners and especially male hospital porters to think that women are physically capable of performing the hospital porter job. The cultural challenge is simply that male hospital porters do not want to clean. It is these very challenges that have caused the most trouble at the hospitals that have already implemented the concept.

Implementing the hospital service concept process also brought about other problematic issues. One hospital saw a very brief strike. At all the hospitals, a few workers resigned, although some of them subsequently applied for a new job. Furthermore, there has been a general resistance to the new job functions. For instance, hospital porters have not wanted to give up their transportation tasks and have often given the hard work to the women, and some of the cleaners have not wanted to have patient contact.

THE DANISH HEALTH CARE SECTOR AND ITS INSTITUTIONS

Health care expenditures in relation to somatic hospitals rose in Denmark from 1995 to 2004, with an average annual growth rate of 2.7 percent (see table 6.3). Total health care expenditures in Denmark are now equivalent to 9 percent of GDP.

In the same period, the number of hospitals in Denmark has decreased by almost 45 percent, and the number of bed days declined by 15.2 percent, with a bed occupancy rate of 82.2 percent in 2004. The table also shows that the number of outpatients has increased dramatically—an astonishing 66.5 percent—during the time span. The average duration of hospital stays has thus been lowered—from 6.2 days in 1995 to 4.7 days in 2004—owing to the growing popularity of same-day surgery. The number of discharged patients has not increased to the same extent as the increase in outpatients; thus, the Danish hospital sector is characterized today by a growing proportion of outpatients compared to the number of employees. The complexity of treatment and care for hospitalized patients is increasing, since a number of the less complicated treatments no longer require hospitalization.

If we compare the per capita health care expenditures in Denmark with other European countries, Denmark is in the top bracket. The annual growth rate, however, has been among the lowest during this period.

If we look at the proportion of the total income (gross domestic

Table 6.3 Health Care Statistics: Somatic Hospital Sector,
1995 to 2004

	1995	1998	2001	2004
Health care expenditure—hospitals	5,920	6,448	6,958	7,494
Number of hospitals	—	76	57	52
Discharges	970	996	1,030	1,089
Bed days	6,014	5,738	5,509	5,111
Number of beds	—	19,472	18,218	16,668
Number of discharged patients	608	606	612	630
Number of outpatients	3,428	3,764	4,663	5,704
Average duration of stay (days)	6.2	5.8	5.4	4.7
Bed occupancy rate	—	79.5%	82.3%	82.2%

Source: Ministry of the Interior and Health (2006).
Note: Health care expenditures are in millions of euros. Discharges, bed days, number of discharged patients, and number of outpatients are in thousands. Healthy newborns are not included.

product) spent on health, Denmark spends only about 9 percent of its GDP compared to the more than 15 percent spent in the United States (see table 6.4). Actually, in 2003 only the United Kingdom spent less of its GNP on health care than Denmark, but the proportion has increased more in the United Kingdom over the period.

According to the World Health Organization (WHO), the public proportion of health care expenditures in Denmark and the United Kingdom in 2003 amounted to 82.9 percent and 85.7 percent, respectively, which are the highest rates in Europe. In Denmark, hospital treatments are covered in full by the government, whereas services such as medicine, dental work, and physiotherapy are covered only partially. With respect to the number of general practitioners, acute care beds, and nurses in relation to the size of the population, Denmark is in the midrange of the six countries.

That health care expenditures do not necessarily affect the life expectancy of men and women is evident if we compare tables 6.4 and 6.5. Denmark and the United States are the countries with the lowest life expectancies, but the total expenditures on health as a percentage of GDP are very different, with the United States spending the most.

Increases in life expectancy in Denmark have been among the slowest in Europe since 1980, resulting in a relatively poor WHO ranking of the Danish health care system. In 2004 the life expectancy

Table 6.4 Total Expenditure on Health in Six Countries as a
Percentage of Gross Domestic Product, 1975 to 2003

	1975	1985	1995	2000	2001	2002	2003
Denmark	8.7	8.5	8.1	8.3	8.6	8.8	8.9
France	6.4	7.9	9.4	9.2	9.3	10.0	10.4
Germany	8.6	9.0	10.1	10.3	10.4	10.6	10.8
Netherlands	6.9	7.1	8.1	7.9	8.3	8.9	9.1
United Kingdom	5.5	5.9	7.0	7.3	7.5	7.7	7.8
United States of America	7.9	10.1	13.3	13.3	14	14.7	15.2

Source: OECD (2006).

was 79.9 for women and 75.2 years for men. From table 6.5 it is also
evident that this relatively low ranking is mainly due to a relatively
high adult mortality rate. According to the Ministry of the Interior
and Health, the most important causes of death among Danish men
and women in 1998 were ischemia and vascular disorder of the brain.
The relatively low life expectancy does not seem to be linked to the
infant mortality rate or the under-five mortality rate.

It is doubtful that the relatively low average life expectancy in
Denmark can be directly attributed to the level of health care funding, although there seems to be a weak correlation between average
life expectancy and the growth rate in health care expenditures (Søgaard 2006).

In the EU as a whole, mortality among both men and women as a
consequence of cancer increased from 1960 to 1994. The increase has
been no greater for Danish men than it has been in other western European countries, whereas for Danish women there has been a relatively higher increase in mortality due to cancer than in the other European countries. Unlike women in the rest of the EU, Danish
women with vascular disorders of the brain have not experienced any
improvement in mortality. Mortality as a result of bronchitis, en-
larged lungs, asthma, and cirrhosis (contracted liver disease) increased in Denmark from 1960 to 1998, although it fell in all other
EU countries.

The clear difference between countries in mortality for certain
types of diseases, as well as differences between genders, can to some
extent be attributed to differences in the quality of treatment and the
prioritization practices in each country's health care system—in

Table 6.5 Basic Health Indicators, 2003

| | Life Expectancy at Birth (Years) | | Probability of Dying (per 1,000) | | | | Infant Mortality Rate (Deaths per 1,000 Live Births) |
| | | | Under Age Five (Under-Five Mortality Rate) | | Between Ages Fifteen and Sixty (Adult Mortality Rate) | | |
	Males	Females	Males	Females	Males	Females	
Denmark	74.9	79.5	5	5	117	72	4.4
France	75.8	82.9	5	4	132	60	3.9
Germany	75.5	81.3	5	5	112	58	4.2
Netherlands	76.2	80.9	6	5	89	63	4.8
United Kingdom	76.2	80.7	6	5	102	63	5.3
United States	74.5	79.9	8	7	137	81	7.0

Source: WHO (2006); OECD (2006).

other words, health system performance (Nolte and McKee 2003). It is evident, however, that behavioral, biological, and social risk factors also have a significant effect on public health (Juel, Sørensen, and Brønnum-Hansen 2006). The performance of the Danish health care sector in relation to the life expectancy of men and women does not, however, seem to affect the level of satisfaction with health care in Denmark. A recent EU study has shown that 90.6 percent of Danes are satisfied with their health care system, and this number by far exceeds the satisfaction level of those living in the other EU countries included in the study (Amtsraadsforeningen and DSI, 2002a). This relatively high level of satisfaction is probably exaggerated, since it is a well-known fact that in general Danes express higher satisfaction (see Johansson and Kristensen 2006).

INDUSTRIAL RELATIONS AND COLLECTIVE AGREEMENTS

This study's target hospital occupations are all highly organized, as are most Danish public employees. However, the unions that organize hospital workers have a long tradition of cooperating with employers about work organization, training schemes, working hours, and the like. In most places, union dominance has been seen as a necessity and a benefit to all. According to the interviews with the target group, almost all nursing assistants are members of the same trade union, the Danish Union of Public Employees (FOA), and all cleaners and service assistants are members of either FOA or the United Federation of Danish Workers (3F).[4] This high degree of unionization is very different from that found in American hospitals, where unionization ranges between 18 and 24 percent. The key aspect of the Danish model is that the trade unions and the Employers' Federation (the social partners) bargain over most of the regulatory issues, while the government is left to "pay the bill" (see chapters 1 and 2). The social partners set wages and negotiate other work conditions; salary issues are therefore settled away from the workplace. The social partners also make agreements on normal working hours and set rules for labor protection with respect to overtime (see also chapter 2). In the hospital sector, as well as in the rest of the public sector, there is a tradition of peaceful bargaining. The fact that employers fully accept union dominance and influence at the workplace leads to cooperative conduct.

Wage Bargaining

While wage setting has been decentralized in the private labor market, public-sector wage bargaining is still highly centralized, with biannual central negotiations. However, a new wage system, called "new-wage," involves many fewer steps than used to be the case. The intention is to pay a larger fraction of earnings as personal add-ons that depend on qualifications, job functions, and individual productivity. Although the purpose was to promote productivity and performance by circumventing the rigid wage system, the system is not fulfilling this purpose because the amounts available for performance-related pay are too limited and in many workplaces are split evenly among the employees.

The public sector, on the other hand, has always had a career system in which to some extent promotions are dependent on seniority. The various employee groups appear to benefit quite evenly from the new-wage system, with average annual nominal growth rates between 3.7 and 4.3 percent from 2000 to 2004. Nursing assistants and cleaning staff experienced average annual wage increases of 4 percent and 4.3 percent, respectively, from 2000 to 2004. In spite of these relatively high wage increases, the workers in our interviews were not satisfied with the wage system, because they claimed it is impossible to differentiate job quality and performance for this type of job function. As a result, the "new wage" does not seem to work as intended in all hospitals. Often the target groups agree to divide the share of individual performance-related pay among the members of a work unit, making it a standardized supplement instead. There did not appear to be any difference in the perception of the new-wage system between the two target groups.

Fewer than 1 percent of the employees in the Danish hospital sector can be considered low-wage workers. The wage level for service assistants, cleaning staff, hospital porters, and nursing assistants is presented in table 6.6.

As the figures show, the cleaning staff has the lowest wage per hour (€13.90, US$19), whereas nursing assistants have the highest wage per hour (€15.40, US$21.06). Service assistants and hospital porters earn a wage increase after three years of employment, whereas the wage for nursing assistants increases only after four years of employment. All groups of employees get the same overtime pay. Thus, employees receive 50 percent of the hourly rate when they work on pub-

Table 6.6 Wage Levels (Euros per Hour) and Pensions for
Hospital Staff, 2006

	Service Assistants	Cleaning Staff	Hospital Porters	Nursing Assistants
Basic wage	14.10	13.90	14.10	15.40
Wage after two years		14.40		
Wage after three years	14.60		14.60	
Wage after four years				15.60
Wage after five years		15.10		
Wage after seven years			16.10	
Wage after ten years	16.30			16.80
Extra pay for work on public holidays	50%	50%	50%	50%
Extra pay for overtime	50	50	50	50
Extra pay for duty on weekdays 5:00 PM to 11:00 PM	29	29	29	29
Extra pay for duty on weekdays 11:00 PM to 6:00 AM	32.5	32.5	32.5	32.5
Extra pay for duty on Saturday 8:00 AM to Sunday 12:00 PM	40	40	40	40
Pension[c]	12.8	12.8[a] 7.69[b]	13.4	12.6

Source: Amtsraadsforeningen and FOA (2005a, 2005b); Amtsraadsforeningen et al. (2005); FOA (2005a, 2005b, 2005c, 2005d, 2005e).
[a] Twenty-five years old and four years of employment.
[b] Twenty-one years old and one year of employment.
[c] The total pension amount in percentage of the salary. One-third of the pension amount is payable by the employee.

lic holidays or other "unsocial hours." Overtime pay for duties on weekdays between 5:00 PM and 11:00 PM is 29 percent of the hourly rate, 32.5 percent for working weekdays between 11:00 PM and 6:00 AM, and 40 percent for working between 8:00 AM Saturdays and 12:00 AM Sundays. Hospital porters have the highest total pension in percentage (13.4 percent). One-third of the total pension amount is paid, according to the agreement, by the employee in order to make them save money for their retirement. Cleaning staff with only one year of seniority have the lowest percentage (7.69 percent). Nursing assistants receive a fairly low percentage considering their high wage level compared to the other employment groups.

A nursing assistant and a cleaner in a Danish hospital are not low-wage workers according to our definition, since the income for a full-time employee excluding holidays, benefits, and pensions is above the low-wage threshold cited in chapter 2.

The average retirement age for the Danish population is 64 years for men and 61.5 for women (Portal om EU og Arbejdsmarkedet 2002). All inhabitants of Denmark are secured a minimum retirement benefit, and most workers in the private sector have no coverage other than that. Hospital employees have always had extra pension coverage as part of their employment package. Since most low-skilled workers had had no extra pension coverage in the private sector, this benefit was an important part of the wage package, and it was an important feature of public-sector jobs compared to similar jobs elsewhere. Since the mid-1990s, all employees covered by a general agreement have retirement benefits as a routine element of their wage package, so in this respect the difference between the public and private sectors will gradually disappear.

THE HEALTH AND SAFETY AT WORK ACT

All Danish employees are covered by the Health and Safety at Work Act, which ensures that employers offer their employees a healthy and safe work environment. The act states that employees are guaranteed a continuous rest from work for at least eleven hours every twenty-four hours. For some jobs—such as shift work—the rest period can be reduced to eight hours. Employees are also ensured a twenty-four-hour break every seven days. For employees in jobs that involve working with people, like the target occupations, it is officially permitted to defer the weekly rest for later time off. In our interviews with staff at the case hospitals, this was not mentioned as a problem when we discussed working hours and schedules, although getting time off may be a problem for the doctors.

Maybe as a result of the Health and Safety Act, all of the interviewed employees in the target group felt that they had the necessary support to perform their job, and no one reported any risks—for example, exposure to cleaning chemicals. Furthermore, the case hospitals emphasize injury prevention in their training and procedures. All nursing assistants have thus been trained in how to lift patients and also have the necessary equipment.

CHANGES IN THE DANISH HOSPITAL SECTOR

The focus of this section on the changes currently taking place in the Danish hospital sector will be changes in governance and changes in hospital financing.

CHANGES IN THE GOVERNANCE OF HOSPITALS

Until January 1, 2007, the Danish public-sector governance structure had three tiers: the state level, the county level, and the municipality level. The counties ran the hospitals, with the financing coming from taxes collected from all the county's inhabitants.

The bill passed by the Danish Parliament to increase the productivity of the public sector (which took effect on January 1, 2007) has had several consequences. First, the size of the municipalities has been increased to a minimum of thirty thousand inhabitants, and the fourteen counties have been abolished and replaced by five regions whose sole purpose will be the managing of the hospital sector. The regions will not have tax collection rights but will get the majority of their financing from the municipalities, which will pay for the hospital treatment of their inhabitants. With the municipalities' increased size, the provision of some long-term care (after, for instance, strokes or seizures) is expected to be transferred from the regional level to the municipalities, since the municipalities will now have an incentive to vertically integrate these services.

CHANGES IN HOSPITAL FINANCING: THE PATIENT'S RIGHT TO CHOOSE

Today patients have the right to choose the hospital where they want to undergo treatment. This right to choose has triggered considerable competition, and a simultaneous increase in the demand for work process rationalization to minimize costs has resulted in a movement toward fewer but larger public hospitals. Thus, the number of public hospitals decreased from 76 in 1998 to 52 in 2004.[5] These 52 hospitals had an average size of 320 beds in 2004, the average in 1998 being around 255.

In this connection, specific hospital departments have become more autonomous, and most hospitals are trying to implement a form of accelerated patient progress. As mentioned previously, from 1995 to 2004 the total number of beds related to somatic diseases decreased by about 15 percent, although the number of discharges rose by 12 percent during the period (see table 6.3). This has been accomplished by reducing the average number of bed days. Furthermore, some surgery that used to require hospitalization is now often done in same-day surgery.

CASE STUDY FINDINGS

In this section presenting the findings of our case study research, our focus is on highlighting the job situation of the two target occupations as well as the changes they are experiencing. In the cleaning function, the primary change is from unskilled to skilled labor. In the other occupation, nursing assistant, the change is one of overall transition.

The Nature of Jobs: Cleaning and Basic Caregiving

Cleaning   Depending on the hospital, cleaning tasks are performed by one of two vocational groups, cleaners or hospital service assistants.

A hospital service assistant's job consists of carrying out tasks such as general hospital cleaning, shifting and making beds, linen service, replenishing products, cooking meals, serving meals, moving patients, and maintaining patients' personal hygiene. In hospitals where hospital service assistants perform tasks closely related to those of the nursing assistants, the hospital service assistants do not have the full responsibility. At the hospitals where the cleaning function has not been expanded to include service functions, cleaners merely clean. Both employee groups perceive their job as physically demanding, despite the fact that the hospitals do have the necessary cleaning aids.

At some hospitals, hospital service assistants and cleaners do work on a rotation scheme according to a prespecified schedule. Employees who perform an integrated service function feel that they often are interrupted in their daily work routines because they have to lend a hand in various service functions, either as a result of a strategic choice or simply due to scarce resources. Such interruptions are perceived as very stressful.

Hospital service assistants generally work from 6:30 AM to 7:00 PM, in two shifts. In addition, former porters often perform twenty-four-hour guard duty. The majority of hospital service assistants work full-time, a proportion similar to findings from the American study.

Compared to hospital service assistants, cleaning assistants have a more restricted job function because basically they only clean. Since cleaning is not that visible to the rest of the organization—except when it is not done—cleaning assistants find it difficult to earn a status vis-à-vis the other hospital work groups. At the hospitals that have decided not to integrate the functions of cleaning, food service, and hospital porters, the cleaning assistants did not get the chance to qualify as hospital service assistants. Most of the cleaning assistants at these hospitals want to take the course because passing it gives them greater self-confidence and actually becoming a hospital service assistant brings them higher status.

Basic Caregiving   The Danish hospital sector employs two types of nursing assistants: sygehjaelper, who are low-qualified nursing assistants (hereafter "nursing assistants [LQ]") with pre-1992 training; and social- og sundhedsassistent, who are highly qualified nursing assistants (hereafter "nursing assistants [HQ]") with a post-1992 education.

After 1992, when the current education was launched, the Danish hospital sector experienced a huge reeducation process: many nursing assistants (LQ) underwent a vocational training program in order to qualify for the new certification as nursing assistants (HQ). Most nursing assistants under age fifty were "encouraged" to enter the vocational training program, and it is now no longer possible to get a hospital job with the old certification. Nursing assistants (LQ) who do not enter the vocational training program now have the choice of either staying in their current position or moving to the municipality care sector.

The basic tasks of the nursing assistants are the same for both groups: nursing patients, monitoring them, and serving them meals.

Nursing assistants (HQ) may also, however, perform some administrative tasks, go on rounds, and fill out the patients' case sheets. In addition, at some hospitals they perform tasks related to nutrition, admission and discharge interviews, and liaison with the municipality. They are allowed to dispense nonprescription medicine. On some wards, nursing assistants (HQ) have been educated and certified in dispensing prescription medicine as well. High-seniority nursing assistants (HQ) also undertake teaching responsibilities and train nursing students.

The work of nursing assistants resembles that of nurses, but they do not have patient responsibility. Nurses tend to get involved in administrative tasks, leaving the care of the patients in the hands of nursing assistants.

Work scheduling is typically delegated to the head nurse and planned in cooperation with nurses and doctors at team meetings. Nurse assistants are involved in the planning of work tasks, but there are still some fixed routines in the daily work tasks. The work tasks are performed both alone and in cooperation with others. Nursing assistants work in teams with nurses, doctors, physiotherapists, and other hospital personnel.

Nursing assistants (LQ) who have not gone through the vocational training program are not as involved in the task slide from doctors and nurses as the nursing assistants (HQ). At the case study hospitals, we found that the supplementary training is usually offered only to the nursing assistants (HQ). Those who have chosen to remain nursing assistants (LQ) have thus done so at a price. All future educational and developmental initiatives for this target group will be aimed at the nursing assistants (HQ); the nursing assistants (LQ) can either remain in their position on the ward, performing their current duties until they retire, or transfer to the municipality sector. Our interviews with nursing assistants (LQ) revealed that they are satisfied with performing their usual duties and not being part of the task slide.

QUALIFICATIONS

Cleaning   Traditionally, cleaners at Danish hospitals have no formal qualifications, although they must attend a course when they begin a hospital job. The introduction of the hospital service assistant concept is an attempt to heighten the skills of some of the vocational service staff groups at Danish hospitals.

Hospital service assistants may qualify in three different ways. The first is to attend a seventeen-week course covering various elements of the service function, but this option is not that common anymore, as it was a forerunner of the two other options. The second option is to take two years of supplementary training at a vocational school, and the third option (available only to individuals age twenty-five or older who have at least two years of relevant work experience) is one year of supplementary training. The one- and two-year educations combine training and work experience.

While attending a training course, a worker under the age of twenty-five gets a grant from the State Education Grant and Loan Scheme (see chapter 2) amounting to €633 (US$865.53) per month. When the worker goes on to practical training under supervision, the wage increases to €917 (US$1,253.90) per month for workers under eighteen and €1,176 (US$1608.05) per month the first year and €1,252 (US$1,711.78) the second year for workers age eighteen and older.

If a worker instead starts with practical experience—for instance, if she already has a trainee agreement—she will not receive the SU grant but instead is remunerated as a trainee throughout the whole course. For workers age twenty-five and older, the wage is €2,204 (US$3,013.39) per month. This is slightly less than the basic wage of a hospital service assistant (€2,230 [US$3,048.94]). If the trainee is already employed as a cleaner at a hospital, she will receive her usual wage.

In March 2005, 1,187 individuals who took the seventeen-week course were employed as hospital service assistants, contributing to a 74 percent increase in the number of hospital service assistants since 1998. In the same period, the number of cleaning staff and hospital porters decreased by 19 percent and 25 percent, respectively. Some of the decrease clearly resulted from the new job category and training. This conclusion is also based on the fact that the cleaners employed today are mainly middle-aged women who, when they retire, will be replaced by trained hospital service assistants. The number of male cleaners used to be limited, but the proportion of men in this occupation seems to be on the rise since the introduction of the hospital service assistant concept (Wiegman, Hjort, and Hvenegaard 2005).

The economic incentives for taking the training course are rather small for high-seniority cleaning staff, as they will receive only a minor wage increase. Hospital porters usually get a wage increase only if it has been negotiated locally. One advantage for cleaners in becoming hospital service assistants is that they get their lunch break paid, which is not the case for traditional cleaners, who are covered by a different agreement.

Besides the small economic gains obtained from attending the course, the education also qualifies as nursing assistant training, but almost nobody does that yet.

A manager from one of the case hospitals said that even though the hospital service assistant course is not compulsory, the hospital management does encourage cleaners to attend it. The reason is not to help them do a better job, but rather to give them more self-confidence, which has been shown to be a common result of receiving a diploma proving one's qualifications.

Basic Caregiving   The education as a nursing assistant (HQ) takes thirty-four months, of which a minimum of fifty-six weeks is theoretical study. The student spends the rest of the time as a trainee at a hospital. The curriculum includes health care and nursing-related courses, medical, social, psychology, and pedagogy courses, as well as Danish, English, and natural sciences courses. The education involves examinations for the theoretical part and mandatory evaluations of the time spent as a trainee.

After fourteen months, the students may leave the program with vocational basic caregiving qualifications. These qualifications do not give students access to a hospital job, but they can, for instance, take a job at a nursing home. The students get paid during their education. For a person age eighteen or older, the salary is €1,160 (US$1,586.10) a month the first year and €1,240 (US$1,695.49) a month the following years.

Nursing assistants (LQ) who have a pre-1992 education can obtain the new certification (HQ) by attending a one-year vocational training program consisting of six months of theoretical education and six months of vocational training. As is the case for the thirty-four-month program, the vocational program includes exams. It is also possible for someone with a different basic vocational education within health care to be reeducated as a nursing assistant (HQ). The length of the training required depends on one's previous education.

Nursing assistants (HQ) who decide to become nurses may receive credit for their work experience as part of their nursing education. However, Danish nursing assistants (HQ) rarely want to study to become nurses, unlike American nursing assistants, many of whom hope to get into higher-paying nursing jobs with additional formal education. Danish nursing assistants' lack of interest in becoming nurses is mainly due to the fact that one must have a high school diploma to register to become a nurse, and nursing assistants rarely have such a diploma.

Nursing assistants said in our interviews that they have opportunities to choose courses they find interesting as long as the courses are relevant to the work function. These courses are paid by the employer and subsidized by the county for up to 20 percent of the cost.

The head nurse consults with each of the nursing assistants about their personal and professional development. However, structured training programs for nursing assistants (HQ) are not that common. Supplementary training is still important as nursing assistants become more flexible and can handle more functions. Hospitals are not very willing, however, to allow them to take other courses of interest that are not directly related to the work function.

EMPLOYMENT IN THE DANISH HEALTH CARE SECTOR

Table 6.7 shows that the number of doctors and nurses has grown continuously over the time span. The increase in health care expenditure seems to have benefited these two occupational groups the most. The number of nursing assistants was on the rise until 2002, but by 2004 it had fallen to a level below that of 2000, as table 6.7 indicates.

The group labeled "other" that includes cleaners and hospital service assistants has decreased in size continuously over the time span. The redundant employees from these groups have moved into other parts of the public sector or into low-skilled jobs in the private sector, and they therefore do not add to the unemployment rate.

The number of full-time equivalent employees in the Danish somatic hospital sector increased by 1.9 percent from 2000 to 2004, as table 6.7 indicates.

Looking at developments in employment for the two groups of nursing assistants, we see that the nursing assistants (HQ) are indeed taking over the jobs of the nursing assistants (LQ). The number of nursing assistants (HQ) increased by 54 percent from 2000 to 2004, and the number of nursing assistants (LQ) decreased by 43 percent, in large part because nursing assistants (LQ) either retired or moved

Table 6.7 Employment in the Somatic Hospital Sector in Denmark

	Full-Time Equivalent Employees					Increase in Employment
	2000	2001	2002	2003	2004	
Doctors	9,161	9,325	9,584	9,830	10,163	10.9%
Nurses	25,834	26,196	26,549	26,653	27,271	5.6
Other nursing	9,577	9,588	9,902	9,663	9,135	-4.6
Other health care staff	14,296	14,335	14,606	14,678	14,873	4.0
Administration	2,418	2,533	2,658	2,661	2,605	7.7
Other	13,180	12,773	12,487	12,276	11,871	-9.9
Total	74,466	74,750	75,786	75,761	75,918	1.9

Source: National Board of Health (2006).
Note: Nursing assistants are included in "other nursing"; cleaners and hospital service assistants are included in "other."

to the municipal care sector. In 2004 there were 5,158 full-time-equivalent nursing assistants (HQ) and 3,011 nursing assistants (LQ).

The picture is the same when we look at the change in cleaners' jobs, which were down by 30 percent from 2000 to 2004. They have also been affected by the emergence of a new occupational group: the number of hospital service assistants who had completed the seventeen-week training course rose by 74 percent from 1998 to 2005. The large relative fall in employment for cleaners from 2000 to 2004 is mostly due to successive cutbacks in the cleaning function at Danish hospitals and has little to do with outsourcing of cleaning services, according to the case study hospitals.

OCCUPATIONAL AND DEMOGRAPHIC CHARACTERISTICS

The majority of hospital employees are skilled, and nearly 80 percent of this workforce has some health-related training. Moreover, the average skill level has increased for both men and women over the last ten years. Doctors are still typically men (although this is changing because many women are now studying to become doctors), and nurses and nurse assistants are typically women. The average skill level for men is therefore somewhat higher than that for women. On average, the total years of schooling for men is 14.6 and 13.9 for women. Women's skill levels, however, have increased more than men's, and that difference obviously has narrowed the gender gap.

The occupations of low-wage workers are distributed as shown in table 6.8. From this table it is evident that hospital cleaners and kitchen hands make up the highest proportion of low-wage workers in the two target groups.

According to the table, most of the cleaners and nursing assistants can hardly be considered low-wage workers. Some of the low-wage work in the target occupations is in positions filled by students, but there is low-wage work in these occupations even when students are exempted.

The hospital sector has generally experienced a large increase in the average age of the workforce. In 1986 the average age was thirty-three, but that had increased to forty by 1999; the majority of those employed in the target groups were age forty or older. A consequence

Table 6.8 Low-Wage Workers in the Hospital Target Groups, 2003

Occupation	Low-Wage Employment Including Students	Low-Wage Employment Excluding Students
Nursing assistants	2.53%	2.25%
Cleaning and kitchen hands	12.37	11.72

Source: Statistics Denmark and Center for Corporate Performance (CCP) data.
Note: The percentage is calculated as the number of low-wage workers within each occupational group divided by the total number of workers within the occupational group.

of this increase in average age has been higher wages, owing to seniority wages. Therefore, Danish hospital services have become more expensive because the experience element in wages is not fully reflected in higher productivity.

WORKING HOURS

In Denmark the length of the workweek is determined during the general wage bargaining between trade unions and the Employers' Federation. The normal hours have gradually been reduced as a consequence of union pressure and the general increase in welfare; the workweek is now thirty-seven hours, and recently vacation time was increased from five to six weeks (see chapter 2).

For the target groups in the hospital sector, however, a thirty-seven-hour week is not the most prevalent form of employment. For instance, a majority of the nursing assistants are not employed full-time but slightly less (as mentioned earlier, a thirty-two-hour week is very common), because, according to most of the case study hospitals, a shorter workweek makes scheduling easier on the wards. This is different from the findings in the American study, which showed that about 80 percent of nursing assistants work full-time.

The advantage of using part-time workers, as put forward by the managers for the target groups, is that more employees are available to fill absences due to illness and vacation. Moreover, weekend duties can be split among more workers. The disadvantage, however, is a discontinuity in work performance.

At most hospitals, the workers can decide whether they want to be employed full-time or part-time. The contracted number of work hours is often age- and gender-specific: usually men want to work full-time, whereas young women with children want to work part-time.

At some hospitals, the target groups work in rather fixed schedules—for example, day-evening or day-night—in order to decrease the discomfort of shifting duties. At other hospitals, the work schedule is more varied and workers sign up for their preferred duty. This enables workers to participate in fixed leisure activities. Weekends are normally equally distributed according to a fixed pattern.

FLEXIBILITY AND JOB MOBILITY

According to table 6.9, mobility between hospitals is fairly low for the target occupations: only 5 percent changed hospital employer from 2001 to 2002, and only 7 percent from 2002 to 2003. Table 6.10 shows that 42 percent of those who entered the hospital sector in the target groups were health and social workers in their previous occupation, and as many as 82 percent of those who took jobs outside the hospital sector entered some kind of health and social work.

Table 6.11 presents the number of low-wage workers who are members of an unemployment fund. As the figures indicate, most workers are full-time insured.

Apart from the unemployment system, Denmark has a fine-meshed welfare safety net. This probably affects individuals' job searches and their sense of security when they change jobs or become unemployed. The Danish welfare state also affects firms' decisions about layoffs and other staff issues. All in all, the Danish labor mar-

Table 6.9 Number of Workers in Target Groups Changing Hospital Workplaces, 2001 to 2002 and 2002 to 2003

	2001 to 2002		2002 to 2003	
	Number	Percentage	Number	Percentage
Workers (excluding students) who moved from one hospital to another	705	5	992	7
Student-workers who moved from one hospital to another	68	26	101	34

Source: Statistics Denmark and Center for Corporate Performance (CCP) data.

Table 6.10 Industries in Which Workers in the Target Groups Changed Jobs, 2001 to 2002 and 2002 to 2003

	Health and Social Work		Other		Total	
	Number	Percentage	Number	Percentage	Number	Percentage
Industry that workers came from (2001 to 2002)[a]	247	42	341	58	588[a]	100
Industry that workers went to (2002 to 2003)[a]	702	82	149	18	851	100

Source: Statistics Denmark and Center for Corporate Performance (CCP) data.
[a] Excluding students.

Table 6.11 Unemployment Fund Status for Target Groups, 2003

	Workers Excluding Students		Students	
	Low-Wage	Non-Low-Wage	Low-Wage	Non-Low-Wage
Full-time insured	83.3%	91.1%	19.1%	16.7%
Not insured, weekly working time more than thirty hours	8.9	4.7	2.1	3.0
Part-time insured	1.5	1.9	n.a.	n.a.
Not insured, weekly working time between twenty and twenty-nine hours	1.4	0.7	n.a.	n.a.
Not insured, weekly working time between ten and nineteen hours	1.6	0.8	27.7	14.1
Not insured, weekly working time between zero and nine hours	1.8	0.4	44.7	63.2
Unknown	1.5	0.2	6.4	3.0
Total number	732	18,079	94	234

Source: Statistics Denmark and Center for Corporate Performance (CCP) data.

ket has very high job mobility and high mobility with respect to wages (see chapter 2 for further detail).

Finally, it should be mentioned that the income tax in Denmark is high for everybody; the lowest marginal tax bracket is about 38 percent, although taxpayers at this level are granted a tax-free allowance of €5,066 (US$6,926.38) (see chapter 2). Thus, for the target groups with an annual income of €28,000 (US$38,282.41), the tax is €8,715 (US$11,915.22), which leaves the employee with €19,285 (US$26.366.62), or 69 percent of earned income. When comparing this amount with incomes in other countries like the United States, it is important to add that rental housing is subsidized for low-income families, most medical services are free, and the educational system is free for everybody.

OUTSOURCING AND INTERNAL AND EXTERNAL AGENCY

CLEANING

None of the case hospitals are planning to outsource the hospital service assistant function or the cleaning function; instead, they see the advantages of keeping these functions in-house: higher flexibility, stability, and quality. In line with the concept of combining cleaning, housemaid, and porter functions into one service function, the jobs now require more multiskilling, and therefore replacing internal employees with external employees becomes more difficult. The hospitals do not use external temporary employment agencies. Instead, they employ an internal agency consisting of employees with non-fixed working hours who are either permanently part-time workers or students. Hospitals use these workers to fill in for regular staff taking time off for sickness or education. Some hospitals even have a permanent internal agency pool consisting of two or three full-time employees who are sent to work in the departments with the fewest resources.

Patient satisfaction is another reason for not outsourcing the hospital service assistant function. A manager in one of the case hospitals stated that the hospital service assistants often contribute to the satisfaction of patients, since they are the ones with the closest contact with the patients.

Basic Caregiving

None of the hospitals that took part in this study outsource the nursing assistant function or plan to do so in the future. Nor do they use external temporary employment agencies on a regular basis, but only in extreme circumstances.

Instead, they call in regular employees to do more shifts, or they draw on nursing assistants from other wards. Most of the hospitals have their own internal agency that covers vacant shifts. In addition to the internal agency, there are part-time workers employed on the individual wards who sometimes are willing to take extra shifts.

JOB SATISFACTION, TURNOVER, AND ABSENTEEISM

Cleaners

This target group is characterized by a high degree of job satisfaction, regardless of whether the hospital has integrated the service function or not. According to the workers we interviewed, their job satisfaction is a result of good cooperation and comradeship among coworkers. At the hospitals that have integrated the service function, the workers get more respect from other work groups and in general have gained a higher reputation in the organization. Both cleaners and hospital service assistants reported a high level of job satisfaction, and no difference between the two groups is discernible.

All workers experience this job as highly stressful. Workers who perform both cleaning and servicing indicated that the job has become more stressful since the restructuring: they perform the same cleaning tasks as before, but now they also carry out service functions. They said that they do not have enough time to get all the different tasks done and so must not only prioritize them but also learn not to take home unfinished tasks in their minds. The stress is also explained by the fact that the service assistants are interrupted in their cleaning work when, for example, they have to assist with patients. Furthermore, the hospital service assistants emphasize that this may be the cause of hygienic problems, as they leave an unhygienic cleaning task behind in order to perform a caregiving function. As hospital service assistants, they must be more service-minded, which requires a more complex job performance. Since both those who have an integrated function and those who only clean perceive their job as stressful, we conclude that the stress stems more from the general time pressure that the target group faces than from the restructuring itself.

Those workers who perform an integrated function do not seem to want to go back to only cleaning tasks. They emphasize that they meet and talk to more people because they get around more—for example, when they are moving patients—and they also like being in contact with patients. In addition to having more varied job functions, they also have more freedom to prioritize and plan their own tasks.

The target group's level of absenteeism varies across hospitals (4 to 9 percent), but no hospital reported a remarkably higher level compared to other groups of employees. All hospitals have an absence policy that includes, among other things, interviewing the worker in question when he or she has had either many absence spells or long absence spells. Absenteeism is mainly caused by employees becoming fatigued. One of the high-productivity case hospitals was able to reduce absenteeism from 7 to 4 percent in one year by implementing an absence policy that involved holding conferences with long-term absentees and focusing on developing the target group's competencies. Apart from this example, there does not appear to be any relation between hospital productivity or hospital size and the level of absenteeism.

All of the case hospitals have a very low turnover in the target group. This might be explained by the generally high job satisfaction, but a relatively high wage compared to other cleaning jobs could also reduce turnover. Moreover, working at a hospital is more prestigious than working at other places. All of the hospitals reported that the work conditions and the advantages of working at a hospital—such as more status—make it is very easy to recruit workers for cleaning and service functions. Some hospitals even have a job waiting list.

BASIC CAREGIVERS

This target group is also characterized by a high degree of job satisfaction. According to the workers in the focus groups, nursing assistants have good working relationships with their colleagues, including nurses. Furthermore, nursing assistants generally find their job interesting and prestigious.

Nursing assistants' level of absenteeism varies across the hospitals, but for all hospitals the level of absence reported is similar to that for cleaners and hospital service assistants. For all the hospitals, absenteeism is mainly explained by fatigue, although stress is also a factor.

Turnover is low for nursing assistants, and it is generally easy to recruit them. Nursing assistants can also find employment in the municipality sector quite easily—at a nursing home, for instance—but the general finding from the case studies is that nursing assistants prefer to be employed at a hospital, primarily because the tasks are perceived as more challenging and because hospital work is more prestigious.

Although the level of absenteeism varies quite a lot across hospitals and wards, most of the hospitals work to reduce absences in a very structured manner. Conducting structured job satisfaction surveys is very common; hospitals also conduct conferences with both employees who have had many recent absence periods and employees who have a long-term absence problem.

One of the case hospitals has just embarked on a new program to reduce the level of absence related to fatigue. It conducted training in lifting technique and now employs a therapist at the department so that employees can get any physical problems attended to before they turn into a cause for a period of work-related absence. If an employee has a problem requiring physiotherapy, he or she can see the therapist and get the problem attended to during working hours. In this way the hospital believes that it can prevent some absences by treating employees' ailments before they become serious enough to cause absence.

CURRENT DEVELOPMENTS AND TRENDS IN CLEANING AND BASIC CAREGIVING

For quite some time now, the Danish hospital sector has been suffering from a shortage of doctors. The increase in demand for this vocational group, as shown in table 6.7, along with an insufficient supply of newly graduated doctors, has led to recruitment problems for many hospitals; in December 2006, according to the National Board of Health, there were 2,789 vacant doctor positions at Danish hospitals—or the equivalent of more than 20 percent of the total number of doctor positions in Denmark.

The insufficient supply of newly graduated doctors is due to a low intake of medical students at Danish universities. Medical education is highly popular, and the universities have to turn down many of those applying for it. It would therefore be possible to increase the number of students significantly if the universities could persuade the government to fund the expansion of programs in medical education.

Meanwhile, hospitals are adopting two strategies to overcome the shortage of doctors. First, doctors are increasingly being recruited from other countries—primarily from European countries but also from outside Europe, including refugees with a medical degree (who receive intensive language training before they are allowed to treat patients).

Second, a doctor-to-nurse task slide has been taking place for quite some time. This strategy has probably had a more significant impact on Denmark's ability to cope with the number of vacant doctor positions than the recruitment of foreign doctors. This task slide is also one of the reasons why the number of nurses has been growing, as shown in table 6.7. It is primarily administrative tasks that nurses are taking over from doctors. This change in responsibilities is slowly changing the nature of the nursing position: from the case studies we find that the change comes at the expense of close contact with patients, which is not only nurses' area of greatest expertise but also the primary reason most of them become nurses in the first place. So the added responsibility comes at a price.

The strategy of encouraging a task slide from doctors to nurses is not a panacea for the doctor shortage, however, since currently there is a shortage of nurses as well. Again, the most important strategy has been to slide tasks from nurses to nursing assistants, since the strategy of hiring foreign nurses simply cannot fill the vacancies. Some foreign nurses have been able to obtain certification to work in Danish hospitals, but between the late 1990s and 2001 hospitals were able to hire only around one hundred of them per year, and more than half of these were from the Nordic countries (National Board of Health 2006).

A wide variety of tasks slide from nurses to nursing assistants. At some of the case study hospitals, nursing assistants have received additional training to enable them to hand out prescription drugs, perform catheterization, and handle other nursing-related duties such as doing rounds with the doctors. The additional training is needed because these tasks are not a part of their basic education.

The task slide does not end at the nursing assistant position. Some tasks are also sliding from nursing assistants to hospital service assistants. At some hospitals, the hospital service assistants have taken over some of the routine nursing assistant tasks, such as replenishing supplies and handing out food to patients.

The Cleaning Function: From Unskilled to Skilled Labor

As previously indicated, the number of hospital service assistants is increasing, and this vocational concept has been implemented very differently in the Danish hospital sector.

Traditionally, Danish hospital cleaners have belonged organizationally to a centralized service department, which took care of all hospital cleaning and where middle managers assigned cleaners to specific wards on a more or less permanent basis. Cleaners have therefore closely identified with the service department, not the wards, and have felt a stronger sense of association with the other cleaners than with the health care workers on the wards where they work.

One of the highly productive hospitals has taken a different approach to the implementation of the hospital service assistant concept. Hospital service assistants are no longer employed by the service department but are assigned to specific wards and report to the head nurse. They take part in the work shifts alongside nursing assistants and nurses, which creates a new identity for these employees. Hospital service assistants at this hospital now see themselves as part of the health care staff instead of employees who merely provide services to health care workers. As a consequence, these hospital service assistants perceive their job function as more important, since they can see their own contribution to the care of the patients. Being able to see themselves as taking part in running the department gives the hospital service assistants generally higher self-esteem. One drawback, however, is that the different occupational backgrounds of those they work with, including their managers, often make the hospital service assistants feel they are in the minority; they also miss the contact with other service assistants. This finding is in accordance with the findings from the American study. Being affiliated with a certain ward, however, helps hospital service assistants to feel a greater responsibility for the general running of the ward.

It is not possible to trace any difference in present job satisfaction between hospital service assistants who work on the wards and those who work in centralized departments.

Some of the cleaners at these hospitals who have undergone training are disappointed that the hospital has been unable or unwilling to exploit their new competencies. After the training program, they returned to their old cleaning job.

Whether the cleaning function is centralized or decentralized at their hospital, all hospital service assistants are organized in work teams. If they are employed in a medical department, they enter the schedule with nursing assistants and nurses; if they are employed in a central unit, they are grouped with other hospital service assistants. There is a high degree of autonomy in the individual teams regarding job performance. The teams follow an overall work schedule, often described by the number of minutes allocated to tasks, but plan their daily work ad hoc.

Although, as mentioned earlier, the implementation of the hospital service assistant concept has been problematic, at some hospitals it is the general perception that this concept will become even more prevalent in the future. The hospitals see the use of hospital service assistants as a way to increase the quality of the service provided to patients and relatives while reducing costs. They also acknowledge that this concept could not have been so widely implemented without the active cooperation of the union, which sees it as a way to prevent future outsourcing initiatives.

According to the case hospitals, not only is the line between what nursing assistants do and what service assistants do fuzzy, but this line has moved. Some service assistants now answer patient calls, something they would not have done earlier. Some nursing assistants also fill the dishwasher and transport patients. At the high-productivity hospital where service assistants are assigned to a specific department, the manager believed that this blurring of responsibilities may have happened as a result of employees now identifying with the department to which they have been assigned, which gives them a higher sense of responsibility for the operation of the department.

Furthermore, one of the case hospitals has dealt with the shortage of doctors by having hospital service assistants take over some of the nurse and nursing assistant tasks, such as assisting doctors at operations by suctioning blood, holding legs, and so on.

NURSING ASSISTANT: A POSITION IN TRANSITION?

The task slide from nurses to nursing assistants has also been documented in another study. A recent investigation conducted by the

Danish Union of Public Employees (FOA) shows that more than 50 percent of nursing assistants report that they go on rounds and that more than two out of three hand out drugs. The investigation also shows, however, that many nursing assistants work with nurses who prevent them from taking over some of the tasks they have been trained for, such as going on rounds, making pharmacy orders, and handing out nonprescription drugs. These nursing assistants report that they are not a part of a defined strategy for fighting the shortage of doctors through task-sliding (Birkemose 2007).

The advantages of having nursing assistants take over some of the nurses' tasks are numerous. It reduces the general shortage of workers in the hospital sector because the training of nursing assistants is shorter; also, patient waiting lists are reduced because patients can be treated sooner. Additionally, this task slide gives nursing assistants a generally better work environment in that it promotes better relationships with nurses and other employee groups and gives them more interesting and varied job functions. And finally, the task slide from nurses to nursing assistants helps hospitals retain nursing assistants.

This last advantage is particularly important considering that in spite of the task slide from nurses to nursing assistants, the total number of nursing assistants in the Danish hospital sector has been declining since 2002. The decrease in the number of nursing assistants (LQ) does not fully correspond to the increase in nursing assistants (HQ), as indicated previously. Thus, there has been a net reduction in the total number of nursing assistants.

Some of the "vanishing" positions may have been filled by nurses, as mentioned in one instance by nursing assistants who participated in the study. Recently one of their colleagues had retired, and the hospital hired a nurse instead of another nursing assistant. At another hospital, a vacant nursing assistant position had been filled with a service assistant. The small difference in pay between nurses and nursing assistants also has an effect, according to one of the head nurses we interviewed. Nursing assistants (HQ) are in pay brackets 18 to 24, and the nurses are in brackets 22 to 31. This means that a nursing assistant (HQ) receives a basic hourly wage of between €15.40 and €16.80 (US$21.05 and US$22.97), depending on experience, and nurses receive a basic hourly wage of between €16.30 and €18.90 (US$22.29 and US$25.84). Since most of the nursing assistants (HQ) leaving a given ward are high-tenured and thus in the highest pay bracket, it is actually cheaper for a hospital to hire a young nurse to replace an older nursing assistant (HQ).

The primary catalyst for the decline in nursing assistants, however, is probably the trend toward fewer bed days for many treatments. Care has become more complex owing to an increasing technification of treatments and equipment. The average number of bed days for a stroke patient, for instance, has gone down by more than 50 percent over the last ten years. As mentioned previously, the average number of hospitalization days declined from 6.2 in 1995 to 4.7 in 2004 for somatic diseases (see table 6.3). This decrease in bed days, combined with the decreasing number of beds, is probably the reason why the total number of nursing assistants has gone down since 2002.

Since the number of nurses has been increasing in this period, the proportion of nurses has gone up. According to some of the interviewed nurses in managerial positions, the higher proportion of nurses gives hospitals greater flexibility in their scheduling, and it becomes easier to plan, for instance, night shifts that require a nurse on duty. These nurses also felt that a number of the tasks performed by nurses cannot be taken over by nursing assistants (HQ), but this is not problematic with a higher proportion of nurses on staff.

Previous research has shown that there are other advantages of a higher proportion of nurses. When nurses perform basic caregiving tasks, they are able to monitor patients and pick up on conditions that require medical attention (Preuss 2003), leading to higher care quality. Nursing assistants are unable to do this to the same extent as nurses. This research was conducted in the United States and may not be directly transferable to the Danish health care sector, since the skill levels of nursing assistants in the United States and Denmark are different. The level of formal education is higher for nursing assistants in Denmark, which probably limits the effect of substituting nursing assistants for nurses.

The finding of the American study is actually in accordance with the experience of one of the Danish head nurses who preferred having nursing assistants perform some of the doctors' administrative tasks instead of the nurses: nurses could thus spend more time with the patients, who would thus receive better care because, according to her, nurses have a better feel for the medical condition of the patients. In this respect, the task slide in this medical department is unique because the emphasis is on having nurses spend as much time monitoring patients as possible.

Most of the hospitals stated that the difference in the proportion of nurses on the individual wards has become larger in recent years because specialization on the wards has increased. The proportion of nursing assistants is relatively high in long-term care departments that take care of, for example, patients recovering from stroke, compared to wards that take care of patients with more complicated illnesses that require a higher degree of nursing competence. This phenomenon has not necessarily caused the total number of nursing assistants to decline but is simply a factor in the changes in the number of nursing assistants on the individual wards. This kind of specialization is found at all hospitals, but there appear to be differences in the extent to which it has been carried out.

Three of the highly productive hospitals, Holstebro, Herning, and Ringkøbing, stand out in this respect. At these three hospitals, the traditional hierarchical structure has been abolished in favor of a matrix organization in which a number of centers operate at all geographical sites. The medical center operates the medical function at these hospitals, and to a large extent it has been able to implement specialization on the various wards at the center. This has led to higher differences in the proportion of nursing assistants on the individual wards, with a high proportion on long-term care wards.

The employees at these hospitals appear to have a positive attitude toward the matrix structure, although the effect on their daily work has been limited. The possibility of knowledge sharing between the different geographical sites has primarily been relevant to doctors and nurses. It has not had a significant effect on the working conditions of nursing assistants or hospital service assistants. One reason for their positive attitude toward the matrix structure despite its negligible impact on their working conditions may be that they see it as a way of maintaining jobs at their geographical site.

Among the nursing tasks that nursing assistants have been taking over from nurses are handing out prescription drugs and performing catheterization. They need additional training to perform these tasks because they are not a part of their basic training, and this training appears to be an up-skilling in their jobs like the up-skilling occurring in relation to the hospital service assistants. There is one distinct difference, however, between the two occupational groups in this development in competencies.

Hospital service assistants are part of a highly structured development whose ultimate aim is to raise the competencies of an entire occupational group. This development enables them to take part in a task slide that, at some hospitals, has them taking over some of the routine nursing assistant tasks, such as replenishing supplies and handing out food. The cleaners at hospitals that have implemented the hospital service assistant concept are encouraged to reeducate themselves, and they receive extensive support from their employer.

The up-skilling of nursing assistants, however, is less structured at most of the hospitals. Most reeducation efforts are decided locally on the wards and are not part of an organization-wide reeducation initiative that includes all nursing assistants. In other words, reeducation is decided at the level of the individual nursing assistant, taking the actual work conditions on the ward into account. Some nursing assistants stated that they have no structured training possibilities, but this is not the case for all. Others stated that they have not attended any reeducation sessions in a long time, although they would like to; others who have had the chance to enhance their competencies stated that this did not change the tasks they perform in their daily work.

The up-skilling of nursing assistants is therefore a lot more varied than that of hospital service assistants. We might say that hospital service assistants are being trained for a completely different job, whereas nursing assistants are redefining their position as it evolves in the hospital setting.

Another difference in today's up-skilling of the two occupational groups is the role of the unions. The union has been very involved in occupational up-skilling initiatives for cleaners and hospital service assistants, but this has not been the case for the more incremental up-skilling of nursing assistants. The union may be involved to some extent at individual hospitals, but it has made no coordinated national effort to raise the competence level of nursing assistants as a whole, as it has done with the up-skilling of cleaners to hospital service assistants.

DISCUSSION AND CONCLUSIONS

In general, the Danish hospital sector is not a low-wage sector, and the incidence of low-wage work in it has declined over the years.

At all the case hospitals, average tenure is high for both target occupations, and there are no recruitment problems. There are several other job opportunities in the municipality or private sector for cleaners and nursing assistants, but being employed in the hospital sector is perceived by both occupational groups as more prestigious.

Both to increase efficiency and improve the quality of patient care, Danish hospitals have been focusing on upgrading the skills of both target occupations, as well as integrating the functions of cleaning, food service, and hospital porters into the new hospital service assistant occupation.

A general task slide is taking place among the different occupational groups involved in the treatment and care of patients, from doctors all the way to hospital service assistants. At some of the case study hospitals, the nursing assistants have received additional training to enable them to hand out prescription drugs, perform catheterization, and perform other nursing-related tasks such as doing rounds with the doctors. Hospital service assistants are taking over some of the routine nursing assistant tasks such as replenishing supplies and serving food to patients.

The number of nursing assistants has been declining since 2002, most likely because of the trend toward fewer bed days for many treatments. Another reason for that decline is that care has become more complex as a result of the increasing technification of treatments and equipment.

The highly productive hospitals seem to be more on the forefront in work organization than the less-productive hospitals. At one of the highly productive hospitals, the hospital service assistant concept was implemented in a new organizational setting (on the wards), and that change allowed this occupational group to develop a new identity consistent with their new job functions, which enabled them to work more extensively with nurses and nursing assistants. At the other three hospitals with relatively high productivity, the traditional hierarchical structure has been abolished in favor of a matrix organization that has led to specialization on the various wards.

One important difference between the two target occupations in the up-skilling of their jobs is that the initiatives directed toward the hospital service assistants have been highly structured, whereas the initiatives directed toward the nursing assistants have mostly been decided and conducted locally. In general, however, the up-skilling of the jobs of nursing assistants and hospital service assistants will enable hospitals to let even more tasks slide from doctors and nurses, and this is one way in which hospitals can overcome the shortage of doctors in a cost-efficient manner.

NOTES

1. The number of public-sector hospitals has been declining for many decades. According to the National Board of Health (2006), there were 154 hospitals in 1945, and the number has been steadily declining since then.
2. We chose medical departments because they are among the most comparable departments across hospitals and countries.
3. Using DEA, the authors estimated the cost-efficiency of seventy Danish hospitals, based on diagnosis-related groups (DRGs). Productivity was measured as total input according to this formula:

$$\text{Productivity} = \frac{\Sigma(\text{rate of the } j^{th} \text{ DRG}) \times (\text{discharges in } j^{th} \text{ DRG})}{\text{adjusted costs}}$$

   All hospitals in the study were ranked according to this ratio.
4. FOA is the third-largest trade union in Denmark, having organized 211,000 members, primarily in the public sector but also some privatized employees in the public sector. The United Federation of Danish Workers (3F) is Denmark's largest trade union: it has organized 362,000 members, both skilled and unskilled, in several sectors, including industry, building and construction, transport, cleaning, horticulture, agriculture, and forestry.
5. The decline in the number of hospitals has been going on for many decades. According to the National Board of Health, there were 154 hospitals in 1945 and the number has been steadily declining since then.

REFERENCES

Amtsraadsforeningen [Association of County Councils in Denmark]. 2001. "Fremtidens plejeprofil: Rapport fra udvalget vedrørende den fremtidige plejeprofil" ["Health Care profile of the Future: Report from the Committee on the Health Care Profile of the Future"]. Copenhagen: Amtsraadsforeningen.

Amtsraadsforeningen and DSI Dansk Institut for Sundhedsvaesen [Association of County Councils in Denmark and Danish Institute for Health Services Research]. 2002a. "Deskriptiv analyse af udvalgte nordeuropaeiske sundhedssystemer" ["Descriptive Analysis of Selected North European Health Systems"]. Copenhagen: Amtsraadsforeningen and DSI Dansk Institut for Sundhedsvaesen.

————. 2002b. "Fokus paa plejepersonalet" ["Focus on Nursing Staff"].

Amtsraadsforeningen and FOA [Association of County Councils in Denmark and FOA — Trade and Labor]. 2005a. "Overenskomst for sygehusportører samt arbejdstidsaftalen" ["Collective Agreement for Hospital Orderlies and Agreement on Working Hours"]. Copenhagen: Amtsraads-foreningen and FOA.

———. 2005b. "Overenskomst for social og sundhedspersonale samt arbe-jdstidsaftalen" ["Collective Agreement for Social and Health Service Staff and Agreement on Working Hours"]. Copenhagen: Amtsraadsforeningen and FOA.

Amtsraadsforeningen, FOA, HK/Kommunal, and Dansk Laegesekretaer-forening/HK [Association of County Councils in Denmark, FOA — Trade and Labor, HK/Kommunal — Union of Commercial and Clerical Em-ployees in Denmark/Municipal Division, and Danish Union of Medical Secretaries]. 2005. "Arbejdstidsaftale" [Agreement on Working Hours"]. Copenhagen: Amtsraadsforeningen, FOA, HK/Kommunal, and Dansk Laegesekretaerforening/HK.

Birkemose, Jan. 2007. "Personalefnidder koster sundhedsvaesenet dyrt" ["Health Care Services: Staff Bickering Costs"]. Ugebrevet A4(3, January 22).

Danish Union of Public Employees (FOA). 2005a. "Arbejdstidsbestemte saerydelser" ["Work Hour-Related Ad Hoc Disbursements"]. Copen-hagen: FOA.

———. 2005b. "Aarsløn" ["Yearly Salaries"] (2006). Copenhagen: FOA.

———. 2005c. "Aarsløn 1" ["Yearly Salaries 1"] (April 2005). Copenhagen: FOA.

———. 2005d. "Kost-service" ["Catering and Cleaning"]. Copenhagen: FOA.

———. 2005e. "Social og sundhed" ["Social and Health"]. Copenhagen: FOA.

Indenrigs og Sundhedsministeriet [Ministry of the Interior and Health]. 2006. "Sundhedssektoren i tal" ["The Danish Health Sector in Figures (January and June)"]. Copenhagen: Indenrigs og Sundhedsministeriet.

Johansson, Edvard, and Nicolai Kristensen. 2006. "New Evidence on Cross-Country Differences in Job Satisfaction Using Anchoring Vignettes." Working paper 06-1. Aarhus, Denmark: Aarhus School of Business, De-partment of Economics.

Juel, Knud, Jan Sørensen, and Henrik Brønnum-Hansen. 2006. Risikofak-torer og folkesundhed i Danmark. Copenhagen: National Institute of Pub-lic Health.

Ministry of the Interior and Health. 2003. Health Care in Denmark. Copen-hagen: Ministry of the Interior and Health.

National Board of Health. 2006. Health Care Statistics Database. Copen-hagen: National Board of Health.

Nolte, Ellen, and Martin McKee. 2003. "Measuring the Health of Nations: Analysis of Mortality Amenable to Health Care." British Medical Journal 327 (7424): 1129–33.

Olesen, Ole B. 2004. "Anvendelse af data envelopment analysis til produk-tivitetsevaluering af danske sygehuse for perioden 2000–2002" ["The Use of Data Envelopment Analysis for Productivity Assessment of Danish Hospitals, 2000-2002"]. Odense, Denmark: University of Southern Denmark.

Olesen, Ole B., and Niels C. Petersen. 2002. "The Use of Data Envelopment Analysis with Probabilistic Assurance Regions for Measuring Hospital Efficiency." *Journal of Productivity Analysis* 17 (1-2): 83–109.

Organization for Economic Cooperation and Development (OECD). 2006. *OECD Health Data.* Paris: OECD.

Portal om EU og Arbejdsmarkedet [Portal on EU and the Labor Market]. 2002. "Pensionsalder i EU-lande og ansøgerlande" ["Pensionable Age in EU Countries and Applicant Countries"]. Accessed at http://www .eu-arbejdsmarked.dk/eu_arbejdsmarked/artikel.html?id=2506#4.

Preuss, Gil L. 2003. "High Performance Work Systems and Organizational Outcomes: The Mediating Role of Information Quality." *Industrial and Labor Relations Review* 56(4): 590–605.

Søgaard, Jes. 2006. "Lav udgiftsvaekst i dansk sundhedssektor sammen-lignet med den øvrige vestlige verden" ["Slow Growth in Expenses in the Danish Health Care Sector Compared to the Rest of the Western World"]. *Tidsskrift for dansk sundhedsvaesen* 81.

Wiegman, Inger-Marie, Signe Roderick Hjort, and Hans Hvenegaard. 2005. "Serviceassistenter: Fremtiden ligger forude—en analyse for køkken og rengøringssektoren teamarbejdsliv" ["Service Assistants: The Future Lies Ahead—An Analysis of the Catering Sector]". Copenhagen: TeamArbejdsliv.

World Health Organization. 2006. *Working Together for Health: The World Health Report.* Geneva: World Health Organization.

CHAPTER 7

Pay and Job Quality in Danish Call Centers

Ole Henning Sørensen

The "call center" as an organizational principle is becoming the primary vehicle for customer interaction. As in the United States and several other countries, including the United Kingdom, the Netherlands, and Germany, call center work has been among the fastest-growing types of employment in the Danish economy since the late 1990s. In 2004 there were an estimated 300 and 400 call centers in Denmark. Approximately 25 percent of these were subcontractors concentrating on selling call center services. Between 20,000 and 25,000 people are employed in Danish call centers, or around 1 percent of the total Danish workforce (Sørensen and El-Salanti 2005).

Historically, service provision has been personal and service labor markets local in certain sectors such as banking and retail. Other sectors, however, such as telecommunications and travel, were using telephone-mediated services long before call centers took off as a dominant model for customer service. Other kinds of companies and sectors, such as utility providers and some publicly owned companies, have had a low orientation toward service, and customer service has generally been much less emphasized in Denmark than in the United States—probably owing to the less competitive market situation (Huber and Stephens 2001)—for both publicly and privately owned companies. In Denmark the increased use of call centers as an organizational principle represents not simply a transformation of traditional meaningful jobs based on local, personal service but the creation of new customer services. These are accompanied by new job functions that are central to Danish companies' aims to survive in an atmosphere of increasingly service-oriented competition and in some cases increasingly deregulated markets. Another difference between Denmark and the United States is size: the greater physical distances in the United States, together with lower telecommunication prices, have made the use of telephone-based customer services much more common there.

According to Rosemary Batt, Larry Hunter, and Steffanie Wilk (2003), the transition from personal service to call centers in the United States has entailed changes from:

- Jobs with variety and personal relations to impersonal, routinized, and monitored jobs

- Local service markets to locality-independent disposable work-places

- Job security with career opportunities to dead-end jobs in remote areas

- Low wages to even lower wages, owing to downward pressure on wages

These trends are of special concern to call centers that focus on the mass-market services in the United States, whereas the exception has been business-to-business centers. Call center technologies make it possible to differentiate service jobs according to function, product, and customer segment and to create large business units that focus on specific segments. Management is thus able to deploy different service management strategies and job designs according to the customer segment (Batt 2000; Wood, Holman, and Stride 2006). The developments in telecommunication technologies and costs make it possible to (re)locate and outsource centers easily. Because the technologies also make it easy to monitor employees and to use industrial engineering principles, call centers have been depicted as new types of factories for white-collar workers (Fernie and Metcalf 1998; Taylor and Bain 1999). The typical employment model for mass-market call centers is based on low wages, low skills, limited training, and high turnover (Batt, Doellgast, and Kwon 2005).

In Denmark, call centers have also had a popular image of providing low-quality jobs with a high degree of monitoring, monotonous working conditions, and insecure employment conditions. The trade unions and the press have used examples of unjust treatment of young people—for example, dismissals without salary—to burnish this image. The critique has been especially targeted at the small telemarketing companies that hire young people on dubious contracts with a promise of high bonuses. But the large in-house centers of prominent companies have also been exposed. Cases have been brought forward in which employees were highly dissatisfied with the close monitoring or were fired on short notice without the promised bonus. Recently, however, the public image of call centers seems to be changing. Some of the large call centers are collaborating with the Employers' Federation and the trade unions to establish a more positive image, and some call centers have dealt with the negative connotation of "call center" by changing the term (and partly the function) to "customer service center."

Even though the public image of call centers in Denmark has been similar to the image that prevails in the United States, the case studies and survey reported in this chapter show a much more positive and varied picture of Danish call centers. The strategy of segmenting jobs is much less used—indeed, the opposite actually seems to be the trend, which is a positive development. In-house call centers are generally not moved to remote areas, and managers often specifically argue that a central position close to headquarters is important. Centers do not seem to be relocated on a whim—in most of the call centers in the study, the existing workforce is considered too important to subject to such moves. The jobs are typically not dead-end jobs, and several of the centers studied use an active retention and promotion strategy. Some of the call centers in the study were distancing themselves from monitoring and trying to involve employees in planning and goal-setting activities.

Wages at Danish call centers are typically well above the low-wage threshold and far better and much more compressed than call center wages in the United States. For call centers serving the mass market, the typical annual wage for a full-time employee averages €32,000 (US$43,601), which is about the same as the median of the Danish wage distribution (see chapter 2). The typical annual wage for a full-time employee at an American call center serving the mass market averages €22,000 (US$29,976), which is around 80 percent of the United States' median wage. The difference cannot be explained by higher formal skills in the Danish workforce. On the contrary, according to the survey of the Global Call Center (GCC) Project, the average educational level of the workforce in Danish call centers is slightly lower than that of the similar workforce in American call centers (Holman, Batt, and Holtgrewe 2007).

Even though the Danish call centers seem to be offering much better pay and better working conditions than American call centers, they are struggling with the same types of issues: relatively high labor turnover and absence, jobs that easily become monotonous and machine-paced, low levels of discretion, difficulties in using teams, limited career possibilities, monitoring and control, noise and climate problems, work during unsocial hours, and low levels of union membership. One of the striking characteristics of a call center is that technology gives managers extremely detailed information about the work processes. As one manager expressed it: "Don't ask me whether we have the figures. We measure everything. The question is how we use it."

STUDY DESIGN AND METHODOLOGY

The empirical evidence for this chapter is based on three different data sources. First, I conducted case studies based on common interview guidelines in eight call centers within the finance and utility subsectors. A second source is a survey conducted in 2004 as part of the Global Call Center Survey (Holman, Batt, and Holtgrewe 2007). The description of the industry is based on a representative sample of 128 Danish call centers described by Ole Henning Sørensen and Nadia El-Salanti (2005). It has been possible to use the Danish and international survey data for additional analysis. Finally, I used register data to compare Danish call center wages to Danish wage standards. I collected case study data through a series of interviews in each case company.[1] I also conducted six interviews with union and Employers' Federation representatives. Table 7.1 shows the total sample, including the number of employees in the call centers.

I selected companies so as to establish variation on two contrasting dimensions: in-house versus subcontractor, and low complexity versus mid-complexity of tasks. I used "time to become competent" and "call duration" for the typical full-time employee as proxies for the complexity of the work tasks. Table 7.2 illustrates the implications of complexity: it takes considerably longer for employees to become competent in "mid-complex" than in "low-complex" centers, and call durations are longer in mid-complex centers.

It was not possible to identify financial call centers with outsourced call center activities. Furthermore, I was unable to identify in-house utility call centers of low complexity or to find any subcontractor with mid-complex utility tasks. In the finance sector, it was

Table 7.1 Size and Distribution of Call Centers

Subsector	Name	Type	Complexity	Size (Number of Employees)
Financial services	BigBank	In-house	Mid	150
	NewBank	In-house	Mid	200
	SmallBank	In-house	Low	20
	DataBank	In-house	Mid	50
Utilities	CityPower	In-house	Mid	100
	RuralPower	In-house	Mid	40
	MultiService	Subcontractor	Low	350
	ServiceUnit	Subcontractor	Low	250

Source: Author's compilation.
Note: Size is approximate to secure anonymity. The size is a calculated full-time equivalent.

hard to identify call centers that had primarily low-complex tasks. A large credit card operator was the best candidate. However, it declined to participate. I decided to include one small financial call center in the sample to increase variation.[2]

In the following sections, I describe how and why the general conditions in the Danish call center industry differ from the United States call center industry, starting with general developments in the Danish industry and conditions in and similarities between Danish call centers. Second, because management strategies and union presence matter in Denmark, I describe places of demarcation, for exam-

Table 7.2 "Time to Become Competent" and Call Duration in Relation to Assessed Complexity of Call Centers

	Low-Complex		Mid-Complex	
Complexity	Competent (Weeks)	Duration (Minutes)	Competent (Weeks)	Duration (Minutes)
Utilities				
In-house	—	—	12–24	3–5
Subcontractor	2–4	¼–3	—	—
Financial services				
In-house	4–6	1–3	12–24	3–5
Subcontractor	—	—	—	—

Source: Author's compilation.

ple, the influence of the product market and differences between in-house centers and subcontractors. The case studies focused on call centers within two subsectors with two different vertical markets: the finance sector and the utility sector. Therefore, special emphasis has been placed on these two sectors.

DANISH CALL CENTERS AND CALL CENTER WORKERS

What is here referred to as the call center industry is a mixture of in-house call center units in companies in different sectors and independent companies that work as subcontractors and specialize in organizing call center activities. I use the terms "independent" and "subcontractor" interchangeably. An attempt to identify all Danish call centers by industry code leads to inconsistent and limited results, since in-house call centers cannot be identified through the industry statistics. The description of the industry here is therefore based on a representative sample of 128 Danish call centers (Sørensen and El-Salanti 2005).[3]

The Danish call center industry is not particularly well researched, and no industry statistics are available. However, Denmark has been part of the Global Call Center Project (Sørensen and El-Salanti 2005). Furthermore, a large EU Social Fund intervention project has been completed with more than eight hundred employees in three large call centers (Wiegman, Møller, and Petersen 2006). This study, entitled "Competence and Organizational Development in Call Centers," has successfully demonstrated how focus on competence development and increased autonomy can improve perceived working conditions and service quality. Results and examples from these research projects are included in this chapter.

The industry is relatively young in Denmark. Because of the lack of statistical material, I have used the age of establishment and references to terms such as "call center" and "contact center" in two national newspapers as indicators of the growth of the industry (figure 7.1). Before 1994, there were very few such references. From 1994 to 2000, there was a steep rise in articles about call centers, then a decrease in the years after the millennium; by 2003, however, the number had reached the level of 2000. The development of a pattern of references to call centers in the newspapers largely corresponds to the year of establishment reported by the centers in the global survey.

Figure 7.1 Growth in the Danish Call Center Industry

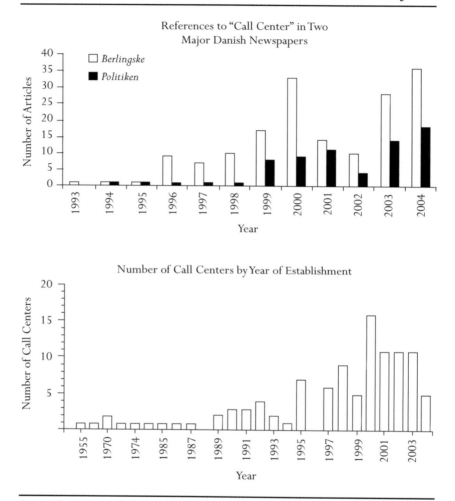

Source: Sørensen and El-Salanti (2005).

THE EVOLUTION OF THE CALL CENTER INDUSTRY

Industry experts agree that the frequency of articles mirrors the rapid expansion in the use of call centers as an organizational model (Sørensen and El-Salanti 2005). The Danish industry was born at the beginning of the 1990s, when the basic technology became available.

Computer technologies made rationalization of service activities possible. The first commercial call centers were established in the areas of hotline and help-desk functions, media and publishing companies, and mail-order–based retail companies.

In the late 1990s, the industry experienced what experts termed "Klondike" growth—development with minimal realism. The telecom companies quickly established large centers after the deregulation of the market. Some of these centers were outsourced as independent call centers. The deregulation of other sectors, such as utilities and transport, encouraged start-ups and mergers and an increased focus on customer service that subsequently led to the establishment of more professionalized customer service units. The subcontractors experienced a pressure on profitability. This pressure and the lack of professional management combined with the growth in small telemarketing companies that had quite dubious sales methods to give the industry a bad reputation. In this period, labor unions started to focus on the industry. The first collective agreement with an independent call center was negotiated in 1998.

Since the millennium, the industry has become more professionalized. The independent subcontractors have consolidated. The explosive growth in the telecommunication companies fell to a more moderate level. The transnational call center companies carried out mergers and takeovers. The independent call centers in particular realized that they needed more systematically economic procedures and better administrative management techniques. Several call center agent curricula were developed at business colleges around Denmark, and a one-year call center education was developed by the social partners. Industry experts believe that there has been a general shift in the Danish industry in the last few years from a focus on expenses to a focus on quality.

CALL CENTER WORKERS

The typical Danish call center worker is a woman (68 percent), which is consistent with the picture in other industrialized countries (Holman, Batt, and Holtgrewe 2007). The larger the call center, however, the lower the rate of women employed (Sørensen and El-Salanti 2005). Seventy-two percent of the employees on temporary contracts and 56 percent of the permanent employees are under thirty years of age. Only 8 percent of the employees are over fifty (IP Teams 2004).[4]

The case studies show that the age level is higher in the in-house units than at the subcontractors. There are, however, sector-specific differences: the average age is higher and the age span is wider in the finance sector, for example, than in utilities.

Call centers primarily employ unskilled workers or workers with a vocational training background related to the service area. In 33 percent of the call centers, the highest education of the majority of workers is secondary school. In 50 percent of the call centers, the majority of the employees have a vocational education, the highest such level being in finance (90 percent). As described earlier, young women in Denmark are better educated than men. The majority of employees in the Danish call centers, however, are relatively young women with relatively little education. This is similar to the education levels found in other industrialized countries (Holman, Batt, and Holtgrewe 2007). Several of the centers in the case study have sought to increase the share of men they hire, but they receive few applications. This indicates that customer service work is predominantly perceived as a woman's job. The global survey indicates that Danish call center employees have a slightly lower educational level than call center employees in other countries, such as the United States and France. The proportion of employees with a vocational education is relatively large (Holman, Batt, and Holtgrewe 2007).

The case studies suggest that call center employees do not view a call center job as part of their career. Several of the full-time employees said that they took the job in the call center as a temporary arrangement, either because they hoped to move on within the organization or because the wanted a job only for a while—for instance, before they started their studies. These motivations are similar to individuals' motivation for taking other low-wage jobs. Compared to other low-wage jobs, call centers offer less physically strenuous jobs and require higher cognitive skills, such as computer, problem-solving, and writing skills. Some of the employees interviewed selected the job because they were tired of what they had been doing (nurse, shop assistant, hairdresser), and one went to work at a call center because she wanted a job with less responsibility and therefore less stress.

Danish call centers employ a fair share of part-time workers. Thirty-five percent of the call center workforce hold part-time jobs. Part-timers work twenty-two and a half hours per week on average. Around half of the part-timers are bachelor or graduate students, who typically work fifteen hours or less. The use of students does not vary across sectors, but outbound call centers are more likely to use students than inbound centers (Sørensen and El-Salanti 2005). The case studies indicate that the qualifications required for call center jobs are often not related to the qualifications students will develop through their university studies. The call centers use only the students' general qualifications, such as cognitive and abstract skills, inner motivation, and computer knowledge. Thus, the jobs usually do not qualify the students for their future career. The case studies show that fewer than 5 percent continue working in the call center or other places in the company after they graduate. The jobs are primarily a supplement to the state student subsidy during a temporary phase of their lives.

Some call center workers are employed through temp agencies. These account for about 5 percent of the total workforce in the Danish call centers, which is low compared to the United States and the other European countries in this study. Temporary workers are mainly employed as buffers for peak periods and unsocial work hours. Temp agencies are also used in the recruitment process; hence, every year 16 percent of the temporary workers are transferred to permanent contracts (Sørensen and El-Salanti 2005).

THE STRUCTURE OF THE CALL CENTER INDUSTRY

In-house call centers typically serve specific vertical markets, whereas subcontractors sometimes serve several markets. The largest sectors in the Danish call center industry are the financial sector and the IT and telecom sector, each accounting for around 15 percent of the workplaces. The call centers within these sectors are generally large, with an average of 80 workplaces in finance and 113 in telecom. Utility, retail, distribution, media, and entertainment each constitute around 7 percent of the industry, and the average number of workplaces in each of these sectors is around 40. The call centers vary greatly in average size. Fifty percent of the employees are employed in 10 percent of the call centers.

Table 7.3 illustrates that there is variation across sectors in the number of inbound calls and the rate at which they are handled by in-house centers. The IT and telecommunication sector has mainly outsourced call center activities. This sector also accounts for the sec-

Table 7.3 Inbound and Outbound Activity in In-House and
Subcontractors Call Centers, by Sector

	Finance	Manufacturing, Utilities, Etc.	IT and Telecom	Distribution, Etc.	Other	Total
How would you describe this center?						
In-house center	100%	95%	35%	75%	64%	73%
Subcontractor	0	5	65	25	36	27
The majority of your activities are?						
Inbound	100	86	80	90	68	83
Subcontractor	0	14	20	10	32	17

Source: Global Call Center (GCC) Project (Sørensen and El-Salanti 2005).

ond-highest rate of outbound calls; only call centers in "other sectors" have a higher rate. The majority of the outbound calls are handled by independent call centers (Sørensen and El-Salanti 2005). The case studies show, however, that several inbound centers have a fair share of outbound activities. Language barriers make offshoring rare in Denmark. There are a few examples of call center operations placed abroad in Ireland or Spain, where Danish employees are hired to work under local wage and tax conditions.

The survey shows that the call centers in Denmark are considerably smaller than many centers found in the United States. It is customary for American banks to establish multiple call centers differentiated by product markets: credit cards, retail banking, mortgages, insurance, and so on (Batt, Doellgast, and Kwon 2005). This sort of horizontal market specialization is not used as much in Denmark. One manager in one of the larger centers in the case study explained that "we simply do not have the size to do that." In other words, country size might be an important factor, simply because functional differentiation is harder to achieve in a small country. The relatively small Danish call center size is partly an effect of its small country size.

Most training is based on on-the-job training and in-house courses that do not provide any formal qualification. On average, Danish permanent call center employees receive twenty-two days of training the first year they are employed, which is similar to the training offered in other industrial countries. Call centers with a collective agreement generally offer more training than call centers without an agreement. Since 2000, several formal courses for employees and leaders have been established in business colleges. A certification program for basic customer service agent skills is also offered. The courses are embedded in the flexible Danish vocational education and training system (AMU), in which half of the expenses are funded by the state. A one-year customer service agent education was established in 2004, but it attracted few applicants. It is not obligatory to take the course to get a job, and young people do not seem to view customer service as an attractive career path.

According to the trade unions, the worst working conditions are found in the outbound telemarketing call centers. According to industry experts, however, the share of these companies is relatively low in Denmark, in large part because outbound activities are limited by a law regulating "home solicitation sales"—popularly called the "door-to-door sales law." The law applies not only to physical door-to-door sales but, unlike in the United States, also to nonphysical sales activities conducted by phone, email, or fax. It puts severe restrictions on "cold calling" directed at selling products directly to private consumers outside of the merchant's place of business. Therefore, most telemarketing companies serve business-to-business (B2B) markets. Independent centers in particular are affected by the law because the majority of outbound activities are conducted by these centers. Exceptions are newspapers, magazines, journals, insurance companies, surveys, and publicly licensed health service providers. Therefore, some of the largest outbound call centers are found in the large survey and media corporations (the "other" sectors in table 7.3). The largest of these media centers make extensive use of students (80 percent of employees).

INDUSTRIAL RELATIONS

Sector-specific relations seem to influence the call center industry, since the working conditions and pay vary depending on the sectoral agreements. The relatively new Danish call center industry is characterized by a fairly weak institutional framework compared to the Danish labor market in general. The finance sector is an exception, because it is rather tightly organized: 79 percent of employees are governed by collective agreements, a rate that corresponds to the na-

Figure 7.2 Percentage of Collective Agreements in Call Centers, by Sector

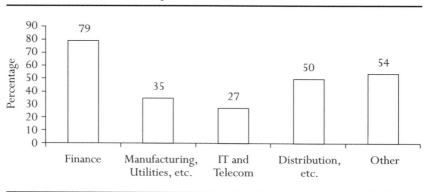

Source: Sørensen and El-Salanti (2005).

tional level of 80 percent. The IT and telecom area has a very low organization rate of 27 percent, which is related to the large degree of outsourcing (see figure 7.2). Fifty percent of all Danish call centers have cooperation boards.

The rather low degree of unionization in this relatively new industry is interesting. Have the employers exploited the situation? Both the survey and the case studies show that call centers provide wage and job conditions comparable to more organized industries. One reason for the comparable wages is the high UI benefits (described in chapter 2). Other reasons are sector-specific traditions and the character of the job.

One explanation for the relatively low organization rate might be that the employees' need for the protection provided by collective agreements is lower in the call center sector than in manufacturing or other service industries. Because of the character of the work (office, service), employees in call centers are categorized as clerical, salaried workers. In Denmark, salaried work is regulated by the Salaried Workers Act, which does not apply to manual workers. Thus, if employees work more than eight hours a week, they are automatically covered by the act, which regulates conditions of employment such as sickness pay, maternity leave, how much notice employees should have, and protection against unfair firing. Wages, however, are not regulated by the act. Furthermore, EU regulation requires companies to draw up contracts for employees who work more than eight hours a week.

Another explanation for the low organization rate is related to the relatively young age of the employees and the high number of part-time workers. The case study interviews indicate that young employees do not find that they need to organize. They typically believe that the employer behaves decently and that if it does not, they will be able to find a new job easily. The relatively high turnover rates in some of the call centers indicate that it is quite easy to find a new job. Often the young employees do not relate improvements in work design and job quality to labor unions but think of them only in connection with unemployment subsidies, legal assistance, and wage negotiations.

The overall picture is that the vast majority of call center workers in Denmark are covered by the Salaried Workers Act and half of the call centers are covered by sectoral agreements that provide further rights and benefits. The case studies indicate that most centers provide wage and working standards close to or even surpassing the wage and working standards specified in the sectoral agreements, even where there is no collective agreement and only a few of the employees are union members. Unionized centers have slightly but significantly higher wage levels (Sørensen and El-Salanti 2005).

There are no special employer or employee associations dedicated to the call center industry. Generally, the employers of in-house call centers are organized in the employers' associations related to the vertical market served by the call centers. Normally, employees are organized according to job functions. Because work in call centers is usually considered clerical work, the Danish labor union HK (Union of Commercial and Clerical Employees in Denmark) organizes most of the call center employees. In some subsectors, the employees are organized differently. Hence, employers and employees in the finance sector are organized by the association dedicated to this sector, with one exception organized in HK. For employees, other company-specific exceptions apply; for example, the telephone operators in the former state-owned telecom company (TDC) are organized by the Danish Metal Union for historical reasons related to the merger of unions. Also, one exception applies here. A previously independent call center now owned by TDC is (still) organized by HK. In both cases, the collective agreement of HK is the least beneficial for employees.

HK has been the most active player in relation to call centers. In 2000 HK stated: "HK is not particularly concerned about the issue of call centers as they either already have a collective agreement in place or the terms and conditions offered to employees follow the same norms as those governing the rest of the labor market" (EIRR 2000). However, this opinion changed. Between 2001 and 2004, HK focused on the appalling working conditions in some telemarketing call centers. HK established a website that blacklisted companies where members had experienced problems. In 2005 the website was closed because it was ruled illegal to expose companies by name. Consequently, HK changed its strategy to focus on well-performing call centers. However, attempts to pressure firms to negotiate collective agreements have largely been unsuccessful. Within the sectoral agreement, HK can force a company to enter a collective agreement only if a majority of the employees are members of HK, but this is far from the reality in the majority of the call centers.

In Denmark, it is not possible for the financial companies to move to a green-field site to escape unions, as it is in the United Kingdom, the United States, and Germany. For example, when CityBank established an operation in Denmark, it tried to avoid the union presence and collective agreement. After a conflict, the industrial relations court in April 1983 ruled that CityBank had to follow the sectoral agreements. After the introduction around 2000 of a new individual wage bargaining system, it became possible to place call centers in the provinces to attract a workforce with somewhat lower absence levels and possibly a lower wage level. A few call centers have been established in—or moved to—rural areas with higher unemployment rates, a more stable workforce, and support from public programs and the local governments. In 2001 one of the largest subcontractors followed such a strategy and moved from Copenhagen to South Zealand. Other subcontractors have considered such a move but find that the availability of young people and students in the large cities is an advantage.

This overview of the Danish call center industry has provided a general description of the changes in the competitive situation from rapid growth to consolidation and moderate growth. In the next section, the business and employment strategies of the industry are further described, with examples and assessments based on eight case studies of Danish call centers in two subsectors, finance and utilities, and two subcontractors serving the utility sector.

BUSINESS AND EMPLOYMENT STRATEGIES

The general picture of the call center industry has been one of mergers and the creation of larger call centers. However, the case companies have managed these changes differently. This section provides examples of how managers have tackled the structural and institutional changes in each of the subsectors and how they assess the related implications for the quality of work. Because the call centers belong to two different subsectors, it is useful to look at the institutional setup in each sector in more detail in order to understand the managerial choices. Subcontractors are discussed in a separate section.

THE FINANCE SECTOR

Labor relations in the financial sector can be characterized by social partnering. The finance sector has not experienced a strike in twenty years. The large majority of call center employees are organized in Finansforbundet (Financial Services Union) and DFL (Danish Insurance Employees). Employers are organized in FA (Danish Employers' Association for the Financial Sector). Traditionally, bank employees have had "lifetime employment," and there is a history in this sector of very close cooperation between the partners.

The finance sector saw a wave of mergers during the 1980s and 1990s that created a few very large players (25,000 or more employees). Several of the mergers in the 1990s crossed previously separate areas, such as retail and mortgage banking, or insurance and real estate chains. This has led to a large potential for cross-sales activities, and the role of call center workers has thus changed from financial advisers to financial sales employees. Furthermore, around 1990 a regular bank crisis was added to the structural changes. As a result, many bank advisers were dismissed or relocated, and many branch offices were closed. Since 2005, the sector has experienced a shortage of employees with a vocational education in finance, partly as a consequence of reduced training activities during the crisis period.

As a response to changing competitive conditions and technology developments, call centers serving as telephone banks were established in the middle of the 1990s. In the same period, computer-based home-banking was introduced. Therefore, many of the organizational units became responsible for both telephone banking and IT support for home-banking products. Some employees were relocated to call centers from branch offices that had been closed or downsized, a move that increased considerably the travel distance to work for many of them. The financial call centers typically grew during the crisis, because they were one of several answers to the productivity problem.

The merging of financial companies has not been the only trend. The competitive landscape also includes quite a few successful small banks, many of which have outperformed the large banks on key economic figures. The small banks typically do not have regular call centers.

In the same period, consumer behavior changed as opening hours of shops were partly deregulated. Increasingly, customers did not want to show up physically within normal working hours (9:30 AM to 4:00 PM). Telephone banks therefore required longer working hours than the normal working hours defined in the collective agreement. Because the sector was so tightly organized, unions were involved in the renegotiations of normal working hours and compensations for working unsocial hours. The "teleconcept" was developed in cooperation between the labor union and the Employers' Federation. Table 7.4 shows the standard additions to the hourly wage. The agreement also secured decent notices of work schedule changes and a decent pay for part-time students.

The sector saw many different responses to the structural changes. In the case studies, two very different responses to the productivity crises in the Danish finance sector were identified by BigBank and SmallBank. BigBank is one of the largest Danish banks. As a reaction to the competitive pressure, it closed many small branch offices and transferred activities to one call center and a number of larger branch offices. As a result, the call center grew rapidly. One of the informants, a shop steward, participated in the work design process. A guiding principle in this center was to avoid any resemblance to the "factories" in the United Kingdom. This principle led to the design of high-profile jobs for full-time employees, with a wide range of responsibilities. Despite this design, two problems arose, and according to the shop steward, both were related to the call center's fast growth. One problem was the workload of training many new employees. The other problem was that employees were "forced" to work in the center because the job was the alternative to a layoff; according to the

Table 7.4 Extra Pay for Work During Unsocial Hours in the Finance Sector

	Time	Addition/Time Off
Weekdays	7:00 AM to 8:00 AM	25%
	6:00 AM to 7:00 AM;	
	6:00 PM to 10:00 PM	45
	10:00 PM to 6:00 AM	65
Weekends and holidays	6:00 AM to 10:00 PM	65
	10:00 PM to 6:00 AM	75

Source: Finans Forbundet (2005).

shop steward, these employees were often not the best bank advisers from the branch offices. Internally, the call center got a bad reputation. According to both the shop steward and management, the problem has been overcome by branding the center internally and by focusing on education, training, and individual coaching. The call center employees now generate more sales than the bank advisers in the branch offices. The employees interviewed were proud of working in the telephone bank.

The small retail bank in the sample, SmallBank, reacted to structural changes in the sector completely differently. SmallBank's branch office network was already relatively small, and it partly relied on net-bank products. The bank's strategy was to be a low-cost bank, and it had already established a telephone bank and support function. However, as a reaction to the excess capacity of bank advisers, SmallBank decided to personalize the interface to the customer by assigning a personal branch office bank adviser to each customer. As a consequence, the call center was reduced to half its previous size, and the tasks of the agents became focused on simple transactions, reception calls, general emails, and net-bank support. After the change, agents needed fewer qualifications, and the jobs became relatively monotonous. To extend the jobs and create more time off-phone, management has sought to attract administrative tasks to the call center.

NewBank was a newly formed finance merger between a large mortgage bank and a small retail bank. The call center was established to avoid creating an extended branch office network after the merger. In this case, the union representatives were not as active in the design of the call center, which might be one reason why the company chose a traditional, functional segmentation that gave the frontline personnel quite monotonous tasks. In 2003 NewBank decided to improve service quality and brand identity by offering the customers a single contact point for all financial products. At the same time, it joined a large EU Social Fund project targeted at improving job quality. During the two years the project lasted, the work organization was radically reorganized from segmented call centers to one unified call center with self-directed, mixed-competency work teams. This change required a major upgrade of skills for most agents. Three levels of formal competency were defined: basic call center skills, basic level within each of the three product-market areas, and expert level within each of these areas. New training procedures were developed with a mixture of classroom teaching, work in a training environment, e-learning, and job shadowing in the team. A career progression within the call center and to other parts of the organization was formulated. Process facilitation was provided for teams and team leaders. The team leader role was changed to a coaching role. Several administrative tasks were delegated to teams—for example, team members now take turns performing the role of coordinator. Research-based evaluations of the project show increased job quality, service quality, and productivity (Mathiesen, Wiegman, and Møller 2006).

The core activities of the last financial call center, DataBank, were not directly affected by the structural changes in the financial sector because it delivers data and customer services related to credit card operations as a sort of subcontractor of data services. In 2003 DataBank sold the least complex credit card activities to a bank (account statements, and so on) and kept the most profitable, mid-complex activities in-house (blocking, fraud, and so on). As a consequence, employees in this center receive a great deal of training and have much discretion in customer interactions. However, DataBank does not use a team-based organization.

All of the financial companies in the case study use students to cover unsocial working hours and peak hours. Student workers in the finance sector are students covered by the standard conditions in collective agreements of FA, with exceptions in certain areas such as the right to pension schemes, education plans, and maternity and parental leave. By July 2005, the agreement specified a minimum hourly wage of €15.40 (US$21), which, at 70.3 percent of the Danish median hourly wage, is a relatively high student wage. The minimum hourly wage for a newly hired full-time employee without experience is the same. The strategies for using the students differ considerably. At BigBank, students are organized in a separate team that handles simple inquiries during peak periods at the end of the month. At NewBank, students are an integral part of each work team. However, they have fewer competencies and less access to training than the full-time employees. Many students are also used for outbound activities. At DataBank, students are fully trained, which takes more than six months. Until they are fully trained, they work on day shifts. After that, they work night and weekend shifts. At SmallBank, students are able to cover all the low-complex work tasks, so they are primarily used to cover unsocial work hours. It is hard to single out an institutional determinant that explains how students are used. The main reason management gives for using students is flexibility, but in some cases recruiting them for the future is another motivation.

Management at BigBank has found that capacity planning related to the peaks at the end of the month is very difficult and that restrictions on scheduling in the collective agreements make this problem worse. For some years they have used students to handle simple inquiries at month's end. But since the collective agreements also restrict work scheduling for students and secure the students a relatively high wage, the center recently started to experiment with temporary agents, an arrangement reluctantly accepted by the local union representatives. DataBank has solved this problem differently. It has negotiated a local agreement that makes exceptions to the scheduling restrictions possible. As compensation, the students are paid on a par with permanent employees when compensations for working unsocial hours are taken into account.

THE UTILITY SECTOR

The utility sector is less organized than the finance sector. Only a minority of technical employees are union members. The administrative personnel are usually organized in company-specific staff associations with affiliation to FTF (Salaried Employees and Civil Servants Confederation). The supply of electricity, water, and so on, must be maintained; hence, as suppliers of these goods, workers in the utility sector are prohibited from striking. This prohibition, which also applies to call center employees, leaves employees with lower negotiation power. HK has tried to recruit members and negotiate collective agreements in the utility call center, with very little success. There is no sectorwide agreement on compensation for work during unsocial hours, which is determined instead by each company. Management in the utility call centers stated that wages and conditions are set in accordance with the conditions in similar jobs in the industry; in other words, the collective agreements in other service areas have some effect. The collective agreements of HK do not specify a special wage level for students in the service area. For the public administration area, HK has a wage scale for students that starts at €13.90 (US$18.96) per hour (as of 2005), which is 63.5 percent of the Danish median wage. This is considerably lower than the level in the finance agreement. There is no minimum wage for full-time employees, but HK will not enter a collective agreement if the lowest wage in the company is below €13.50 (US$18.41) per hour.

The markets for electricity and water have been deregulated since 1999. Before that, most power companies were publicly or cooperatively owned. At the beginning of the 1990s, call centers were established based on local service offices, often as part of local municipalities. The deregulation process resulted in a wave of privatizations. Competition increased, and mergers and consolidations led to fewer and larger utility providers. The consequence for the utility call centers has been mergers and relocations to new office facilities. Large resources have been consumed to merge and upgrade customer database systems and administrative IT systems.

One aim of deregulation was to give consumers their choice of provider. This possibility has primarily been used by companies and public administration. Most private users still use the local provider, and few utility providers focus on this segment. Thus, the main activity in the utility call centers is inbound customer service. Several utility providers have diversified into related product areas, such as cable and Internet networks. The consequence for call center employees has been a growing demand for cross-sales activities.

CityPower is a relatively large power provider in the Copenhagen area. The case studies were performed in a relatively stable period after a merger in late 2002. A new merger was scheduled for late 2006. After the first merger, activities were centralized, and workers from several local offices were moved to one relatively large call center. There was an intake of many new and relatively young employees. Management decided to employ young, inexperienced team leaders to create a dynamic work environment. After a year, the call center was experiencing wide dissatisfaction with the monitoring and control of employees. An experienced call center manager from the telecom sector who was hired to tackle the problems introduced coaching and sent the young team leaders on courses. Gradually, the employees gained more influence. At the time of the interview, the management strategy was based on employee involvement, team influence, and coaching.

Ironically, in 2005, after conditions had started to improve, the union initiated a press campaign against the center based on testimony from forty present and former employees, even though HK had organized only a few employees in the center. The center was exposed in the national press as one of the worst call centers in Denmark and as a workplace where even toilet visits were timed and measured. According to some of the CityPower employees who were interviewed, however, many of them were offended by the campaign against their workplace, and subsequently HK became unpopular. Nevertheless, these employees conceded, the campaign had an effect and became an occasion to improve on some problems. Because of the threat to the image of the otherwise well-regarded company, top management initiated an internal investigation.

The other utility operating an in-house call center, RuralPower, is a power utility provider in the provinces. It was also the result of several mergers. According to the manager, the merged call center was based on the best practices of the previous call centers. The employee representative noted that the merger got rid of some problems with work-related stress that had been an issue at one of the previous call centers. Since the merger, experienced employees have participated in the development and testing of the new, unified customer relation system. To avoid heavy workloads, the center has used long-term temp agents and outsourced some functions. The call center is organized in teams with low influence and makes limited use of coaching.

CityPower has decided that the complexity of the tasks and the training requirements are too high to make it economically feasible to employ students who work only fifteen to twenty hours a week. In part because it is situated far from universities and lacks the option of hiring student employees, RuralPower aims to create full-time, permanent jobs to attract a stable workforce. The opening hours of both centers are from 8:00 AM to 6:00 PM on weekdays only, so the number of unsocial hours is limited.

SUBCONTRACTORS

The use of outsourcing has been quite different among the sectors (table 7.3). Whereas several utility providers have experimented with outsourcing, it has not been possible to identify a single financial company that has outsourced call center activities. The risk of compromising data security is the reason given by managers in the financial case centers. However, a manager of an independent subcontractor complained that the financial companies in the EU have an exemption on value-added tax that cannot be transferred to an independent call center. This means that outsourcers have to add 25 percent VAT to the price of their services, and the financial company is not able to balance the VAT expense on incomes because the financial sector is neither paying nor collecting VAT at all. Currently, the EU is trying to find a solution to this problem. In Germany, there are subcontractors that specialize in financial call center service and are subsidiaries of financial corporations, which is a way to avoid the VAT issue. But as long as VAT is an issue, outsourcing's downward pressure on wages in the finance sector will be limited.

In industrial relations, there are large differences in Denmark between in-house call centers and independent subcontractors. Independent call centers have a much lower organization rate than in-house centers (see figure 7.3). Centers with collective agreements pay higher wages and provide more education (Sørensen and El-Salanti 2005).

Because subcontracted call centers emerged outside of the traditional sector-specific industrial relation patterns, certain sectors, such as telecommunications, have partially managed to escape the traditionally strong unionization through outsourcing. The clerical, unskilled character of the work makes HK the "natural" organization for call center employees. HK has focused on the large, influential subcontractors and the telemarketing centers, but, as mentioned earlier, with limited success in establishing traditional collective agreements. As a consequence, HK recently changed strategy. A new type of "collaboration agreement" that does not involve wage negotiations is now being promoted. If a company wants such an agreement, it is obliged to find and involve a shop steward in decision processes. The company has to pay a fee to an education fund that can be used by the company's employees. The company promises to adhere to a certain code of conduct—for example, to contact HK to solve conflicts. The

Figure 7.3 Collective Agreements at In-House and Independent Subcontracting Call Centers

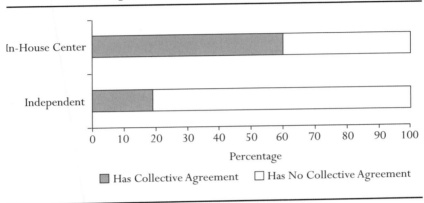

Source: Sørensen and El-Salanti (2005).

benefit of such an agreement for the company is that it is allowed to use the HK logo when advertising for new employees and to use the HK job database. In May 2006, one such agreement was signed, and according to the union representative, several other companies have expressed interest. Such agreements have become attractive to companies partly because of the negative exposure of the call center industry in the press and the emerging shortage of labor. But at the time of the study, collective agreements were the exception, and wages were determined by each individual company. The same applies for working conditions except for what is secured through the Salaried Workers Act and the Working Environment Act.

As described earlier, the competitive situation was very hard from 2000 to 2004. The subcontractors were undercutting each other such that it was almost impossible to be profitable. Two managers from different subcontractors stated that a common understanding had developed in the industry that the situation had to change because of the low profits and the bad industry image due to problems with service quality and poor working conditions, which made it hard to recruit people.

MultiService, a relatively large independent subcontractor with many different contracts, has reacted to the hard competitive pressure by focusing on cost reduction. One element of this strategy has been to minimize training expenses (by conducting minimal and primarily internal training quickly and on the phone), minimize wage expenses (by hiring young people at low pay to work flexible hours), maximize time on the phone (by monitoring and following up and encouraging a mixture of customers), and minimize absenteeism through increased control and economic incentives. One of the methods used to increase productivity and job variety has been to assign agents to several product areas with a mixture of low-complex tasks (reception calls) and mid-complex tasks (utility calls). Paradoxically, the human resource department in this company has very high expressed values for work design. Realities are different, however, owing to cost-driven management and very young and inexperienced team leaders. To establish a career path, capable agents are promoted as team leaders. However, because turnover is quite high (about 50 percent) and employees are young (age twenty to thirty), team leaders often have no managerial potential, experience, or training. According to employees, this leads to all sorts of unpleasant situations characterized by detailed monitoring and control. Recently, the company sent all the team leaders on external leader training. Many of them had been leaders for a long time without training.

The other subcontractor, ServiceUnit, is a relatively small unit in a large corporation that has taken a different management approach. It has invested more in training than MultiService, but less than the in-house centers. The pay is relatively low, but not the lowest. ServiceUnit provides more benefits and uses monitoring less extensively than the other subcontractor. The manager said that one reason for this is the culture and corporate personnel politics of the large service company of which ServiceUnit is a part. He explained that the reason for its relatively good performance was that its average employee tenure is "exceptionally" high (two and a half years in comparison to one and a half years at the other subcontractor).

To increase numerical flexibility and circumvent some of the restrictions on planning imposed by the Salaried Workers Act, MultiService operates with the concept of using "freelancers." A freelancer is guaranteed fifteen hours of work per week. Each week the freelancer must offer the company a window of at least forty-five available working hours and a desired number of work hours (more than fifteen). By doing this, the subcontractor avoids the requirement of four weeks' notice on major schedule changes and creates a high degree of numerical flexibility, which employees appreciate, according to the human resource manager. The support for this claim found in the employee interviews can be explained by the young workforce and selective recruitment. Interestingly, this model makes it impossible for the freelancers to use the UI system if the company cannot offer the desired work hours. The monthly wage for freelancers is equal to that of full-time employees, given the same experience and working hours. However, the median salary is lower for freelancers because of lower seniority. The introductory wage is so low that students are not a special category. Sixty-seven percent of the employees work as freelancers. However, the company is trying to increase the ratio of full-time, permanent employees in response to retention problems. The issues of workplace flexibility and low introductory wages, not the general wage level, appear to be the main reason MultiService has avoided making a collective agreement with HK.

ServiceUnit primarily employs full-time employees. It does not experience problems with scheduling restrictions in the Salaried Workers Act. According to the manager, the scheduling flexibility issue is handled easily enough if both management and employees show flexibility. Students are also used to flexible schedules, especially at unsocial hours. Both subcontractors use many students for outbound activities such as telemarketing, but the share of students on inbound teams is only around 10 percent. Periodically, ServiceUnit experiences fluctuations in demand for employees, owing to large changes in customer contracts. During such periods, it uses temp agencies to avoid hiring permanent employees who would have to be dismissed a few months later. The Salaried Workers Act is more restrictive concerning dismissals than the general agreement for manual workers (see chapter 2).

Both CityPower and RuralPower have outsourced 5 to 10 percent of their call center activities. At CityPower, the purpose of the outsourcing was to get an external benchmark and eliminate some of the simplest transactions. In reality, this meant that low-quality jobs were exported to the subcontractor. At RuralPower, the tasks were outsourced primarily to free up resources in the post-merging period. In this case, the subcontractor was supposed to handle all requests. In reality, many of the complex customer interactions ended up in the in-house center. To create comparable service quality, both in-house centers have arranged on-site training for the subcontractors' employees and set up direct lines to coaches and supervisors. However, the subcontractor employees receive considerably less product- and system-specific training than the agents in the in-house center. The subcontractor employees said that this is a problem, because the IT systems are very complex. Often customers ask for more information than they are trained to handle, and it is frustrating when they cannot give proper customer service because they are not trained sufficiently. This sometimes leads to angry customers. The lower training activities are probably a consequence of the competitive situation and the different focus and strategic situation of the subcontractors compared to the in-house centers. The subcontractors do not have a specific focus on the utility sector. The dominant markets for these companies are telemarketing and IT and telecom.

As mentioned earlier, offshoring in the Danish call center industry is limited owing to language barriers. Recently, however, a new model for offshoring has been introduced. A multinational subcontractor has relocated fifty Danish positions to Barcelona, Spain, or around 15 percent of the company workforce. The center has a mixture of Scandinavian employees targeting the Scandinavian countries. The Barcelona center tries to attract young people who want to spend at least a year working in Spain. This may not compare favorably to average tenure rates in Denmark of one and a half years, but the advantage is that in Spain the employer pays 20 percent less to the employees and the tax for the employee is less than half of the Danish tax. This model could put some pressure on wages, but the trade unions still do not consider it a serious outsourcing threat.

Interfirm Variation in Pay and Job Quality

The foregoing descriptions show that most of the in-house call centers' reactions to structural and institutional changes have been quite disparate. Both NewBank and CityPower have taken a high-performance, work organization approach, although CityPower initially took a cost-focused approach. The call centers in the study have made many attempts to improve job quality, and the primary aim of management seems to be to achieve higher service quality. The financial union has had quite a lot of direct influence on job design, whereas HK has only been able to exert external pressure with limited success. It is evident that some of the low-complex aspects of the jobs are exported to subcontractors or left to students. In this section, we examine the concrete consequences for pay and job quality.

Table 7.5 illustrates that there is a reasonably clear relation between pay and job quality at the call centers in the sample. The call centers have been listed according to increasing job quality, from left to right. The qualitative ranking in the table is based on an evaluation of interview statements, observations, and measures provided by the managers. The figures for tenure and turnover are imprecise because it was difficult to get exact numbers. Furthermore, in some cases low tenure reflects large growth within the last few years; in other cases, it reflects high turnover. Wages are calculated as a percentage of the median full-time hourly wage for the entire economy in Denmark. For full-time call center employees, the hourly wage is estimated based on a conversion of the monthly or yearly salary using the weekly working hours and the number of working weeks per year.

PAY

The typical average annual salary for core employees in Danish call centers was about €35,000 (€20.60 per hour; US$28.09), which is 95.4 percent of the median of the full-time hourly wage distribution for all Danish workers. The lowest typical salary for full-time workers in the survey was €23,333 (€13.70 per hour; US$18.68), which, at 63.4 percent of the overall median, is just under the low-wage threshold of two-thirds of the median of the full-time hourly wage distribution for all Danish workers (see chapter 2). The typical wage falls below the low-wage threshold at only 3 out of the 128 call centers in the survey. The finance sector has the highest salaries, whereas the utility centers are in the middle of the wage distribution. There are no differences between in-house centers and subcontractors, and no differences in relation to size. Sixty-two percent of Danish call centers use individual or group-based performance pay or pay for overtime (Sørensen and El-Salanti 2005). None of the case companies offered performance-based pay, but overtime was normally paid. Normal working hours are thirty-seven hours a week in all the case companies.

Table 7.5 shows that the typical wage for permanent, full-time employees of the call centers in the study is about the same as the typical wage in the call center industry. Low wages are paid to the employees on temporary contracts, mostly students. Only in one case, at MultiService, is an introductory wage for new employees under the low-wage threshold (60 percent of the overall median). The financial call centers generally pay full-time employees more than average and the utility call centers, including subcontractors, pay around average,

Table 7.5 Pay and Job Quality for Employees at the Eight Case Call Centers

	Low-Complex			Mid-Complex				
	Subcontractor			In-House				
	Utility		Finance	Utility		In-House	Finance	
Case Name	MultiService	ServiceUnit	SmallBank	CityPower	RuralPower	NewBank	BigBank	DataBank
Employees became competent (weeks)	1–3	2–4	1–3	12–24	12–24	12–24	12–24	24+
Average tenure (years)	1.5	2.5	1	5	5	2	2.5	10
Annual turnover	50%	35%	50%	13%	5%	13%	20%	15%
Annual number of sick days	14	13	10	13	15	12	9	10
Training	Low	Middle	Middle	High	High	High	High	High
Promotion	Low	Low	Middle	Middle	Middle	High	Middle	Middle
Work environment	Low	Middle	Middle	High	High	High	High	High
Team discretion	Low	Low	Low	Middle	Middle	High	High	Middle
Temporary agents	67%	38%	43%	28%	0%	5%	20%	62%
Wage (permanent)	73	98	86	92	107	99	105	110
Wage (temporary)	66	64	70	76	—	67	73	112

Source: Author's compilation.
Note: Wages are reported relative to the median of the hourly wage distribution among full-time Danish employees. Evaluations are based on statements from employees and managers and on case study observations.

which is in accordance with the survey results. One case, DataBank, is notable for paying relatively high wages to both permanent and temporary employees. In reality, DataBank is a B2B center, and all employees have high levels of responsibility and relatively wide discretion. Student employees typically stay in the center for more than three years. As expected for a firm with low-complex job tasks, SmallBank has the lowest pay for permanent, full-time employees. The nature of the work also explains the relatively high turnover among full-time employees in this call center.

For permanent employees in the utility sector, there is no difference in wages between in-house and independent subcontracting call centers, a finding also in accordance with the survey (Sørensen and El-Salanti 2005). For temporary employees, the pay at the subcontractors is lower than at the in-house call centers. This difference is very important, because the figures hide the fact that subcontractors have a considerably higher number of temporary workers. At Multi-Service, whose wages are below the low-wage threshold, the proportion of temporary employees (freelancers) is 67 percent. Many of these employees are not students. They work full-time, or more and their contracts are "flexible" and not really temporary. It was my impression that a fair share of these employees on semi-temporary "freelance" contracts work more than thirty-seven hours a week, possibly to compensate for the low wage. The other subcontractor, ServiceUnit, does not have similar flexible contracts but instead employs many students. CityPower pays temporary workers relatively well because the students it employs are typically experienced workers who worked full-time before starting their studies.

WORK ORGANIZATION

Internationally, the main problems cited with call center jobs are limited discretion, fast pace, and health problems related to overuse of phones and video display units, such as sore throats, voice loss, deteriorating eyesight, headaches, and hearing difficulties (Mason 2008). Only a few of these problems were mentioned by employees in the case studies.

All Danish call center employees are covered by the Work Environment Act, the Vacation Act, and the Salaried Workers Act. But as discussed in chapter 2, Danish call centers appear to follow a set of "institutional norms" that surpass the regulatory requirements. The call centers in the study generally have decent or good facilities and offer several benefits, such as ergonomically sound and electrically adjustable tables and chairs[5] (better than the EU legal minimum requirement), provision of daylight (more than the legal requirement), decent, good, or even superb canteens (typically also serving headquarters staff), and decent or tasteful interior design, as well as other benefits such as free coffee, tea, sandwiches, and so on. Moreover, due process in case of dismissals, decent wages following industry agreements, organized and fair planning of work schedules, and pension schemes on top of public pensions are common work conditions and benefits. Students and temporary employees do not receive all of the benefits (such as a pension and maternity leave).

In the interviews, the employees were asked about the positive and negative aspects of their job. In all of the call centers except MultiService, the employees were quite loyal to the employer. The majority seemed satisfied and did not want to put a lot of emphasis on problems. This might be an indication of bias in the selection of informants, but this was not the impression of the researcher after further observations and informal talks. The most common complaints were noise and stressful peak periods. At the subcontractors, especially MultiService, employees also complained about monitoring, low discretion, short breaks, and aggressive customers. Harassment from customers was related to unpleasant tasks, inadequate training, and poor organization. Some of the student workers in the financial call centers BigBank and NewBank had similar complaints. On the positive side, employees mentioned flexible schedules, well-organized working conditions, clear work-family separation, and, most frequently, good colleagues. The stress put on the importance of good colleagues reflects the fact that call center employees help and support each other, often despite the individual character of the work and individual performance measures.

All call centers in the study use some kind of team organization, but they compose and use their teams very differently. At the subcontractors, teams are primarily structured around a portfolio of contracts, with one team leader or supervisor assigned to each group. The teams have low discretion, and work is essentially individual except for the training of colleagues. At the utility in-house centers, several teams are assigned to the same work tasks but have different team leaders. Teams here have more discretion, and one role of the team leaders is coaching. The financial call centers SmallBank and

DataBank use teams only as a way of grouping employees. On the other hand, BigBank and, especially, NewBank put great stress on teamwork. In all of the centers, managers and planners emphasized that planning is important and very complex. In NewBank's experience, contemporary planning systems are a barrier to team discretion and do not make employee influence easy. The overall picture is that team discretion is substantially higher in the mid-complex call centers than in the low-complex ones.

The most frequently mentioned motivational issue for managers was how to vary the work to make it more interesting. Several managers and employees explained that it is hard to be on the phone all day. Therefore, several of the call centers vary the jobs by adding other types of tasks, such as mail processing, quality control, system tests, training of colleagues, email, letters, fax, and packing. To create variation in tasks, call centers also train employees to handle several product markets, as opposed to creating specialized teams for each product market. The extent of these arrangements varies depending on the nature of the case company and the complexity of the product. At SmallBank, the manager tries to attract email screening, whereas at BigBank the manager is planning to expand into B2B. In some instances, job variation initiatives have also been managerial attempts to increase productivity and functional flexibility. Nevertheless, most of the employees interviewed appreciated job variation, especially chances to get off the phone.

FLEXIBLE EMPLOYMENT PRACTICES

One of the challenges for call centers is to maximize productivity and accessibility by matching workload to capacity. The structural changes and increased competition in both sectors have challenged the call centers to extend opening hours and respond to increased demands for accessibility in peak periods. The case companies provide a variety of examples of how managers try to meet these challenges—from automation and restructuring to different kinds of flexible employment practices. The employment of part-time student workers is the most typical answer to this challenge. Table 7.5 shows that 50 percent of the case companies use relatively many students (30 percent or more). Five to 10 percent of permanent employees work part-time, but working part-time is often their own preference and not one welcomed by the managers.

Surprisingly, the young employees in the low-complex call center are not considering taking advantage of the UI system. Many are not even insured. Several young employees were of the opinion that they could easily find another job. And as described in chapter 2, the Salaried Workers Act makes the threat of being "flexibly laid off" not as acute as it would be in other parts of the Danish low-wage labor market. In the mid-complex centers, a much larger percentage of employees are insured in the UI system, despite the fact that their risk of being laid off is lower. The high proportion of insured employees is mainly due to the high organization rate in the finance sector.

Day shifts are normally covered by full-time employees. In most companies, full-time employees must sometimes work during unsocial hours, that is, from 4:00 PM to 8:00 PM on weekdays and from 9:00 AM to 4:00 PM on Saturdays or Sundays. However, the work is usually shared between full-time and temporary employees, and since the workload generally is lower during these periods, each full-time employee works unsocial hours only a few times a week. As described earlier, the collective agreement in the finance sector has developed a system for additional compensations during these hours. In the utility sector, where the companies have no collective agreements, compensations are also given, but rates are lower.

Nearly all of the call centers have used temp agencies. In the majority of the call centers, temp agents are trained to occupy full-time positions, either because it is part of a "try and hire" arrangement or because an organizational change, such as a changing order situation or a merger, has created a need for a long-term temporary worker. Up to 10 percent of the employees in the case companies were temp agency workers.

TRAINING, JOB MOBILITY, TURNOVER, AND ABSENTEEISM

Several managers and employees were of the opinion that employees cannot or will not work in a call center for more than two to four years. The challenges mentioned by most of the managers were ensuring sufficient training, establishing carrier paths, bringing turnover down, and lowering absenteeism. Yet another challenge was managing not to invest too much in volatile employees. Most of the managers saw these areas as interrelated.

Training is typically a mixture of classroom training, e-learning, and job shadowing. Most of the call centers rely on internal training, but some utility-sector centers have started to use external providers, especially for team leaders. At the case companies, employees in the low-complex centers receive around one to two weeks of training, whereas employees in the mid-complex centers receive several months of training. The case studies clearly demonstrated that subcontractor employees receive considerably less training for the same tasks as their colleagues in the in-house call centers who outsourced a share of the same tasks.

It is generally acknowledged that the call center industry has a relatively high labor turnover. However, compared to the United States, the labor turnover in the Danish call center industry does not seem very high (Batt, Doellgast, and Kwon 2005). Within a year, about 10 percent of Danish call center workers quit their job. About 5 percent are fired, and 7 percent are promoted or transferred. However, if we remove from the analysis some of the large call centers of former state monopolies, where employees had civil servants' protection and the union presence is high, average tenure falls from around four years to one and a half years.

The turnover at the subcontractors is markedly higher than at the in-house centers. The case studies indicate that this might be closely related to complexity. Table 7.5 shows that the turnover in low-complex call centers is as high as 50 percent, whereas it is around 10 percent in mid-complex call centers. From a human resource management point of view, this is not surprising (Wood, Holman, and Stride 2006). Apart from job design issues such as monotonous work, turnover in the low-complex call centers might also be high because employees do not consider call center jobs a proper career and the career possibilities of such work are very limited.

In the mid-complex financial call centers, some of the employees have actively chosen a call center career. Their choice was influenced by meaningful job content and the training possibilities in the center (BigBank and NewBank). Turnover in these centers is now increasing because the labor market situation is so tight that experienced call center workers can change to positions as financial advisers in other financial companies based on their call center training and without acquiring a formal banking education. According to NewBank, the loss of employees to other financial companies has become a large problem for call centers that provide substantial training.

All of the financial call centers are actively trying to establish career paths for employees within the organization. Even the Small-Bank center is well aware of the labor shortage and tries to find ways to retain employees and their expertise within the organization. This retention policy also applies to students. The utility call centers are less concerned with these issues. Both subcontractors have tried to establish career paths for employees by inventing quasi-management positions and assigning increasing responsibility to the industrious agents who fill them. In the interviews, employees did not express satisfaction with the results of this approach.

The average number of absences for employees in the Danish call center industry do not differ significantly from the general industry, where nine days a year per employee is the mean level. There are some differences between sectors (Sørensen and El-Salanti 2005). Table 7.5 shows that the same tendency can be seen in the case study. The absence level is higher in the utility sector than in the finance sector, and it is not related to complexity. However, the case interviews indicated that the independent subcontractors were fighting a harder battle against absenteeism than in-house companies. One of these centers has implemented a complex incentive structure that gives benefits to teams, based on a profit-sharing scheme, if team absence levels are kept below 7 percent. Several call centers have introduced a "welcome back" talk with the team leader or the human resource department after an employee is out sick for two days or more. BigBank and NewBank have also focused on absence, but primarily because the branch offices have very low absence levels (five to six days per year per employee). At SmallBank, the manager explained that they deliberately keep the work pressure relatively low because they know that the job is relatively monotonous and that this might lead to absence if the workload becomes too high.

REFLECTIONS ON INTERFIRM VARIATION

An important explanation for differences in work conditions between the eight case companies clearly lies in the different sectors. Pay and job quality are undoubtedly better in the financial sectors than in the utility sector. One reason may be related to the different roles of the call center agents. In most of the financial call centers, the employees are central to the core work functions of the company—selling financial products—whereas the utility call center employees are servicing established customers. Another reason is the long Danish tradition of social partnering and union involvement in the finance sector.

A plausible explanation for the relative success of the financial labor unions in shaping the development of the financial call centers lies in the historical development of the sector. When the labor unions saw their core members being transferred to newly established call centers, they sought influence and became involved in job design and working time regulation from the beginning. The managers appreciated this interaction. In the utility sector, the call centers were often established as an expansion of the service offered to customers. Many employees were newly hired and had a different educational background from the rest of the organization. The weak labor unions in this sector therefore did not take any particular interest in this new area, and the newly hired young employees were generally not affiliated with unions.

Another explanation for differences between the sectors in job quality and pay relates to different competitive positions and ownership, as well as different strategies. MultiService has faced tough competition as an independent subcontractor under different international owners. It followed an expansion strategy of competing on price for contracts. The result has been pressure to minimize expenses and focus on cost. ServiceUnit has acted differently. According to the manager, it has focused on service quality and has not accepted contracts with margins that are too low. Part of the explanation for the lower job quality at the subcontractor call centers in comparison to the in-house call centers may also be that the in-house centers export low-complex tasks to subcontractors to improve job content for their own employees and these are the least complicated tasks to outsource. The contract managers of the subcontractors were aware of this problem, and they tried to attract contracts with the highest possible job complexity.

Generally, temporary workers, especially students, get the jobs with the lowest complexity, the lowest job quality, and the lowest pay. But this outcome varies according to the policy of the company and, in some cases, the negotiations between union representatives and management. For the mid-complex call centers, this issue does not seem to be relevant to the competitive position and the cost and quality objectives of the call center. At the BigBank and NewBank call centers, students have low-complex tasks. At DataBank, they have mid- or even high-complex tasks and earn pay comparable with that of permanent employees.

DISCUSSION AND CONCLUSIONS

Across sectors and firms, the case studies and the survey indicate that Denmark has not experienced a "race to the bottom," despite the fact that Danish call centers have a lower organization rate than Danish industry in general and the competition between the independent call centers has been relatively strong. Compared to the relatively low standards in American and British call centers (for descriptions, see Batt, Hunter, and Wilk 2003; Fernie and Metcalf 1998), the general job quality in Danish call centers is considerably higher.

Therefore, it is tempting to conclude that Danish call centers constitute an exception to the trends described for the United States. Managers have generally not selected a low road to job design. In fact, in all of the call centers in the study managers were trying to create variation and improve job content one way or another. The jobs are not highly monitored or routinized. All the jobs considered are monitored, but only one case company uses the statistics intensively for disciplinary reasons. Workplaces are fairly stable except for those involved in mergers in the sector. Jobs are typically not dead-end; most of the case companies try to establish career paths for employees, although a clear career path can only be seen in some of the financial call centers. Considering that call centers predominantly employ relatively young women with little or no education, wages are not low compared to the Danish mean for full-time employees.

There is, however, a bias in the sample. The case companies were selected from two of the better sectors in the Danish call center industry. Nevertheless, the scores on discretion and pay in the global call center survey also indicate that Denmark is faring better than most other countries (Holman, Batt, and Holtgrewe 2007).

It is clear from the study that the subcontractors constitute the low end of the spectrum, which is not surprising. Subcontractors have been used to increase competition, and they often primarily get the low-complex tasks. The deregulation of service markets has put pressure on job quality and pay in other service industries in Denmark. One of the subcontractors in the sample shows many of the characteristics of the situation for American call centers. This subcontractor also provides the only example of low-wage employment in the sample. It is apparent that this company has gone out of its way to circumvent regulation by using freelancers. But the managers of the company are also aware of the problems related to turnover and service quality and are trying to reverse the situation. It seems plausible that regulation, high UI benefits, and a highly organized labor market are what keep call center job quality and pay at decent levels.

APPENDIX

Table 7A.1 The Case Study Call Centers

Case Name	Subsector/ Complexity/ Type	Owner-ship	Collective Agreement	Coopera-tion Board	Local Unemploy-ment	Size[a] (Number of Employees in Utility Teams)
MultiService	Utility/low/ subcontractor	SE	No	No, roundtable	6 to 10%	350 (6)
CityPower	Utility/middle/ in-house	DK	No	Yes	6 to 10%	100
ServiceUnit	Utility/low/ subcontractor	DK	No	No	6 to 10%	250 (8)
RuralPower	Utility/middle/ in-house	DK	No	Yes	6 to 10%	40
SmallBank	Finance/low/ in-house	DK	Yes	Yes	6 to 10%	20
BigBank	Finance/middle/ low/in-house	SE	Yes	Yes	0 to 2%	150
NewBank	Finance/middle/ low/in-house	DK	Yes	Yes	0 to 2%	200
DataBank	Finance/middle/ in-house	DK	Yes	Yes	0 to 2%	50

NOTES

1. Typically I spent one and a half hours with a manager, one hour with an employee representative and a supervisor or team leader, two hours with two to four employees (typically in a focus group), and forty-five minutes with a human resource representative. I recorded all interviews and transcribed some of them. I observed and photographed planning systems and office locations and made some field notes. Finally, most of the case companies provided additional statistical data. All of the call centers were very supportive, open, and friendly. Visits were conducted over the course of two days, and the planning of the activities was well structured. Subsequently, I systematized the data and produced eight case reports, which were validated by the contact person in each com-

Type of Contract	Main Hours	Main Working Patterns	Pay/Hour, Permanent (Percentage FT)	Pay/Hour, Temporary (Percentage FT)	Training/ Promotion	Work Environment
FT (33%)	10:00 AM	37 hrs/	€16.00	€14.50	Low/low	Low
PT (67%)	to 5:00 PM	week	(73)	(66)		
FT (88%)	10:00 AM	37 hrs/	€20.20	€16.70		
PT (12%)	to 5:00 PM	week	(92)	(76)	High/middle	High
FT (62%)	10:00 AM	37 hrs/	€21.50	€14.10	Middle/low	High
PT (38%)	to 5:00 PM	week	(98)	(64)		
FT (100%)	10:00 AM	37 hrs/	€23.50	n.a.	High/middle	High
PT (0%)	to 5:00 PM	week	(107)			
FT (57%)	8:00 AM	37 hrs/	37 hrs/	€15.30	Middle/middle	Middle
PT (43%)	to 9:00 PM	week	37 hrs/(86)	(70)	High/middle	High
FT (80%)	8:00 AM	37 hrs/	€22.70	€16.00		
PT (20%)	to 8:00 PM	week	(105)	(73)		
FT (51%)	8:00 AM	37 hrs/	€21.60	€14.70	High/middle	High
PT (49%)	to 9:00 PM	week	(99)	(67)		
FT (38%)	11:00 AM	37 hrs/	€24.00	€24.60	High/high	High
PT (62%)	to 2:00 PM	week	(110)	(112)		

Source: Author's compilation.

Note: FT: full-time, permanent employment; PT: part-time, temporary employment; SE: Sweden; DK: Denmark.

a. Size of the call center is approximate to secure anonymity. The size is a calculated full-time equivalent. The figure in parentheses is the number of employees working with utility calls.

pany. Employee statements were validated by the involved employees before they were used.

2. The intention of the case study design was to select case companies of the same size to keep this factor constant. But because it was not easy to get access to companies in the utility sectors, selecting call centers of the same size was not an option. In finance, it was difficult to find a center with low complexity. Most low-complex financial call centers were smaller than the cutoff size of twenty-five employees. However, two of the mid-complex centers turned out to have a substantial number of students who performed low-complex tasks that were very sim-

ilar to those performed by the full-time employees in the low-complex center.
3. In this context, a call center is defined as "an organizational unit where a minimum of five employees as their primary work task provide service to customers, potential customers, or citizens with the help of integrated telephone and computer technology" (Sørensen and El-Salanti 2005). The call center industry is defined as the totality of in-house centers and subcontractors.
4. These figures are found in a consultancy report based on a management survey of 120 call centers.
5. When several people use the same computer workplace, tables and chairs have to be adjustable.

REFERENCES

Batt, Rosemary. 2000. "Strategic Segmentation in Frontline Services: Matching Customers, Employees, and Human Resource Management Systems." *International Journal of Human Resource Management* 11(3): 540–61.
Batt, Rosemary, Virginia Doellgast, and Hyunji Kwon. 2005. *The U.S. Call Center Industry 2004: National Benchmarking Report—Strategy, HR Practices, and Performance*. Working paper 05-06. Ithaca, N.Y.: Cornell University, Center for Advanced Human Resource Studies (June).
Batt, Rosemary, Larry W. Hunter, and Steffanie Wilk. 2003. "How and When Does Management Matter? Job Quality and Career Opportunities for Call Center Workers." In *Low-Wage America: How Employers Are Reshaping Opportunity in the Workplace*, edited by Eileen Appelbaum, Annette Bernhardt, and Richard J. Murnane. New York: Russell Sage Foundation.
European Industrial Relations Review (EIRR). 2000. "Call Centers in Europe, Part 1." *European Industrial Relations Review* 320(September): 13-20.
Fernie, Sue, and David Metcalf. 1998. *(Not) Hanging on the Telephone: Payment Systems in the New Sweatshops*. London: London School of Economics, Center for Economic Performance.
Finans Forbundet. 2005. "Standard Collective Agreement Between the Danish Employers' Association for the Financial Sector (FA) and the Financial Services Union on Salary and Working Conditions in the Banking and Mortgage Credit Sector." Accessed at http://www.finansforbundet.dk.
Holman, David, Rosemary Batt, and Ursula Holtgrewe. 2007. "The Global Call Center Report: International Perspectives on Management and Employment." Global Call Center Network.
Huber, Evelyne, and John D. Stephens. 2001. "Welfare State and Production Regimes in the Era of Retrenchment." In *The New Politics of the Welfare State*, edited by Paul Pierson. Oxford: Oxford University Press.

IP Teams. 2004. *Den danske CallCenter undersøgelse [The Danish Call Center Survey]*. Copenhagen: IP Teams.

Mason, Geoff, editor. 2008. *Low-Wage Work in the United Kingdom*. New York: Russell Sage Foundation.

Mathiesen, Karin, Inger-Marie Wiegman, and Niels Møller. 2006. *Udvikling af arbejdet i callcentre: Saadan gik det [Development of Work in Call Center: The Results]*. Lyngby, Denmark: Den Europæiske Socialfond.

Sørensen, Ole Henning, and Nadia El-Salanti. 2005. *Call Centers in Denmark 2004: Strategy, HR Practices, and Performance*. Lyngby, Denmark: Technical University of Denmark.

Taylor, Phil, and Peter Bain. 1999. "'An Assembly Line in the Head': Work and Employee Relations in the Call Center." *Industrial Relations Journal* 30(2): 101–17.

Wiegman, Inger-Marie, Niels Møller, and Jeus Voxtrup Petersen. 2006. *Drivsel: Drift og trivsel i callcentre [Drivsel: Productivity and Well-being in Call Centers]*. Lyngby, Denmark: Department of Manufacturing, Engineering, and Management (IPL), Technical University of Denmark.

Wood, Stephen J., David Holman, and Christopher Stride. 2006. "Human Resource Management and Performance in U.K. Call Centers." *British Journal of Industrial Relations* 44(1): 99–122.

Index

unemployment rate: and flexicurity model, 23; immigrants, 58; in Netherlands, 12; regional differences, 59–60; trends, 35–36, 47–48; vs. U.S., 36–37; for young people, 36–37, 43–44

Union of Commercial and Clerical Employees (HK), 40, 147, 271–2, 277–8, 279, 280–1

unions and unionization: in call center industry, 265, 269–72, 273, 277–8, 280, 293; in Denmark, 14, 17, 19–21, 37–42, 175; electrical goods retail employees, 147; food processing industry, 112, 117–8; food retail industry, 147, 162–3; in France, 11, 22, 38; in Germany, 22, 40; hospitals, 227; hotel industry, 40, 194–5, 211; in Norway, 39; retail industry, 147, 174; and unemployment insurance, 46; in U.S., 174, 227. *See also* collective bargaining

United Federation of Danish Workers (3F), 40, 112, 227, 255*n*4

United Kingdom: health care expenditures, 224, **225**; health indicators, **226**; low-wage labor market, 11; low-wage work incidence, 6, 11; minimum wage, 11; social model, 9

United States: call centers, 259; educational attainment, **62**; employment rate, 35–36; health care expenditures, **225**; health indicators, **226**; labor force participation, 35–36; low-wage work, 6, 29–30; part-time work rate for women, 54; retail industry, 174–5; unemployment insurance, 29; unemployment rate, 28–30, 36–37; unionization, 174, 227

universal health care, 27, 45

upstream production, 108–9

utilities industry call centers: complexity of, **262**; inbound vs. outbound activity, **268**; industrial relations, 277–8, 293; industry deregulation, 278; outsourcing, 280; as percentage of call center industry, 267; size and distribution of, **262**; wages, 285, 287; work organization, 278–9, 288

Vacation Act, 88, 287

vacation pay, 43

vacation time, 55

VAT (value added tax), 45, 188, 216*n*3, 280

vocational education, **73**, 81, 82, 119, 167, 269

vocational education and training system (AMU), 81, 82, 119, 269

wage bargaining. *See* collective bargaining

wage dispersion, low-wage work as reflection of, 5–6

wage distribution, 16, 51–52

wage gap, gender, 21, 54

wage growth, and employee turnover, 43

wages: of call center employees, 260, 276, 278, 285, 287; of electrical goods retail employees, 170; of food retail employees, 161–2; of hospital workers, 228–30; of hotel workers, 188, 198–9, 202–3, 207, 216*n*13; and market competition, 7–8; of meat processing industry, 128–30; in retail industry, 147, **161**; of slaughterhouse workers, **123, 124**. *See also* minimum wage

WEA (Working Environment Agency), 87, 116, 128, 197

welfare: incentive problems, 86; political issues, 17; receipt by low-wage workers, 77; system specifics, 37; vs. UI system, 24–25; and unemployment, 48–51

Westergaard-Nielsen, N., 43, 64, 78, 88

white-collar workers, 23, 42, 43, **72**, 88

WHO (World Health Organization), 224

Wilk, S., 259

women: in call center industry, 265, 266; in confectionery industry, 124; in electrical goods retail industry, **168**; in food retail industry, 156; hotel industry employment, 199, **200**; labor force participation, 35, 52–54; low-wage work incidence, 13, 69, **70, 71**; low-wage work probability, **73**; part-time employment, 53–54; as percentage of low-wage workers, **53**; wage distribution, **51**

work conditions and organization: call